THE VANDALS' CROWN

HOW REBEL CURRENCY TRADERS OVERTHREW THE WORLD'S CENTRAL BANKS

GREGORY J. MILLMAN

THE FREE PRESS

NEW YORK   LONDON   TORONTO   SYDNEY   TOKYO   SINGAPORE

The Free Press
A Division of Simon & Schuster Inc.
1230 Avenue of the Americas, New York, N.Y. 10020

Printed in the United States of America

printing number

1 2 3 4 5 6 7 8 9 10

Library of Congress Cataloging-in-Publication Data

Millman, Gregory J.
    The vandals' crown : how rebel currency traders overthrew the
world's central banks / Gregory J. Millman.
        p.   cm.
    Includes index.
    ISBN 0-02-921287-1
        1. International finance.   2. Financial services industry—
Technological innovations.   3. Foreign exchange futures.   4. Money
market.   5. Capital market.   6. Banks and banking,   Central.
7. Brokers.   I. Title.
HG3881.M535   1995
332'.042—dc20   94-41125
                                                         CIP

FOR MARTINE

NO WONDER OF IT, SHEER PLOD MAKES PLOUGH DOWN SILLION
SHINE . . .
                    —GERARD MANLEY HOPKINS, "THE WINDHOVER"

CONTENTS

A NOTE TO THE READER

The Japanese stock market began to fall in 1990, and its fall continued for two years, much to the astonishment of the Japanese government. In 1992 and 1993, the European currency exchange rate mechanism disintegrated in the face of a speculative attack, despite the efforts of European governments to hold it together. In the spring of 1994, devastating losses on so-called derivative investments rocked some of the world's biggest industrial and financial corporations. In the autumn, when this book was just about to go to press, Congressman Henry Gonzalez, chairman of the House Banking Committee in the 103rd Congress, and Congressman Jim Leach, likely chairman of that committee in the 104th, had made clear their determination to bring the markets to heel with legislation.

These incidents are all related, and there will certainly be more like them. The past two decades have witnessed a revolution in finance comparable to the discovery of nuclear power in physics. Until recently it has been largely a secret revolution, little noticed beyond the financial industry. Now people far from the markets are being affected. This book attempts to explain how and why this revolution has taken place and what its consequences may be.

The financial markets are nonlinear. So is this book. The 1992–1993 speculative attack on the European exchange rate mechanism forms a sort of gravitational center or nucleus around which the chapters cluster, like electrons,

vii

more or less tightly bound. The brief "interregna" following chapters 2, 4, and 6 sketch this attack from several perspectives.

The story of the new financial markets is largely a story of incompatible, colliding perspectives. In order to put the markets in their historical context, chapters 2 and 3 provide a brief history of the centuries-old struggle between governments and financial interests. Chapter 4 begins the story of the radically new markets that have transformed the contemporary world. Readers with a particular interest in how corporations trade currencies and derivatives, and in the hidden risks that have led to recent well-publicized losses, will find these issues discussed in some detail in chapters 5 and 8. Thus, although the chapters are numbered sequentially, readers need not be bound by that linear order. The full story must take into account many different characters and events, since each participant in the new international financial system provides a context for the others' behavior. So, too, the chapters of this book.

GREGORY J. MILLMAN
Plainfield, New Jersey
November 18, 1994

PROLOGUE

RUMORS OF WAR

MARCH 27, 1992. The Cold War was over; democracy and capitalism had won. But the world was not a safer place. On this day, in the western regions of what had been the Soviet Union, a ground-to-air missile hit an Aeroflot jet. Before the news flickered on blue computer screens or flashed across the long black electronic boards hanging above their heads, currency traders had passed garbled rumors by telephone from continent to continent. These traders were arguably the most powerful people in the world, for they controlled the only power that really mattered anymore, the capital that made capitalism: the dollar, the yen, the deutsche mark.

In a modest suite on the ground floor of an office mall in Englewood Cliffs, New Jersey, Andy Krieger felt a buzz. He reached into his shirt pocket and withdrew a black box slightly smaller than a cigarette pack. He pressed a button, and a gray screen on the box flashed the most recent currency price quotations. Something very strange was going on—the deutsche mark was plunging. He slid his chair back from the heavy, hand-carved teakwood conference table and asked his guest to excuse a momentary absence. The guest watched him as he walked into a room across the hallway where computer screens blinked on a trading desk. Krieger spoke with a young woman seated by one of the screens. The early, ominous word: war between Russia and the Ukraine.

What chance would there be of containing such a conflict? The Red Army, riven by factions, still had soldiers based in East Germany, where the euphoria of liberation had vanished in a hangover of inflation and unemployment. Stretched across the potential battlefield, oil and gas pipelines that supply much of the energy for German industry were vulnerable. War between Russia and the Ukraine could cripple Germany, the strongest economic power in Europe.

The falling deutsche mark was an omen. Currency traders knew that investors would flee war. Seeking a safe haven for their capital, they would sell what they owned in Europe to buy dollars and invest in the United States, far from the fighting. There would be panic in Frankfurt, Paris, and London as jittery investors raced to sell European assets for dollars before prices fell further and found all prospective buyers hanging back to see just how far prices could fall before reaching bottom. European currencies would plummet. Meanwhile, the surge in demand for safe U.S. investments would push the dollar's value up and drive commodity prices down. Thus, the rumored war on the steppes posed a threat to Latin American and African countries that depend on commodity exports, and even to farmers in the United States.

So the global markets trembled as the rumors raced around the world and traders positioned themselves for currency chaos.

Krieger was no longer the biggest of the currency traders, but he had a reputation for being the boldest. He alone had reportedly caused panic at New Zealand's central bank in 1987, when he sold the money of that country short. In that year he earned $300 million for Bankers Trust Company. Then he suddenly quit the banking industry and went to work for the plutocrat George Soros.

There Krieger refined his technique. In 1988, he fought the Bank of England.[1] On a hunch that Britain was about to register a horrendous trade deficit, Krieger began to borrow pounds and sell them. If a shocking trade deficit caused the pound to fall, he would buy back pounds for less than the price at which he had sold them and repay his loan but keep the profit. He had sold £900 million when British authorities announced that their trade performance had been much better than anyone had supposed. The pound moved up instead of down. Despite this evidence, Krieger stuck to his conviction that the pound would fall. Instead of cutting his losses, he doubled his bet, continuing to borrow and sell until he had sold short nearly £2 billion.

A colleague turned green and nearly vomited into a wastebasket when he saw how much risk Krieger had taken. The pound was continuing to move up instead of down. All indications were that Krieger was about to take massive losses on his short sales. Then, unexpectedly, the Bank of England began to sell pounds. Apparently, the bank feared that sterling was moving too far too fast and wanted to push it down. It almost seemed as though Krieger and the central bank were on the same side. But Krieger wasn't on anybody's side but his own.

When the Bank of England's sales had forced the pound down to a level that assured him healthy profits, he quickly bought a billion pounds back. The billion-pound order hit the market like a shot of speed, causing chaos and panic in the trading rooms. Sterling rocketed on the sudden, massive demand from one trader—Krieger. The Bank of England fought the surge, pushing more and more pounds onto the market in order to keep the currency stable, but Krieger had already done his trade and the chaos he had caused was the least of his concerns.

Now running his own trading firm, in the New Jersey office, Krieger slipped into a chair and tapped at a keyboard. The Reuters wires brought a confirmed report that a dud rocket had been fired off by an irregular band of Azerbaijani separatists. This was no war. The currency values were quickly moving back to where they had been before the jolt of those terrible rumors.

It did not take him long to find his positions satisfactory: no need to pick up the phone to give a buy or a sell order. He returned to his seat at the conference table, sipped a Diet Pepsi, and spoke softly of a financial system in crisis. "There's a net exposure that is absolutely mind-boggling," he said. "It's worse than what people imagine because it's not reported."

———————

Every day, the currency traders move $1 trillion around the world at the speed of light. Add up all of the Saudi oil, Japanese cars, American wheat, and European aircraft, and throw in the rest of the things that countries buy and sell from each other, and you will get only a small fraction of the $1 trillion. The rest is traded for profit in a fast-moving market where "the long run" means ten minutes, and that's plenty of time to win or lose millions.

Like masterless samurai in an unceasing struggle to capture even greater wealth, the traders battle constantly—among themselves and against any vulnerable government authority. The battlefield is the international capital markets, their weapon is money, and their fighting styles are as diverse as the Asian martial arts. "Fundamental traders" analyze basic economic data to calculate supply, demand and price. "Technical traders" look for predictive shapes in the graphs of past price trends. "Quants" rely on heavy computer power to calculate probabilities of price moves based on small changes in relationships between markets. "Judgment traders" try to think like their opponent, imagining all the options open to a central banker whose currency they plan to attack, and systematically closing them off. Most of the great financial warriors are adept in several different styles, because different styles work under different circumstances.

The currency market is connected to all other financial markets, influences them, and is influenced by them. In fact, the influences are so strong that it is probably archaic to speak of the currency market, the stock market, the bond market, and the commodities market as though there really was a neat boundary between each of them. Financial innovations of the past twenty years, especially the development of financial derivatives, have dissolved the barriers of geography, regulation, and custom that once divided the world's financial system into separate markets. Now traders move capital quickly and quietly along a multitude of channels that link markets in subtle and scarcely understood ways. Low interest rates in the United States can cause stock prices to rise in Malaysia, futures contracts traded in Singapore and Chicago may undermine the Japanese Ministry of Finance, and when American homeowners decide whether or not to refinance their mortgages they stir up a storm in the treasury bond market. The financial world has changed, and that means the whole world has changed.

In the not so distant past, economists believed that a country whose manufacturers were efficient and competitive and whose government managed its finances soundly could theoretically expect to enjoy a stable currency. Now, however, it doesn't matter how efficient and competitive a country's manufacturers may be, at least in the short run. Traders determine the value of currencies by bidding for them. And since currency values determine the prices at which manufacturers will sell their products on the world markets, currency traders can indirectly determine whether auto workers in America, Japan, or Germany will build cars or be unemployed. During the 1970s, for example, a weakening dollar made American products relatively cheap in foreign markets. In the early 1980s, as American interest rates rose, traders poured massive amounts of capital into the American markets, bidding up the price of the dollar. Because the dollar became more expensive, American tractors, cars, machine tools, and many other products became more expensive too. Journalists coined the term "Rust Bowl" to describe the effect on once thriving American manufacturing centers.

Like the vandals who conquered decadent Rome, the currency traders sweep away economic empires that have lost their power to resist. Time after time in country after country, when governments can't cope with the new financial realities, traders are the agents of creative destruction. Although investors have always had to take into consideration the quality of a government's management of its economy, traders now have an unprecedented degree of power to sweep the financial foundation out from under poorly managed, politically unstable, or uneconomic governments before the bureaucrats even know what has happened.

Like bounty hunters in the Old West, the traders enforce the economic law, not for love of law, but for profit. They have only one goal—making money. No political ideals or immaterial values can ever distract them from this goal. When the governments of Europe decided to implement a common monetary policy, they had a long-term program in mind to overcome centuries of division by establishing a historic union. Traders didn't care about that dream. For several years during the 1980s, the European monetary system was a profitable trading opportunity. Then in 1992, European governments showed by small words and acts that they might not be quite as committed to the program of unity as they originally said they were. Traders immediately reversed course, sold off some European currencies, bought others, and in the process demolished the European monetary system. Some European officials saw in the activities of the traders evidence of a conspiracy to wreck European unity. But that view gives traders credit for being more broad minded than they are. If European unity had continued to be a profitable project, the traders would certainly have supported it.

Is it a bad thing, this single-minded concern with safety of capital and profits? Well, no, at least not entirely. It matters how profitably our pension funds are invested, how safe our banks and insurance companies will be, whether or not the companies that employ us have the financial discipline to compete in world markets. The traders have perfected an efficient mechanism for delivering rough economic justice: Things sell for a true, free-market price. What's more, the traders can react quickly to change, and the world in which we now live is a world of dramatic, sudden, and astonishing change. Opinion remains sharply divided, however, on the merits of the world they have shaped. Milton Friedman praises the freedom and economic logic of the new order. On the other hand, former Federal Reserve Board Chairman Paul Volcker decries their vigilante economics as chaotic, disruptive, and serving only to enrich an already rich elite.

For better or worse, since the collapse of the Bretton Woods international monetary order, traders provide the only financial discipline the world knows. They are financial vigilantes. Because governments could not provide financial law and order, traders took the law into their own hands. They sell protection at a price.

And what a price. George Soros made $1 billion in a few days during 1992 by helping to push Great Britain out of the European monetary system. Clearly, traders who know how to seize an opportunity find fantastic riches. Most of them, unlike Soros, shun publicity and are happier working in the shadows. Hardly anyone outside the financial derivatives markets knows the names of Joe and Mark Ritchie, the founders of the powerhouse options trading firm CRT. They were just born-again Christian prison guards and bus drivers before they discovered the magic of the marketplace. They set up a small trading operation in 1977, and a decade later they sold it to Nations Bank for $225 million. The Ritchies were parvenus, but so were the great banks and investment banks of the 1980s, institutions like Bankers Trust and Salomon Brothers that eclipsed the blue-chip financial houses that had prospered in a more stable world. The world of the traders is a pure meritocracy. Here, at least, the race is to the swift, rather than to the well born, properly schooled, or decently acquainted.

It is only a little more than twenty years since the Bretton Woods system definitively fell, and just more than ten since financial engineers began to design the mysterious and powerful new tools called *derivatives*. This book will introduce the people who have reshaped the international financial world and explain what they have done. Like junk bond traders of the 1980s, the traders in financial derivatives and currency of the 1990s have reaped both wealth and controversy from their activities. This book will take readers behind the scenes of the exchanges, corporations, and hedge funds to see how and why money moves as it does.

This book does not purport to be an exhaustive economic analysis, a textbook of financial theory, or a study of financial history. It is a journalist's report. My objective is to explain the gist of complex and difficult financial events in language understandable to any reasonably literate lay person. In order to do that, of course, it is necessary to give some background. In presenting this background, I have elected to put the interests of the lay reader before those of the trained economist or financier. This book contains no graphs, formulas, or other such impedimenta of financial exposition. It does not analyze theories with all of the subtle exactitude that economic jargon makes possible. Instead, it offers the reader a series of scenes and incidents and anecdotes that together form a picture of this new financial world—a world in which change is the only constant, risk the only certainty. With apologies to Winston Churchill, it is governed by the worst financial system possible—except for all the others that have been tried.

THE VANDALS' CROWN

Philadelphia Stock Exchange, September 1993

The light here is difficult. It trembles and seems almost gray, though it is not dim. The very profusion of different kinds of light is what confuses the eye. It would be so much easier if there were but one single source. Instead, a luminous melange shivers from the shifting screens on vast banks of cathode ray tubes; blinks from the yellow news-spelling bulbs on the wallwide Reuters board; flashes red from telephone signal beacons on twisted, gangly necks atop each black-walled booth; fluoresces from the ceiling tubes far above. Yet the many colors all blink and wink at different tempos, and mixing together they form something like a bright shimmering twilight that is half-absorbed by black walls, black booths, black frames suspending the price screens, black floor that mutes not only light but also steps and sounds.

In a distant corner of the big black room, a CNN anchorman announces the unemployment numbers from a television screen mounted high above. Unemployment is lower than expected! The red lights flash like Christmas as every clerk in the black tiered booths grabs blinking phones. Receivers cocked to their ears, they shout, and men the size of linebackers sprint to the broad open space at the base of the tiers where a tall bald trader jumps up and down, bellowing hoarsely,

1

"Ten thousand marks, ten thousand marks." Gathered in a close ring, the traders shake their fists in each other's faces, faces torqued tight, twisted, red behind the beard stubble. The ring has the intensity of a dockyard crap shoot. Above, in the tiered booths, a short blond woman stands on a chair waving, shouting, "I want two, I want two." The scaffold-mounted screens flicker and blink as markets move in London, New York, Chicago. Shouting gets more intense, roaring and echoing despite the sound-absorbing tiles, as the decibels crash in waves and the ears ache from the noise.

Fingers flail; arms thrust; the ring knots, bunches, turns. Now and again, a taut tired face turns inquisitively toward the black booths with their flashing beacons. There a tall spectator waves two fingers, three, shakes his head, nods, waggles his hand just above his hair. Turning back, the tired face shouts the hoarse name of new numbers. Tempers flare. A clerk with hair like General Custer's stomps his feet and hollers, "Fuck! Fuck! Fuck!" The ring roars more. Then there are few voices, then two, then one. The ring dissolves. Individual men walk away a little distance to stand with hands in pockets, or scratch, talking in low but still-tense voices about the numbers. The calm is short.

On a black desk in the top tier of booths, a phone rings, a red light flashes once, and a big man grabs the phone before the light can flash twice. He listens. "Yeah. OK. When? How much? We'll look for it."

He scans the loose mill of men at the perimeter of the trading floor. They are waiting. "A call from Chicago," he mumbles curtly to a visitor. "A big deal just went down on their floor. Maybe someone will try to lay it off here."

"They just called you to tell you that?"

"Yeah. A favor." The favor could be worth a million. A big order in Chicago can almost immediately move every market in the world. It's in the space *between* "almost" and "immediately" that the traders make their money.

Now a phone rings on another desk. Someone is a bit too slow, a bit too careless, and over a shoulder a competitor sees something valuable, the name of the caller. It's a French multinational, looking to move money out of French francs at a good price. The order is for twenty-three thousand put options, representing the right to sell nearly a billion dollars' worth of French francs. Everyone knows the franc is in trouble. The French government has been telling everyone about its firm commitment to protect the currency. That's a bad sign. Five or six centuries of experience have taught the markets that when the state makes reassuring noises, it's time to dive for cover. But to know that now, this particular French corporation will try to move a multibillion-franc option order through the markets is to know something truly valuable. Superior knowledge allows traders to seize that space between almost and immediately.

So brokers and traders are constantly on the watch for clues about the party behind each order telephoned to their competitors on this trading floor. Most of these firms assign each of their important clients a dedicated telephone line, but it doesn't take long for the competition to figure out who calls on each line. "If somebody comes up with a new customer, you find out who it is and go after them," says a young mother who works the floor here from 3:00 A.M. until the market closes. "We might be friends with these people after work, go for a drink together, go to a movie together, but at work I'll cut your throat and you'll cut mine: whoever gets there first wins." Brokers, traders, and clerks crane their necks over each other's shoulders to see whose light is blinking on which phone. If that doesn't work, they look for clues in the trade itself. To those in the know, trading styles are as distinctive as animal tracks. For example, if the Shearson floor broker comes to market with a big order for "60-delta" options, the rest of the floor can be reasonably sure that Batif, a French fund management company, is the customer behind it.

The big man is picking up his phone, this time to make a call. He knows about the order that hit the floor in Chicago. He knows about the order from the French corporation just now moving through Philadelphia. He has an idea of which way the markets may move, and he's phoning a customer who might be interested in the other side of that trade.

The big man's name is Gene. He earned his college degree through night school while working as a journeyman printer, but printing didn't pay. He drifted to the Philadelphia exchange because he knew someone who worked there. Now he's a broker, running floor operations in currency options for the Bloom Staloff brokerage firm. He hits a button on the speed dial. Gene has programmed into the telephone a list of customers to call when big orders come to the floor. Because he is a broker and does not trade for his own account, he must have a customer lined up before he sends anyone onto the floor to trade. He'll give the customer, usually a bank or investment bank, a window into what is happening on this floor. If the customer likes the action enough to place a bet, Gene's firm will pocket a commission. If he's right, and if he's first, he'll have a chance. Three or four other brokers from other firms are hitting their speed dialers at the same time to call the same customer.

Most of these customers don't depend on Philadelphia. They trade far more frequently in the interbank market, where the biggest banks, insurance companies, and investment houses deal directly with each other. The money that moves through Philadelphia is nothing compared to what moves through the interbank markets. In 1992, the Philadelphia exchange celebrated its anniversary with the slogan "Trillion Dollar Decade." In the interbank market, over $1 trillion changes hands every day.

Yet the interbank market traders make their money in the same place as these floor traders—between *almost* and *immediately*. They're linked to the exchanges through men like Gene, always on the lookout for a chance to buy low or sell high. As a result, the prices in Philadelphia are always close to those in London, Chicago, or Tokyo. The law of one price is everywhere enforced. If the interbank traders want to keep a really big trade secret, they spread it around—do a piece with a bank, a piece with an investment house, a piece in Chicago, a piece in Philadelphia. Too big a piece in any one place might tip their hand and move the market against them.

Gene reaches an interested customer and quickly recaps the action on the floor. The customer tells him where the price has to be for an option position of this size, this type. Then the conversation turns to Greek. Gene is talking about delta, a mathematical abstraction relating the price change of the option to the price change of the currency underlying the option. Numbers, expiration dates, time values. Everything feeds into the interbank trader's computer. Only seconds have passed since the French corporation's order came in; Gene already has someone who'll buy part of it. He sends a trader sprinting to the floor. The ring closes, shouts; fists and fingers fly.

The traders here are not the stuff legends are made of, the market millionaires. "There's not a millionaire on this floor," says Gene. Their incomes range between $50,000 and $100,000 a year, though outstanding performers like Gene can take home half a million in a good year. Working stiffs from Philadelphia's neighborhoods, most look and talk as if they'd be just as much at home in a steel mill or dockyard, like the guys who graduated from high school with them. Some have college degrees, some don't; some go to night school, some don't bother. Hairstyles range from greasy punk spikes to baldness, and beer guts bulge over broad leather belts. To break the tension, a fat, crew-cut wit chaws a doughnut, washes it down with a Coke, and burps loudly enough to be heard over the shouting—then burps again, louder, just in case anyone thought the first was an accident.

These are the infantrymen of finance. Their work is face to face, hand to hand, and intimidation is a big part of success. "If I can get you to doubt yourself, back down, wander out of the ring, I can eat your lunch," says a young trader who has recently moved to Philadelphia from Chicago. In the riot of trading, misunderstandings happen. They are never harmless. The trader looking to fill a thousand-contract order in the heat of shouting and waving may miss his count and buy twelve hundred instead. Or the seller may only think he sold that two-hundred lot. Or two traders may bid for the same deal at the same time. A mistake can cost $100,000 a minute if the market is moving fast. Someone will win, and someone will lose, every time. It helps to be the kind of man no one will challenge. Not all of the traders top six feet, 250 pounds, but it helps if they do. Few women trade on the floor. The action gets so rugged that one of the most successful floor trading companies sends all of its new hires to a special intimidation training course to prepare them for the fray. "I've seen people walk off the floor and almost want to quit, and a lot of people do quit this business after a couple years. The tension isn't worth it, the payout isn't worth it, it's not worth it in the long term for health reasons," says Gene.

Like infantrymen, the floor brokers here execute orders without knowing the greater scheme into which the orders fit. Sometimes it's not clear for days why a customer took a certain action. When several big banks phoned in orders for put options on the yen in August 1993, the floor brokers just executed them. Put options gave these banks the right to sell yen, and would increase in value if the price of yen fell. It was unusual to see that kind of action in the yen, Gene says. The reason became clear a few days later, when the U.S. Treasury, the Fed, and the Bank of Japan intervened together to stop the strengthening of the yen and push its price down. That made the put options more valuable and brought handsome profits to those astute enough to know beforehand what the regulators were about to do.

At other times, it's all too clear why customers are calling. In the autumn of 1992 and the summer of 1993, the interbank currency option markets broke down. As Italy, Britain, and finally France abandoned their long-standing commitments to the European Monetary System's Exchange Rate Mechanism (ERM), option traders at some banks simply stopped answering the telephones. They knew that customers were calling to buy put options that would allow them to insure against the falling lira, sterling, and franc by giving them the right to sell the currencies at a favorable price. But selling put options during the collapse of the ERM would be like selling storm insurance in the middle of a hurricane. Those currencies were going in only one direction—down—and everybody knew it.

Meanwhile, the options exchange in Philadelphia kept running. So did the currency futures exchanges in Chicago. These exchanges typically function as a small adjunct of the interbank markets, but crisis magnifies their importance. In a trading pit, where traders are face to face, it's always possible to get a price. The price may not be good, but at least it's a price.

It was far from inevitable that the rearmost back room of the stock exchange in Philadelphia should play such an important role in the international financial system. Indeed, it was a role no one planned. The oldest organized stock exchange in the United States, the Philadelphia exchange was dying in the late 1970s, when a staffer invented the currency option. Now it is a major node in an international network of financial power. The network is a sort of vigilante posse strong enough to shatter the plans of pin-striped Ph.D.'s in Europe's capitals, breach the walls of Japanese financial protectionism, confound the U.S. president, and enforce the law of supply and demand wherever money moves.

On the last days of September 1993, the Philadelphia traders gathered together in Paris. It had been a triumphant year for them. To celebrate, they rented the Musée de Cluny, site of the world's finest collection of medieval art. Odine Pope's Philadelphia saxophone choir blew jazz through the millennial chambers where Roman colonists once cooled themselves after a dip in the bathing pools and where now the traders of Philadelphia dined. Above their heads, in an upper room, suspended from small gold chains, hung the crowns of the old Vandal kings.

Uncomfortable in their tuxedos, these traders had nonetheless fairly won their place beneath the crowns. They had taken a great risk and reaped a great reward. It was the option that made Philadelphia strong again.

Not since the invention of paper money has financial history seen an innovation with such impact. Central bankers compare the option to nuclear energy. It is unquestionably the most powerful and versatile of the new financial tools developed by the private markets to cope with economic chaos.

Yet the idea of options is older than Aristotle.[1] The first option was invented by a Greek philosopher named Thales of Miletus. Ridiculed for his poverty, Thales set out to prove that he was poor by preference, not by necessity. By reading the stars and the weather, Thales forecast a bumper crop of olives one year. Before the fruit began to form, he went around to all owners of olive presses and offered them a payment in advance for the right to rent their presses during the harvest, if he should need them. He also negotiated in advance the rent he would pay. When the great harvest came in, Thales paid the press owners the rent he had negotiated and charged the olive growers whatever he pleased, because he controlled all the presses. That ended the ridicule.

It is a short step from Thales of Miletus to the currency options at Philadelphia. Because Thales had negotiated the rent he would pay for presses well in advance of the bumper crop, and because no one else foresaw the great demand that would come at harvest time, he was able to negotiate a low rent. He didn't begin to pay the rent immediately. Instead, he paid a one-time fee for the right to rent the presses at harvest time. If by chance the crop failed, he was not obligated to rent the presses. He would have lost only the one-time payment.

Similarly, a currency option is merely the right to buy or sell a currency at a certain price at some point in the future. If the currency strengthens—that is, grows more valuable—the right to buy it cheaply is like Thales's right to pay a bargain rent for olive presses.

It's also possible to negotiate an option to sell. Suppose an owner of olive presses had feared a poor harvest. He* might have offered to

---

* *A note on gender and usage:* Some readers may question the use of the pronoun *he* or the syllable *man* used as a description of the human race, as a prefix (e.g., *mankind*), or as a suffix (e.g., *salesman*). Throughout this book, the pronoun *he* refers exclusively to men only when it is preceded by an identified male antecedent. Where the identified antecedent is female, the pronoun *she* consistently follows. In cases where there is no identified male or female antecedent, the pronoun *he* and the syllable *man* are used by default and, as it were, androgy-

buy an option from Thales. This option would give the press owner the right to rent his press to Thales. Then, when the harvest came in rich, the owner could have chosen not to exercise this option. In finance, an option that gives one the right to sell something is called a put option. If a currency weakens—that is, becomes less valuable—then the right to sell it for a good price is worth a lot. The option is a valuable right, but it is a right whose owner has no obligations to exercise.

Thales did not have to contend with government policies regulating the price of olive presses. In the financial world, traders do. In fact, a desire to evade inconvenient regulations has been one of the driving forces in the growth of the new financial markets.

For example, during the breakup of the European Exchange Rate Mechanism, when the French government had taken various measures to prevent speculation against the French franc, some of the most active buyers and sellers of French franc options were French corporations. At times, French multinationals initiated as much as half of the currency options business on the Philadelphia exchange. They could use options either to insure their balance sheets against a collapse of the franc or to speculate against their government's stated currency policy. All anyone in France had to do was pick up a phone and call a broker, and the order went to Philadelphia; the French government didn't have to know anything about it.

Philadelphia is not unique in this respect. Slightly different options traded in Chicago provided much the same advantages. But Philadelphia is where currency options were born.

Arnie Staloff, a self-described exchange bureaucrat, deserves the credit for bringing these powerful financial tools into the world. A short, round, genial man, he attributes his success to the fact that he didn't know any better than to try something new.

An outsider from the start, Staloff grew up in the only Jewish family in the small northern New Jersey town of Kenvil.[2] His father started out delivering newspapers for a living and eventually owned several trucks and a small convenience store where Staloff worked as a child. On a family trip to Florida, his father noticed a very successful off-price shoe store and decided to open a similar store in New Jersey. "We had

---

nously, to include both sexes. The reason for this choice is that the alternatives (*he/she, he or she, he and/or she, personkind,* and so forth) seem labored and awkward to this writer.

a two-story house, and the upstairs tenants moved out, so my father decided to put the shoe store there. On the first Easter, there were people waiting in line all the way down the street," Staloff recalls. The shoe store moved to a warehouse, but shortly after the move, his father had a heart attack. In those days, the only treatment for heart attacks was retirement in Florida, so the family moved south. But the old man couldn't rest. He bought a vending-machine route, and died of another heart attack just a year after the move.

Staloff was a mediocre student but a hard worker, holding down three jobs to put himself through the University of Miami. He also developed an interest in the stock market and spent his rare free time in a local stockbroker's office watching the tape and trading with a small stake. When he graduated from college in 1967, the height of the Vietnam War, he became draft bait. Because government regulations required companies to keep draftees' jobs open for them, most private companies weren't hiring draft-eligible young men. Staloff took a job with the U.S. Commerce Department's Bureau of the Census, and his draft board took so long to decide whether he was still draft eligible that by the time they made up their minds that he was, a new draft system was in place. The new draft lottery freed Staloff from any obligation to serve in the military. He shifted from the Census Bureau to the Securities and Exchange Commission (SEC), where he worked on the first inspections of stock exchanges in the United States.

Staloff had long been starstruck by Wall Street. But his eyes were opened as he saw how the exchanges struggled against progress. "When my wife and I had gotten engaged, we drove from Miami to New York to buy a wedding ring. I visited the New York and American Stock exchanges, and I was in awe of them and in awe of Wall Street. Now a lot of that awe was stripped away. They were close-knit old boys' clubs, closed shops, difficult to break into, and very poorly managed," he says.[3] For nearly two centuries, the stock exchanges had been neat little cartels, undisturbed by outside forces, conferring wealth and a comfortable if somewhat dubious status on their members. Now market pressures were beginning to destroy the old fixed-commission system that was essential to the survival of these cartels. Meanwhile, New York Stock Exchange member firms were failing left and right as they botched their efforts to automate, buying expensive computers that either didn't work properly or else required unattainable levels of business to break even. One firm, after putting all of its customer records into a new computer, fell apart when someone accidentally hit the wrong key and deleted everything.

Staloff left the SEC in 1971 and joined the Philadelphia Stock Exchange to handle automation and new product development. In order to learn more about new products, he went west to Chicago. What Paris was to art in the 1920s Chicago was to finance in the 1970s. The Chicago traders were breaking new ground in fields that no one had even imagined could exist, inventing new securities and new ways of trading them, putting ideas together with bold strokes of imagination.

One of the boldest was the equity option, also known as a stock option. This new security let investors get all the benefits of buying and selling stocks without actually buying or selling them. There were many disadvantages to buying or selling stocks. Buyers faced a risk that the stock price might fall and their stock would be worth less money. Sellers faced a risk that the price would rise after they sold. If they had "sold short," that is, borrowed shares in order to sell them, a rise in prices could be very costly, for the Wall Street wisdom about short selling is "He that sells what isn't his'n/buys it back or goes to prison." Options offered a way around all of these risks.

The buyer of a call option on a company's stock paid for the right to buy the stock at a certain price, called the strike price. If the price of the stock rose above the strike, the option buyer could demand delivery of the stock and sell it for a profit. Or he could skip the step of demanding the stock and just sell the option for about the same profit. The converse was true of options to sell—put options. If the stock price fell, the option holder could buy stock at the cheap market price and exercise the option to sell it at the more lucrative strike price. Unlike the old-fashioned short seller, the put option buyer risked only what he paid for the option. The short seller's potential losses could be huge. Yet buyers of put options enjoyed the same potentially unlimited gains while limiting their potential losses.

In effect, the option buyer paid the option seller to assume all of the risk. So options not only gave investors new ways to buy and sell stocks but also provided a form of insurance. For example, the owner of a big position in a stock could buy put options as insurance against a fall in the stock price. If the stock price fell, the put options would be more valuable, and the investor's losses on the stock would be cushioned by profits on the options.

"In Philadelphia, we always had to have some sort of gimmick to stay alive. Options seemed to be a reasonable way to go," Staloff recalls.[4] Unfortunately, by the time Philadelphia got the necessary regulatory approvals to introduce equity option trading, the Chicago Board Options Exchange and the American Stock Exchange had already listed options on most of the best stocks. "The biggest stock we had was Louisiana Land," he says.[5] By the late 1970s, options on such picked-over stocks weren't going to keep the Philadelphia Stock Exchange from following other regional exchanges into the twilight of history.

Staloff began to think about options on other things. Precious metals seemed a reasonable candidate in the inflation-bedeviled 1970s. But in 1979, the Hunt family of Texas used silver futures contracts in a scheme to corner the silver market. This scandal made it unlikely that regulators would approve new ways of speculating in silver and gold. That left currencies.

There had always been a need for international investors and businesspeople to buy and sell currencies. Often they bought and sold for future delivery. For example, an American company that sold a large order to a customer in Germany might well be paid in German marks. In order to turn the marks into dollars, the company (knowing when it expected to receive the marks) typically made an agreement with its bank to buy marks forward. The so-called forward agreement obliged both the bank and the company to exchange dollars for marks at a set price on a certain date.

Until 1971, there had been no way to buy and sell currencies without going through banks. However, in 1971, the International Monetary Market of the Chicago Mercantile Exchange was founded and began to trade currency futures. Futures were similar to forwards, in that they provided for future delivery of currency at a fixed price, but they did not require a bank to be involved. Like forwards, the futures contracts were firm commitments—there was no freedom for either side to reconsider. Getting out of a futures contract could be accomplished only by selling it to someone else.

It would have made sense to introduce currency options in Chicago, but the Chicago traders weren't about to do that. Why not? The Chicago exchanges were still dominated by agricultural commodity traders, and options on agricultural commodities had been illegal since 1934. "We felt we could have a niche in options," Staloff says.[6]

So he began working on currency options in the late 1970s. He confronted two major obstacles to introducing the product. The first was a complex regulatory labyrinth designed to meet the needs of the past and incapable of coping with the future. The second was bankers' reluctance to participate in the new market.

The explosion of new financial instruments out of Chicago had blown a gaping hole in the traditional framework for regulating markets. Until the 1970s, securities exchanges and commodities exchanges had been two entirely separate worlds. Commodities exchanges were regulated by the Department of Agriculture until 1974, when the Commodities Futures Trading Commission (CFTC) had been established. The Securities and Exchange Commission (SEC) had been set up by Franklin Roosevelt's New Dealers after the great market crash of 1929, to regulate the exchanges where stocks, bonds, and similar securities traded.

When the Chicago exchanges introduced financial futures, the two worlds collided. Stocks and bonds traded in New York, but stock and bond futures traded in Chicago. The SEC regulated the New York Stock Exchange and other securities exchanges, while the CFTC regulated the Chicago futures exchanges. However, a futures contract is really just another way of buying something. What's the difference between buying a stock today or agreeing to buy it for a certain price next month? The first transaction would be regulated by the SEC, the second by the CFTC. Conflict was inevitable. Both regulatory agencies were fiercely jealous of their powers, and both had powerful, wealthy constituencies behind them. The Chicago exchanges were already trying to block trading of options anywhere else.

Staloff's proposed currency option sailed directly into this political storm. It eventually took an act of Congress to allow the trading of currency options by a securities exchange. The Futures Trading Act of 1982 endorsed a compromise reached in 1981 by the chairmen of the CFTC and the SEC, known as the Shad-Johnson Accord. In essence, the compromise awarded to the CFTC jurisdiction over futures contracts and options on futures contracts. The SEC retained its jurisdiction over stocks and bonds, and also the power to regulate options on securities. Because the Philadelphia Stock Exchange was regulated by the SEC, before it could trade currency options, its attorneys had to prove to the satisfaction of Congress that options on currencies were securities even though currencies themselves were commodities.

While the legal battle was still unfolding, Staloff began to approach potential users of the new product. Banks were obvious candidates. But the idea of an option was something too new and too strange for most of them to consider. "In some cases, I was almost thrown out of their offices," he says.[7] Banks thought the product was complicated and difficult, even though they sometimes admitted that customers needed some form of protection against increasingly volatile exchange rate moves. In 1982, a consultant introduced him to Dennis Weatherstone, then treasurer and destined to become chairman of J. P. Morgan. "Dennis said that one time a very big customer had twisted the bank's arm and forced them to do a currency option as a form of protection against currency swings. They had no idea how to price it and ended up losing money," Staloff relates.

His big break came on February 17, 1982. For some time, financial executives of about twenty major multinational corporations had been meeting monthly in New York. They met in closed sessions, usually over dinner, to discuss problems that affected them all. In order to join this elite group, one had to be at least an assistant treasurer of a Fortune 500 corporation. Among the regular members of the group were financial executives from Mobil Oil, Colgate, Monsanto, Nabisco, Rockwell, Union Carbide, CBS, Kodak, Gulf, Johnson & Johnson, RCA, United Technologies, Schlumberger, and others. Outsiders attended by invitation only. Bankers and other vendors were not made welcome. But the group invited Arnie Staloff to talk about the new currency options.[8]

For American executives, the pressing financial problem of the day was the mercilessly strong dollar. In 1979, Paul Volcker had taken control of the American banking system as chairman of the Federal Reserve Board. His objective was to check the inflation that raged like jungle fever as a result of the Vietnam War. Volcker approached his task with unwavering determination. Appointed by President Carter, he tightened money severely, bringing on a deep recession that helped cost Carter the 1980 election.

The popular definition of inflation is "too much money chasing too few goods." It's fairly accurate. Until Volcker, the Federal Reserve had aimed to keep interest rates more or less stable. Volcker abandoned this old objective and focused his attention on shrinking the money supply. When the supply of anything, including money, shrinks, the price is apt to go up. The price of money is the interest rate, and it soared. But Volcker didn't seem to care how high interest rates went, so long as the money supply targets were met.

America's high interest rates caught the attention of international investors, and funds poured in to U.S. securities.

Demand for dollars surged, driving up the dollar's value on the currency markets. That meant real trouble for American manufacturers. Caterpillar provides one of the most vivid examples of just how much damage the strong dollar caused.

Finning Tractor & Equipment Company sold Caterpillar equipment to miners in the cold, mountainous wilds of British Columbia. The machines were so good that miners gladly paid 15 to 20 percent more than the price of a Japanese Komatsu tractor in order to own a Caterpillar. To say that business was strong is an understatement; Finning's chairman said, "You have to be an absolute genius to lose money as a Caterpillar dealer."[9]

Yet when the dollar strengthened, the bottom fell out of Finning's business. In order to buy Caterpillar tractors, the Canadians had to come up with dollars. Dollars, though, had gotten expensive, so expensive that a Caterpillar tractor now cost half again as much as a Komatsu. So even though Caterpillar hadn't changed its price in dollars, it seemed to have jacked them up massively in export markets that used other currencies. All over the world, the currency markets gave Komatsu a massive competitive advantage, almost as if Komatsu had cut its own prices in half.

Caterpillar was not alone. Soon journalists coined the phrase "Rust Bowl" to describe what had once been America's steel-making centers. Japanese and German automobiles became a familiar sight on American roads. Camera buffs decided to try Fuji film instead of Kodak. The strong dollar spared no American industry. No one had ever seen anything like it. It was impossible for business planners to draw up reliable budgets without knowing how currency exchange rates were going to affect prices and competition.

No wonder the news of the Philadelphia option stirred such strong interest among the financial executives who met in New York. Here was a product that could neutralize their biggest business risk. If they were doing business in Germany or the United Kingdom, they could buy an option that would guarantee them a rate of exchange six months or a year in the future. Just as they could buy insurance to protect their businesses against fires or floods, now they could buy insurance to protect their businesses against the rampaging dollar. They could plan with confidence again.

After the dinner, the corporate executives began to call their bankers. "Each major bank got a call from the dozen or so executives who were at that dinner," says Staloff.[10] The banks could no longer say that options couldn't be done. The corporate treasurers knew where and how they could be done, and they told the banks that they expected to be accommodated.

On December 10, 1982, the Philadelphia Stock Exchange began to trade the first currency options. The contracts were designed so that retail investors could use them to speculate on currency moves. Staloff continued to promote the new product. It was a humbling experience. When a small cable television station in California invited him to do an interview, he flew out to that coast and walked into a brightly painted room decorated with balloons. His hosts told him that they had just switched programming strategies: until a few days before, they had produced a children's program, but that wasn't making money, so they decided to become a round-the-clock financial news program instead. "The fellow who interviewed me had been the clown on the kid's show," Staloff says.[11]

A decade later, no one was laughing.

The markets invented by Staloff and others soon grew so big and powerful that all the governments of the world proved incapable of controlling them. Like the vandals who conquered Rome's empire, they broke down the bureaucratic empire that once controlled international finance. It was apt, then, that Philadelphia traders sat beneath the golden Vandal crowns in Paris, celebrating their trillion-dollar decade.

As they drank and danced, the interbank markets worked, moving a trillion dollars a day, every day, totally unregulated, largely beyond the reach of any law.

The Interbank Market

About the time that Arnie Staloff was promoting the new Philadelphia currency options, Lisa Polsky introduced options to Citibank.

She didn't quite fit the stereotype of a New York banker. In fact, she was something of an outsider. She had originally planned to be an anthropologist, and was studying at the University of Wisconsin when she met a student who interested her more than her coursework. A jazz drummer, he was studying painting but taking a course in economics just to learn something about the subject. "I took the economics course so I could sit next to him," she now admits.[12] The course changed her life. She switched her major to finance, changed her college to New York University, and married the drummer.

Her finance professor, Richard Levich, was a newly minted Ph.D. from the University of Chicago. There, on the windy shores of Lake Michigan, the boldest academic minds in economics and finance had built an intellectual temple in honor of free markets. Milton Friedman had been a voice in the wilderness for decades, crying out against the Keynesian decadence of the economic policy establishment. Now, in the 1970s, his prophecies had come true. The Bretton Woods system had failed, proving the Keynesians wrong about international economic planning. The United States was in the grip of a new phenomenon, called stagflation. This historically unprecedented concurrence of inflation and economic stagnation refuted core Keynesian ideas about government spending and social prosperity.

Friedman had taught the world that free markets worked better than government planners. Any society faces a multitude of choices about what it should do with its resources. Keynesians had believed that the choices were best made by an elite group of economic philosopher-kings. Friedman disagreed. He believed that the choices were best made by independent, free people. In his brand of economics, the market was a kind of parliament in which people voted on the value of different choices. Prices tallied the votes.

Younger, even more radically skeptical economists were now turning their attention to the details of how that parliament worked. Applying analytical techniques derived from nuclear physics and computer science, they scrutinized a hundred years of stock market prices in an attempt to discern some predictable pattern of behavior. But no pattern was evident. Out of their work came a theory that said stock market prices are utterly random and therefore impossible to forecast. They are random because they reflect all available information about the future. The only thing that changes them is surprising new information, but by definition, surprises are impossible to forecast. The stock markets were therefore efficient because they accurately and almost immediately reflected any new information about supply and demand for resources. Lisa Polsky's professor at New York University had chosen to study the currency markets in order to find out whether they were also efficient.

She graduated in midyear 1977. In her search for work, she learned some useful tricks, like calling companies late in the evening when only the top managers were likely to be working, or going in during the lunch hour when the receptionist was out and she could actually get to see a decisionmaker. That's how she got in to see the owner of a small company named Predex. Predex had developed a forecasting model and published a monthly magazine to predict exchange rates for corporations that needed such information in order to plan their budgets. As Lisa was talking about her undergraduate work at NYU, the owner of Predex picked up the telephone and called her professor, who happened to be a friend of his. On the strength of the professor's recommendation, Lisa received an immediate trial assignment. One of the magazine's contributors had written a half-page on the future direction of the British pound sterling. The publisher needed a full page. He asked Lisa to expand the pound sterling forecast.

Soon she was writing forecasts on a broad variety of currencies. "He paid by the country, so I expanded the number of currencies," she says.[13] Some countries weren't covered by the company's model, so Lisa used her own best judgment about the future in order to make predictions. In effect, her job was to prove her professor wrong by accurately forecasting the future direction of the currency markets—a feat that would be impossible if those markets were efficient and price changes random.

After six months, her professor telephoned. General Electric Corporation had called him looking for a Ph.D. student to help analyze currency exchange rate moves as part of a risk-management project. He recommended Lisa for the job, and although she had only a bachelor's degree, GE hired her. With the two part-time assignments from Predex and GE, she earned enough to live on and enjoyed much more independence than the average young New Yorker launching a financial career. When her professor called again and asked her to give a lecture at a conference he was organizing, she naturally consented. She spoke on currency forecasting. In the audience were two people from Citibank who were working on economic research to support the bank's currency trading activities. They offered her a full-time job, but she didn't want to work for a big, boring bank.

"I offered to take them on as a consulting client. But they made me an offer I couldn't refuse—$23,500 per year," she laughs.[14] The year was 1980, and Lisa would spend the next decade at Citibank. She was one of a handful of young New York currency traders who founded the interbank currency options markets.

At Citibank as at other banks, the currency trading function had traditionally been a sort of career Siberia. Young bankers with good prospects and valuable connections typically launched their climb to upper management through the ranks of the commercial lending officers. Real banking was all about arranging loans for important corporations. At J. P. Morgan, out of fifty newly hired bankers in the 1976 training program, only one chose to go into trading. At Bankers Trust, a manager recalls a trading-room atmosphere of "guys from Brooklyn who kept a picture of a naked lady by their phone and drank forty-two beers at lunch."[15]

Bank currency traders were rough, uneducated, backroom functionaries with no real prospects for advancement. The job demanded little more. Currency trading did not require much intelligence or perception during the Bretton Woods era. Banks bought and sold currencies on behalf of customers at official rates, and there was little room for creativity. Occasional crises in the system presented profitable trading opportunities, but they were not frequent enough to build a business around.

After the collapse of Bretton Woods came inflation, volatile interest rates, and currency turmoil. Important corporations were less and less likely to rely on bank loans, because they could borrow directly from investors in the new commercial paper markets. Banks also lost their main source of lendable money, because depositors flocked to money market funds and other high-interest-rate investments. At the same time as their traditional activities became less profitable, the currency and interest rate markets were becoming more volatile. Taking risks in the financial markets could replace corporate lending as a major source of revenue. But in 1980, bankers didn't really understand how the markets worked or whether it was possible to make money consistently by taking such risks. Two people who worked on Citibank's desk during Lisa's tenure recall one outstanding trader whose performance was so impressive that management even tolerated his cocaine binges and furniture-throwing tantrums. He was making money, and no one knew how to replace him.[16]

Lisa's first assignment at Citibank was to design a model of the markets that could forecast movements in exchange rates.

In six months, she put together a basic model and tested it on paper. It worked. She was introduced to the bank's treasurer, who was skeptical about her "paper profits." In order to get a real-life test of the model's performance, he offered her $20 million to trade, allowing her to place bets of up to $5 million on each of four major currencies.

"I was the only trader on the floor with a computer," she recalls, "a Radio Shack TRS 80." By today's standards, that was a laughably primitive, awkward box of a machine. Yet the other traders on the floor rightly saw it and Lisa as a threat to their way of life. "If she does well, who gets the bonus—IBM?" the head trader asked derisively.[17]

Then one day someone from Nestlé called with a problem. Based in Switzerland, Nestlé could only benefit from what looked like an endless strengthening trend in the U.S. dollar. Yet corporate policy required foreign currency revenues to be hedged. Was there a way to buy insurance to protect against a weak dollar but keep the benefits of a strong dollar? Lisa's boss liked the idea. He offered Nestlé a price at which the Swiss company could exchange dollars for Swiss francs, at its option, for five months in the future. Nestlé got its protection, and the bank pocketed a fee for what looked like a no-risk proposition.

In fact, the bank's risk was infinite. Although neither Lisa's boss nor Nestlé expected the Swiss franc to get stronger, they could easily have been wrong. If it had strengthened, the bank would have had to buy it at whatever price the market demanded in order to provide Nestlé with francs at the agreed-upon price.

When she heard about the deal, Lisa told the trader, "You've just done a currency option, and I have that model on my PC."[18] In 1973, three financial economists—Fischer Black, Myron Scholes, and Robert Merton—had published formulas for analyzing and quantifying the risks of trading options. It stood to reason that if options gave the buyer unlimited potential gain with very limited risk of loss, the seller was assuming all of the risk of loss. The so-called Black-Scholes model helped options traders understand what that risk was worth and how to protect themselves against loss. Polsky suggested that the head trader use the model to hedge his option trade.

At first, the head trader brushed her off. He thought that buying hedges against option positions was a waste of money. But it soon became clear that seat-of-the-pants option pricing would indeed expose the bank to massive risks. More and more corporations were demanding currency insurance. Options became a booming business. Science and math and computers were indispensable.

Meanwhile, a few other financial institutions had also begun to deal in currency options. Like Lisa at Citibank, the people responsible for the new activity were usually maverick outsiders. "If you come from an unconventional background, you find an area where you can make it on merit," Lisa says. "That's why there are a lot of women in this business. We went into a startup area, where no one had staked out a turf."

They were a tight-knit group, used similar option pricing models, and relied on each other for help in difficult circumstances. "If we called each other to buy an option, it was because we were up against a risk limit and really needed a hedge," she recalls. In such cases, the callers were vulnerable, and it would have been easy to take advantage. But gouging did not occur. "In the early days of the market, we needed to be able to trust each other," Lisa says.[19]

The interbank traders worked closely with the exchange. In fact, they were all really part of one market. Lisa and her peers at other banks often routed their trades through brokers at the Philadelphia exchange in order to have the protection of the exchange's clearinghouse. This was necessary because if they did business directly with each other, they were subject to credit limits. If the exchange clearinghouse stood between them, credit was not an issue.

As the options business grew, more institutions sought a piece of the action. In 1986, Bankers Trust Company hired a young currency options trader from Salomon Brothers. The young man's name was Andy Krieger. His trading would focus international attention on the hidden risks and heretofore-unimagined power of these new financial tools.

Krieger's background was eclectic. He had majored in philosophy as an undergraduate at the University of Pennsylvania, and went on to graduate studies in Sanskrit. He soon shifted to business, graduating with an MBA from the Wharton School in 1984.[20] When, years later, he had become a powerful and notorious force in the international currency markets, his early studies thickened the aura of mystery about him. British news accounts of a spectacular attack on the pound would describe him as a vegetarian, teetotaling devotee of Eastern religions.[21]

Krieger's trademark was big trades. Although the usual risk limit for a currency trader at Bankers Trust was about $50 million, McKinsey consultant Dominic Casserley says that Krieger's limit reached $700 million, almost a quarter of the bank's capital.[22] What's more, by using options, Krieger could leverage that $700 million into even bigger numbers. With a $100,000 investment in currency options, he could actually control $30 to $40 million in currency.

In his book *The Money Bazaar*, Krieger hints that in 1987 he used options to sell short the entire money supply of New Zealand.[23] Even allowing for some hyperbole in that account, independent press reports about the trade said that the central bank of New Zealand had telephoned Bankers Trust to complain about Krieger's extraordinary speculative attack on the kiwi.

Although Krieger never claimed to be able to move markets over the long term, his trading brought into the glare of publicity an old technique for causing short-term market moves. Called "ramping," this technique is illegal on most organized exchanges but impossible to control in the unregulated interbank currency markets. Traders who concentrate massive sums of capital on thinly traded markets, such as the market for the New Zealand kiwi, can actually make the market jump or fall in the direction they want it to go. Other traders, seeing the sudden move in prices, may join in. The move may last less than a day, but the trader who initiated it has already planned how to profit when it snaps back again. Justifiably or not, many traders in the currency markets believed this was Krieger's trading style. So whenever otherwise inexplicable moves occurred in exchange rates, rumors circulated of another Krieger coup. In 1990, for example, the newsletter *International Reports* identified him as the force behind a puzzling move in the German mark.[24]

However, he did more than simply demonstrate how a trader could use options to attack a major currency with very little risk to himself. He also exposed a serious weakness in the banking system. Krieger left Bankers Trust shortly after the New Zealand incident, reportedly dissatisfied that a $3 million bonus for the year did not adequately reward his contribution to the bank's bottom line. After his departure, federal auditors discovered some discrepancies in how Bankers Trust had valued its options portfolio. The regulators forced the bank to knock about $80 million off its reported earnings for 1987. Even after the write-down, Bankers Trust emerged with over $500 million in currency trading profits for the year.[25] But the fact that the bank was so obviously incapable of understanding Krieger's complex options positions was a serious embarrassment, especially since trading of such positions was on its way to altogether replacing lending as the bank's main business.

Krieger has left a clear mark on the history of the new financial markets. He proved that in the quest for speculative profits, even the world's biggest and most important banks would allow a trader to commit vast sums to trading strategies whose risks his managers could neither measure nor understand. The incident raised serious questions about how much risk traders at other banks may have taken and who, if anyone, was in control of the international financial system. Regulators remembered the collapse of a Viennese bank that some economists blamed for precipitating the Great Depression, and wondered whether the world might be teetering at the brink of another financial collapse.

Rocket Science

In his small, sparsely furnished office at Goldman Sachs, Fischer Black does not share those concerns. Tall, pale, and thin, he has a deliberate manner of speech and a curious, mute laugh that makes one think of a merry undertaker. In fact, he has been a sort of grim reaper: a reaper of grand illusions. Black's career has been one of quiet, methodical demonstrations that strip away investment errors and illusions. His accomplishments neatly recapitulate most major themes in the development of the science that has enabled private risk markets to replace the coordinated plans of government functionaries as the world's best hope for economic stability.

Born in 1938, Black developed an appreciation for risk at a young age. As a boy, he made rockets, mixing his own gunpowder from potassium chloride, charcoal, and sulfur and stuffing it into cardboard tubes. He rigged batteries to make a launcher that allowed him to keep his distance from the rocket as it ignited, went up, and then exploded. One day, though, Black heard that a friend mixing gunpowder in a glass bowl had somehow set off an explosion that drove shards of glass into his abdomen. After assessing the risk and the return of his hobby, Black decided to pursue other interests.[26]

Most of them were bookish. Although he didn't hesitate to experiment with the things he read about, young Black was inclined to skepticism. While in his early teens, he read Aldous Huxley's *Doors of Perception* and was so impressed by the author's account of consciousness-expanding hallucinogens that he went to a neighborhood druggist with a friend and they ordered some mescaline sulfate. "In those days, nobody knew anything about this stuff," he relates. "It was perfectly legal, but it was expensive. The druggist gave us some little white crystals, and we both ceremoniously consumed them. My friend said he had all these perceptual things that Huxley had described. I didn't feel a thing."[27]

He applied to only one university, Harvard, because he liked to sing and Harvard had a glee club. He found precious little glee in it. "They did all these old baroque pieces, and I was more casual about it. Barbershop quartet appealed to me," he explains.[28] On the academic front, he bounced through several majors, trying French, psychology, social relations, math, and chemistry before graduating in 1959 with a degree in physics. In graduate school, he worked on artificial intelligence, completing his thesis on a deductive question-answering system. He took his Ph.D. in 1964, and after a short stay at a computer research firm designing an electronic equivalent of a library, he moved on to applied work with the consulting firm Arthur D. Little. There he met Jack Treynor, one of the seminal figures in the new financial science.

Besides practical consulting work, Treynor was doing research on the Capital Asset Pricing Model, a theory to explain the relationship between risk and securities prices. He spoke with Black about his work, and Black was entranced by the notion that a multitude of investors, with a multitude of expectations about the future, some seeking risk, some seeking safety, eventually cause prices to reach a state of equilibrium in which risk and return are perfectly balanced. "The notion of equilibrium in the price for risky assets had great beauty for me," Black later said.[29] So he changed disciplines again, from computers to finance.

In 1968, he began to work with Myron Scholes, who had recently received a Ph.D. in finance from the University of Chicago and was teaching at the Massachusetts Institute of Technology. Robert Merton, who had done graduate work in engineering mathematics, soon made the duo a trio. Although he had not yet earned his Ph.D., Merton was on the faculty at MIT's Sloan School of Business. He brought a more sophisticated understanding of mathematics to the work of Black and Scholes and helped them explain the importance of time in the pricing of risk. The Black-Scholes option pricing model appeared in 1973.

Black almost immediately took his work to the markets, selling sheets of scientifically determined option prices to traders on the newly established Chicago Board Options Exchange. Over the next two decades, the option pricing model he had codeveloped would be much refined. Other researchers would expand and adapt it to cover a much wider array of risks than Black, Scholes, and Merton had ever considered. Like the original modelers, these researchers would draw on a variety of sciences to engineer a flexible yet strong tool for exploiting profit opportunities while defending against risk.

Their work would quickly make its way from academia into the "real world." Once risk could be measured and priced, it could be bought and sold. This was a most subtly subversive contribution.

Andy Krieger's attack on the New Zealand kiwi was but a small precursor of the massive pressures brought to bear in 1992 and 1993 on the European Monetary System.

An entire economic empire fell to the vandals like Krieger. In its place came an open, unsystematic financial donnybrook whose "only sure beneficiaries are those manning the trading desks and inventing the myriad of new devices to reduce risk—or to facilitate speculation," as former Fed chairman Paul Volcker put it.[30]

In the nineteenth century, an aide to Bismarck wrote, "High finance trembles in its boots whenever there is some political complication." But in the 1990s, it is the politicians who tremble at financial complications. Whether the politician is French prime minister Balladur, stunned by the muscle that forced his country to abandon its commitment to the European Monetary System; or U.S. president Bill Clinton, unable to halt the weakening dollar; or China's Deng Xiao Ping, crushing political dissent while rolling out a red carpet of incentives for international investors; or Boris Yeltsin, promising to put the Russian people through painful economic reforms in order to secure loans from the International Monetary Fund, politicians these days have no doubt where the power lies.

It has been a quiet but momentous revolution, and a long time in coming.

Transitions

The shift in power from government to the markets has been under way for hundreds of years, although it has become most dramatically irreversible only recently. In the distant past, control of money was a royal prerogative, and kings did not hesitate to manipulate the currency when it suited their purposes. Although currency manipulation, usually by debasement, brought short-term revenues to the crown, it played havoc with the economy because it led to higher prices. Foreigners were also unwilling to accept money from countries whose sovereigns were inclined to debase the coin, which made commerce difficult. So merchants occasionally bribed their sovereigns in order to prevent debasement of the coin of the realm. It was cheaper for the merchants to make a single large payment—in the form of a bribe—rather than cope with inflation and commercial payment problems.

As time went on, though, merchants and traders gradually gained power. The Enlightenment saw a new philosophy of government, one that restricted the powers and prerogatives of royalty. As power shifted from the aristocracy to the plutocracy, the kings were corralled by laws or gotten rid of altogether. By the nineteenth century, the gold standard governed the monies of Europe. Under the gold standard, governments had very little leeway in monetary matters. It was the age of laissez-faire and of booms and busts. The gold standard provided stability, but the poor paid a high price.

Then another power shift occurred, this time from the wealthy capitalists to the poor. The breakdown of international order in World War I, combined with the spread of marxism, threatened to demolish civilization as Europe knew it. It was clear that if the masses did not have a stake in the system, the system could not survive. Keynesian economic theory provided the intellectual justification for abandoning the gold standard. Once again the safety and soundness of currency were in doubt. By 1971 the breakdown of the Bretton Woods agreements removed the last vestiges of discipline over the international financial system.

For three decades after World War II, markets vied with states for power over money. Like the kings of medieval Europe, governments debased their currencies, and traders scrambled to protect themselves. But in the 1970s, the invention of financial futures gave the markets historically unprecedented sway over the value of currencies. The development of international communications and easy access to powerful computers allowed traders to anticipate government actions. The old kings who debased their coins got a short-term advantage from doing so. Now, states that choose to inflate their currencies gain nothing: the discipline of the market immediately reduces their currency to an appropriate value.

Because money is so central to the function of a state, it is difficult for governments to accept the fact that they no longer really control it. The breakdown of the European monetary system was the most dramatic recent example of the new power of the markets.

The following few chapters will explore the historical background of the contemporary financial system.

CHEATERS

The language of finance and economics has always borrowed from the physical sciences. We speak of the circulation of capital by analogy to the circulation of blood, of equilibrium by analogy to Newtonian physics, and so forth. Most of these analogies are rooted in the science of the seventeenth and eighteenth centuries, and common to the science of those centuries was a tidy assumption that forces beneath a reasonable magnitude could be safely ignored. The assumption lasted well into the twentieth century and continues to guide much good scientific work. Thus, a young girl skipping double Dutch in Vancouver need not be factored into the equations of seismologists attempting to predict the next great earthquake on California's San Andreas fault. Recently, though, scientists engaged in chaos research have called into doubt the proposition that the negligible can safely be neglected. Perhaps, they say, it is even true that the flapping of a butterfly's wings in Beijing can cause tornadoes in Texas.

Certainly, a brief glance into the history of finance demonstrates that few actions are so minor as to be safely ignored in all cases. Without stretching the point too far, it may even be suggested that a young man removing his shirt in London toward the end of the seventeenth century caused the collapse of international financial order in the twentieth.

Three centuries ago, on a hot summer evening, the young man lounged on the grass in Kensington Gardens, London. The fifth of many children in a destitute but ancient family, poor Edward Wilson was unaware of the woman who had been observing him as he sought to cool himself, or of her desire. She directed her maid to approach him and converse lightly about things of no importance before proposing that he go to St. James Park the following night, at midnight, for an assignation. Wilson could not possibly have imagined the consequences of his consent when he agreed to make the rendezvous.

When he arrived, the lady awaited him, wearing a mask. She hid no more than her face from him. "My Lady was so charmed with her lover that till two of the clock she did not think of retiring," the maid later wrote.[1] A few days later, the maid appeared at the hovel where young Edward Wilson slept. She gave him a fortune in gold—1,500 guineas—and instructions from her mistress that he should obtain the most luxurious accommodations there were and spare no expense on servants and livery. "Be everything that's great and noble," she said. "To those that have money all things may be performed with expedition."[2]

The gift came with two warnings. "All you have to perform on your part," said the maid, "is to reserve yourself entirely for her, and never by an indiscreet curiosity endeavor to discover her. If you enquire and succeed in that enquiry, you must not only lose her but your life also."[3]

Finally, there were instructions for further meetings. Wilson was to meet the maid at midnight, at Pall Mall, and would be led by her into his lady's chamber. Within the chamber would be a single light. It was forbidden for him to use this light to see his lady's face: "Be satisfied that she's young, and by some thought the handsomest. Make use of your good fortune. I suppose sleep will not be your business. When the clock strikes two, rise and be gone! A chair will wait to carry you home. Thus may you be blessed both by riches and beauty. And for the continuation of both that entirely depends on yourself." With these words, the maid left him.[4]

Young Wilson followed the instructions as well as any man might, and was soon the subject of innumerable conversations throughout the coffeehouses of London. His wealth astonished all. He maintained a household suited to the richest nobleman, provided dowries for his sisters, and kept coaches and horses and one of the finest tables in the city. No one could discover the secret of his fortune. He did not gamble; nor was he ever seen with women. When asked, he would say only that no matter how long he might live, he had enough money to maintain himself in opulence. Some speculated that he was a jewel thief who had let another man be executed for his crimes; others, that he was a spy for France's Sun King; and still others, that he had discovered the philosophers' stone and could turn base metal into gold.

His mistress did not demand so much of his time as to become an annoyance to him. But she succeeded, perhaps too well, in piquing and holding his interest. One evening he swore to her in her chambers that no matter what the cost, he must know her identity. She refused to divulge it. He demanded, as a test of love, that she reveal herself. She would not, and after his departure cried to her maid, "Is he not satisfied that I love him more than I ought, without I love him as much as I can?"[5]

The next evening, the maid appeared at Wilson's splendid house. His lady could see him no more, she said, yet would graciously maintain him in the style to which he had become accustomed. Wilson, in a fatal outburst, declared that he had already discovered the lady's identity. During one of their trysts, he had given her a ring. Riding through Hyde Park, he had seen that ring on the finger of Elizabeth Villiers, as her carriage passed and she leaned out of the window to look at him.

Thirty-seven years of age, more intelligent than beautiful, Elizabeth Villiers was the favorite of the reigning British monarch, William III, and would one day become the countess of Orkney—but not if it were known that she had made the king a cuckold. She did not trust Wilson to keep her secret.

Also resident in London at the time was a young man named John Law.

The son of an Edinburgh goldsmith, Law had begun working in his father's business when he was only fourteen. His father, William Law, was one of the most prominent citizens of Scotland. Like others of his profession, he appeared in public wearing a scarlet cape, a cocked hat, and a cane. In the shop, he worked with his sleeves rolled up, making articles of gold and silver. However, the work of the goldsmith was beginning to consist less of metal crafting and more of money lending. In Scotland, the goldsmith shops were about to give birth to something new in the world: the banking industry.

Young John Law was a math prodigy and quickly mastered the calculations of risk and return involved in lending. Then he plunged into the theories of money and credit and the mathematics of probability.

Not long after John entered the business, his father developed a serious case of gallstones, traveled to Paris to consult a famous surgeon, and died, probably from an infection contracted during surgery. John inherited a splendid estate.

He put his mathematical talents to work calculating odds in the gambling houses of Edinburgh and found he could win consistently.[6] He also learned tennis and fencing and, according to one contemporary account, became "nicely expert in all manner of debauchery."[7] A favorite of the ladies, he earned the sobriquets Beau Law and Jessamy John. Edinburgh soon proved too small to contain him, and he made his way south to London.

There he continued to gamble successfully. He also installed a mistress in his lodgings at St. Giles-in-the-Fields.

Another apartment on the premises was occupied by the sister of Edward Wilson, whose sense of propriety was offended by Law's domestic arrangements. Wilson moved his sister to other quarters, giving a blatant and dramatic snub to Law and his lady.

Whether at the instigation of Elizabeth Villiers, who wanted to be sure Wilson would never betray her secret, or of the landlady, who feared for the reputation of her house, or simply because he wanted to avenge the insulting snub to his mistress, Law challenged Edward Wilson to a duel.

Law and Wilson met in the deserted neighborhood of Bloomsbury Square, and Wilson died there. As he lay bleeding, he handed his house keys to a friend and directed him to burn all of his papers. When the friend entered the lodgings, however, he found no papers at all. Had an agent of the king's mistress preceded him? No one knows for certain.

This duel was a critical point in the financial history of Europe. Law was promptly arrested, convicted of murder, and sentenced to be hanged. Perhaps the king's mistress interceded for Law, or perhaps the king considered dueling an honorable way for gentlemen to settle their differences. Whatever his reasons, he granted Law a royal reprieve. Yet an ancient, nearly forgotten statute allowed the family of a murder victim to challenge the king's pardon, and they did so.

While Law was in jail waiting for the court to decide whether or not the pardon should stand, he filed through four bars of his cell window. Before he could escape, he was caught and put in irons. His friends, possibly with the help of Elizabeth Villiers, smuggled in new files, and drugged the guard. On New Year's Day 1695, John Law slipped out of his cell and dropped thirty feet from the walls to the street. He sprained an ankle, but someone helped him into a waiting coach and drove him to a hideout near the sea.

Within days, he was on a ship headed for Amsterdam.

In Amsterdam, he made a living from cards and dice. But he also began to develop a theory of banking and money creation that anticipated Keynes by two centuries.

Money had traditionally meant gold or silver.

In Law's time, it often meant not physical gold but a piece of paper given as a receipt by a goldsmith. The paper could be exchanged for gold by the bearer. Since the notes were receipts for gold, the amount of notes in circulation did not exceed the amount of gold in vaults. The notes were as good as gold, and easier to carry. After a while, people didn't necessarily bother to take them to the goldsmith and exchange them for gold. They paid their bills with notes. Everyone believed in them, accepted them, and used them.

As long as people believed that the notes were as good as gold, they would use them instead of gold. It was the belief, not the gold, that mattered. Law figured that it ought to be possible to dispense with gold altogether and develop a money based just on belief. There would certainly be advantages in such a scheme. For example, when an economy lagged, bankers could crank up the money supply by issuing more money, whether or not they had gold. As people spent the money, they would create more jobs, more production, more employment, more prosperity. This was roughly the same sort of logic that led Keynes to propose massive public spending to help the world out of the Great Depression of the 1930s. However, Law was the first economist to work out and put in practice a theory for a managed money supply. He suggested that money could be created, just like that—out of nothing but faith. This meant that the state could actually make itself prosperous by managing the money supply.[8]

When Law returned to Scotland in 1700, after thinking about this idea for several years, he proposed that the Scottish Parliament take a first step toward his vision by chartering a national bank that could issue paper money. The paper money would be backed, in a sense, by land. Money would be printed in proportion to the value of the land in Scotland. Unlike gold and silver, land did not change in quantity, so the money supply would not be compelled to grow and shrink unmanageably according to the supply of metal. Parliament rejected his proposal. Meanwhile, in London, the family of Edward Wilson still demanded his execution on the old charge of murder, so he could not propose his plan to the English Parliament. Law ached to test his theory. He returned to the Continent.

He spent fourteen years gambling in the capitals of Europe, thinking and rethinking his theory of money, and looking for a monarch who would be enlightened enough to adopt it.

Certainly, monarchs had good reason to look for some alternative to metal money. History had proven that gold and silver were inconvenient. Law offered an appealing solution to this dilemma. In order to understand the eventual appeal of Law's system, it helps to consider how powerfully gold and silver had influenced the development of society and the lengths to which kings had already gone to slip their golden fetters.

The supply of gold and silver ebbed and flowed over the centuries, and the fluctuations in supply of these precious metals had changed history. When bullion was scarce, as in the so-called bullion famine of the fifteenth century, Europe literally ran out of money. All of money's roles—store of value, medium of exchange, regulator of economic activity—had to be filled somehow. In order to get money, people melted down their household silver and gold. Others were forced to resort to barter. In Germany, pepper became a substitute money to fill the role that bullion had played. *Pfefferman*, or "pepperman," was a synonym for *banker*.[9]

Then, when the Spanish conquest of the Americas loosed a flood of silver into the markets of Europe, the bullion famine suddenly ended. Now there was a glut of money. In fact, the easy availability of money destroyed the old feudal order. Instead of paying obligations to one's lord by spending time in his service, a vassal could pay a tax in coin instead. The abundance of gold and silver dissolved the old feudal ties, eroded the very basis of society, and indirectly set the stage for the revolutions that occurred three centuries after Columbus.

Oddly, though, whether gold was scarce or plentiful, there never seemed to be enough of it to satisfy the needs of the government. For from the years of the bullion famine to the present day, in whatever form money had existed, and whether the government was in the hands of kings or bureaucrats, states could be relied upon to be consistent in this: they regularly attempted to deceive the public about the value of their money. While the money supply was constrained by the link to gold and silver, that deception required some elaborate trickery.

The Hundred Years' War, which lasted from the 1330s until 1453, provides some of the most dramatic examples of monetary sleight of hand ever recorded in history. The medieval dictum that "the king should live off his own" was but one bright spot of light emanating from what are somewhat unaccountably called the Dark Ages. The phrase refers to the fact that, as late as the fourteenth century, the French king had very limited powers to take money from the people. He had the right to collect rent on his own land and could collect a few time-honored taxes: a poll tax, a salt tax, road tolls, and a mint tax. However, any other taxes had to be approved by the representative assemblies.[10] This made it difficult for the French kings to raise money, buy arms, bribe allies, and finance the unceasing wars they fought either to gain new lands or to defend their own right to the throne. A French king could not borrow, because no banker trusted him to repay loans. He could not tax, because the French representative assemblies refused to consent to taxes.[11] So in many cases, the kings raised money by means of a royal confidence game.

On St. Crispin's Day 1415, England's erstwhile playboy prince, Henry V, smashed the armies of France's crazy King Charles VI at Agincourt. As Henry moved south toward Paris, he benefited greatly from internal strife between France's two major factions, the Armagnacs and Burgundians. The Armagnacs and Burgundians tried to patch up their differences at a peace conference, but instead of talking, they fought, and the Armagnacs killed John the Fearless, duke of Burgundy. The new duke of Burgundy promptly threw his support behind the English king. This isolated the dauphin, heir to the French throne, who had supported the Armagnacs. The dauphin's isolation soon grew worse, when his mother, the queen, declared that the king was not his father. As a bastard, he had no right to the throne.

The dauphin withdrew from Paris. His coffers had already been a casualty of the struggle between the Armagnacs and the Burgundians. The Burgundians abolished taxes that had previously been approved for the Crown and cut him off from the royal rents on lands in Normandy and around Paris. He needed around 500,000 livres to fight the war, but his income was down to about 60,000. So he levied a tax that didn't have to be approved by the assembly—the inflation tax.[12]

The dauphin had lost a great deal, but he still controlled some of France's twenty-four mints. He persuaded people to bring silver to the mint to be coined. How? Traditionally, a certain number of coins had been struck from a given weight of silver. Some of the coins had been kept by the king, as his compensation for the service of making the coins. The dauphin offered to give people more coins for their silver. Of course, there's a limit to how many silver coins can be made from a given weight of silver. Moreover, the dauphin was trying to raise money. So instead of giving people pure silver coins, he mixed the silver with base metal. People with bullion to sell didn't object. They used the base coins quickly to buy supplies or pay debts.

What about the people who received the coins as payment for goods or in settlement of debts? They didn't realize, at first, that the coins they received contained higher and higher quantities of base metal and less and less silver. This was because the dauphin didn't publish or announce the actual silver content of the coins. All people knew was that the price of silver had gone up—it was worth more coins per unit of weight. In order to determine whether the coins they received had been debased, people would have had to "assay" their coins. This was a complicated process that required the skills of a silversmith. The dauphin made it more difficult by changing not only the fineness of coins but also their weight and by timing his debasements carefully. Debasement did not always accompany the announcement of a change in the mint price of silver. Sometimes there was a lag, so the public was kept off balance.[13] Between 1418 and 1423, the dauphin raised the nominal value of the currency by 3,500 percent.[14]

The dauphin was not alone in debasing the currency. His adversaries also used the tactic. In 1418 alone, debasement had provided more than 500,000 livres to Burgundy and Charles VI.

Of course, pumping more money into an economy usually leads to inflation. Inflation certainly did come, but the public was slow to recognize that bad money was responsible. A Paris merchant's diary blames price increases on war, shortages, the siege of Paris, and almost incidentally the weak currency. Even the mint masters seem to have been taken in. Although they knew full well how little silver was in the coins they were making, they did not press to have their wages indexed to the price of silver until 1419.[15] Others were, of course, slower to recognize why their wages, payments, rents, and receipts—in short, their money—didn't buy enough to live on anymore. Eventually, though, the public did catch on. By 1421, Paris was in the grip of hyperinflation. People no longer trusted coins and didn't want to carry them.

Debasing the currency worked in the short term, though, and that lesson was not lost on other monarchs.

The dauphin exploited the power to coin money more than any of his ancestors or any of his contemporaries. No one had ever debased a currency with such vigor. Although the kings of England also took some liberties with the pound sterling, they seemed almost timid by comparison with the dauphin. Then Henry VIII took the throne in England, and in his voracity managed to eclipse even the dauphin—so much so that he is remembered by economic historians as the perpetrator of the "Great Debasement."

Henry VIII inherited from his father a reasonably stable currency, and during the early years of his reign, he was a model of probity, in economic as in other matters. This was the king who received the title "Defender of the Faith" from Pope Leo X for writing *Assertio Septem Sacrementorum*, a lucid critique of Martin Luther's new religious doctrines. There was no one to award him the title of "Defender of the Money," but he deserved it. He has won the praise of monetary historians for his restraint; other monarchs in other lands looked on currency debasement as a routine source of royal revenue. Not he. Henry VIII had scruples.

But Henry seems to have abandoned all scruples when he abandoned Catherine of Aragon, the first of his six wives. He not only turned from but vehemently turned against all that he had built and defended in the morning of his reign. Breaking with the pope, who refused to approve his divorce of Catherine, Henry launched a bloody persecution of Roman Catholics that would endure for centuries. He confiscated monastic lands and silver to enrich his treasury and fund new wars in France. When he could not confiscate enough, he turned against the currency. Monetary historians who praise the young Henry condemn the mature king for the Great Debasement. "If we could forget that he certainly began it as a deep-laid scheme in time of peace, we should be compelled to point out that he did no more than inflate his currency when England was engaged in a serious war," wrote Sir Albert Feavearyear in his history of the pound sterling.[16]

By 1542, a rumor was going around London that the coinage might be altered. Word had apparently leaked out of the mint, where officers had received orders to obey the Privy Council's forthcoming directions with respect to coinage even if they were contrary to the law. Nothing had yet been publicly announced, but the king was secretly buying silver. It was a classic case of trading on inside information. In fact, the king planned to raise the price of silver, and so he was buying all that he possibly could before the price went up. After the king had stockpiled all the silver he could lay his hands on, he announced an increase in the mint price.

Before the price increase, the mint would stamp 145.94 groats out of a pound of silver. They were worth £2.43. The mint returned groats worth £2.38 to the owner of the silver and kept £0.05 as a tax (called seignorage) that went to the king. The newly announced price for silver was to be £2.64 per pound. But the announcement left something out—the new groats contained 30 percent less silver than the old groats. The king kept the difference.[17]

What did he do with the money he had thereby swindled from his people? By the mid-1540s, Henry was at war on two fronts, on the Continent and in Scotland. He was borrowing at interest rates as high as 16 percent. He sold off the confiscated church lands, mortgaged the royal domains, and eventually seized all the lead in the kingdom to sell it for export. Debasing the currency was just another source of easy money. However, he didn't just swindle the people who brought silver to the mint. He also swindled people who were putting their lives on the line to defend his kingdom. Henry VIII used some of the first of the debased coins to pay the soldiers fighting for him on the Scottish front.

The tactic worked so well that Henry repeated it several times during the latter years of his reign. By the end, coins contained so little silver that they had to be "blanched," or coated with silver, so that they would shine. The shine soon rubbed off when they passed into circulation, and the red base metal showed through. A rhyme of the period goes, "These testons look red, how like you the same?/'Tis a token of grace: they blush for shame."[18]

Henry VIII made over £1 million in direct profits on the Great Debasement. The inflation caused by the debasement gave him an added windfall: he had borrowed heavily and could repay his debt in nearly worthless coin. Henry died in 1547, but the inflation did not die with him. The burden of paying for his excesses fell most heavily on those least able to carry it. In 1549, in Norfolk, Devon, and Cornwall, the peasants revolted. Their complaints: the cost of living, the enclosure laws, and the religious changes. Henry's heir, Edward VI, attempted to fix the prices of grain, butter, cheese, poultry, and other commodities, but conditions continued to deteriorate. By 1551, prices had doubled.[19] The inflation set in motion by Henry VIII raged for almost two decades. It was finally checked in 1560 by Queen Elizabeth, with the counsel of the redoubtable Sir Thomas Gresham.

Debasement continued to be an expedient recourse, however, and over a century later, when John Law escaped from prison, the value of the nation's money was again under attack.

In 1695, the philosopher John Locke, author of *An Essay concerning Human Understanding* and *The Reasonableness of Christianity*, applied his rational, empirical skills to the analysis of the monetary standard of Britain in a pamphlet entitled *Further Considerations concerning Raising the Value of Money*.

At the time, much of Britain's money supply consisted of clipped coins. It was very common for entrepreneurs to cut away the edges of coins, collect the scraps, and eventually melt them down to recover the precious metal.[20] Thus, although the face value of a coin might have indicated that it was worth a certain amount of gold or silver, in fact, by repeated clipping and trimming, the actual amount of valuable metal in the coin had been reduced. In addition to the clipped coins, an immense volume of paper banknotes had been issued by the newly established Bank of England. Inflation had taken hold, commodity prices had begun to soar, and a frenzy of speculation occurred in the stock market.

In this context, a proposal had been made to recoin the nation's money, and there were two schools of thought about how to value the new coins. One group, noting that English money had in fact depreciated and would buy less silver than previously, suggested that the new coins be valued according to what the old coins could actually buy. In other words, since a pound didn't buy what a pound used to buy, no one should pretend that it was worth as much as a pound used to be worth. Debtors had had their load lightened by depreciation because most of the debts had been drawn up when the pound was worth more. The king was the biggest debtor, of course, but there were others, notably the tenant farmers who paid their rent in accord with old agreements.

The other school of thought was led by John Locke. On his side were most of the major landowners. They resisted any such admission that the value of the nation's money had in fact fallen. Locke argued that a depreciation would rob landowners and creditors of their just receipts. He overlooked or refused to recognize that depreciation had in fact already occurred. He was really advocating a reversal of the currency's decay, in order to restore the virtuous old standard. Locke brought something new to the way people thought about money— the idea that money should have some stability, some enduring value, so that agreements and contracts denominated in money would mean the same thing from year to year.

This idea was unprecedented. Never before had people thought of the value of the coin as somehow sacred and unchangeable. The king was all-powerful. He made the coins, using however much silver or gold as he pleased, and changed his mind about it whenever it suited him. No one had the right to dispute him.

After Locke, however, the pound sterling became a fixed, immutable quantity of gold bullion, even when the pounds in circulation were paper notes. The gold value of the pound would be defined by Sir Isaac Newton in 1717. "The sovereign, by these reforms, saw his monetary prerogatives diminished to that of a keeper of weights and measures," says one commentator.[21]

This may be the single most graphic example of the fading power and prestige of the throne. In both political and economic spheres, the sovereign had failed to deliver a constant and reliable rule. John Locke recognized the need for a sort of justice and clearly saw that justice was not forthcoming from the king. The king had abused his allegedly divine right to rule and had trampled on the natural rights of his subjects. The subjects rose up and hemmed him in with laws. The struggle between ruler and ruled would continue, though, both in England and abroad. The course of this battle for power could always be discerned most clearly through an examination of the state of the money.

If the power of the English throne was waning, that of the French had never been stronger, and in his wanderings through Europe's casinos, John Law happened to make the acquaintance of certain French nobles. Through them, he promoted his banking and paper money scheme to the Sun King, Louis XIV. The monarch shrugged off the proposal because Law was Protestant, but a few years later, the Sun King died. His successor was more tolerant; Law's plan offered France a way out of a tight financial bind.

The glittering balls in the Palace of Versailles, the theaters, operas, paintings, monuments, wars, and other indulgences of the French royal vanity—all were financed by what we now call deficit spending. The Sun King died in 1715, leaving behind a national debt of 3 billion livres and only 3 million of income to pay it down. The king's revenues were 145 million a year, but the costs of basic government took 142 million of that.[22] Fearing revolution, some nobles suggested declaring national bankruptcy. Instead, there was a resort to more traditional means. The government debased the currency, forced holders of government bonds issued at 7 percent to exchange them for new securities that paid only 4 percent, slashed salaries and pensions for civil servants, and launched an inquisition against tax cheats and other financial frauds. The effect of these measures was to wreck the economy of France.

One day during these dismal times, a group that included John Law was conversing in the Palais Royal. Someone happened to mention the philosophers' stone, and Law shocked all by casually observing that he had discovered it. "I can tell you my secret," he continued. "It is to make gold out of paper."[23]

In order to test Law's proposal, the regent authorized him to establish a bank and agreed that the state would accept the bank's notes as legal tender for payment of taxes. Meanwhile, Law declared that all notes issued by his bank could be exchanged at his bank for the coin current on the date they were issued. Thus, even if the regent debased the coin, people were protected from damage if they held Law's notes. This inspired such confidence that his notes quickly became more valuable than gold or silver. Law's notes traded at a premium of 15 percent above their face value. Meanwhile, the notes the government had issued to secure its own debts traded at a discount of almost 80 percent below their face value. Law's bank succeeded so well that the regent established it as the Royal Bank of France, the first real state central bank in history.

Law then attempted, by managing the money supply, to put the decrepit finances of France back on a sound footing. He devised a clever scheme to extinguish the debts of France. He established a new company, the Mississippi Company, and the regent granted him a royal monopoly on trade with the East Indies, China, the South Seas, and all possessions of the French East India Company. Law issued shares in return for the *billets d'état*, promising an effective return of 120 percent from gold mines in Louisiana and other anticipated riches. Law was offering something for nothing. The *billets d'état* were cheap because it was no sure thing that the French government would actually pay them. By tendering this cheap, risky government debt to John Law, an investor got in return a piece of the dream of the wealth of the Indies.

Because Law controlled the money supply, it was easy for him to manipulate the price of Mississippi stock. Often, just before the Mississippi Company issued more stock, the bank issued more money. The gullible public rushed into the market, borrowing money to buy stock, pushing Mississippi stock prices up even higher.[24]

One of the greatest speculative manias in history was thus launched. Nobles thronged the streets in front of Law's door, jostling for a chance to buy shares. At night, troops were called out to drive them away. Titled ladies waited day and night in Law's antechambers, willing to do nearly anything in order to have their names put down for a subscription of stock. In the street outside, a hunchback rented his hump as a writing desk for stock transactions in the secondary markets. Commoners who managed to scrape together enough to buy a few shares or to set up as brokers became richer than dukes. Mississippi stock prices rose hour after hour, day after day, for a year. Over three hundred thousand people poured into Paris from the provinces, and the city's economy boomed.

Not everyone was taken in. Richard Cantillon, an Irish banker residing in Paris, had been watching the growth of Law's system with suspicion. Cantillon saw through the ruse. He had made a fortune in the early stages of the Mississippi bubble, even though he sold his shares well before the mania peaked. Now he started to speculate against the French currency by exchanging as much of it as he could for Dutch guilders. Once the public caught on to the fact that the whole Mississippi scheme was a bubble and the French currency nothing but a paper fiction, Cantillon knew French money would be worthless.

Law paid Cantillon a friendly visit to discourage this speculation against the currency. Like central bankers today, he did not object to some speculation, so long as it went his way. However, he considered Cantillon's speculation to be unwarranted, annoying, potentially destabilizing, and therefore a threat to his plans. Law did not waste many words on the actual economics of the situation but struck right to the point. He told Cantillon, "If we were in England, we would be able to talk and reach an agreement; but in France, as you know, I can tell you that you will be in the Bastille this evening if you do not give me your word to leave the country in forty-eight hours."[25] Cantillon saw that Law's logic was compelling, and departed for London.

Meanwhile, though, the prince de Conti had also called Law's bluff. Law had refused to sell him fresh shares. Miffed, the prince sent three wagonloads of banknotes to the Royal Bank of France, demanding to exchange them for gold and silver. Law paid. But the regent recognized that if others followed, the entire scheme would collapse, and forced the prince to refund the precious metals.

Nonetheless, in the spring of 1720, Law had to face the fact that his system was teetering at the edge of an abyss. He announced a reduction in the issue of Mississippi stocks and also in the money supply. He attempted to demonstrate that this reduction did not in any way diminish the wealth of his investors or of those who held the French currency. The public did not accept his reasoning.[26] It was now clear that there was nothing behind Law's notes except more paper. In fact, the paper money of the Royal Bank of France was backed by nothing but the vapors of popular confidence, and a chill wind of doubt was blowing. People scrambled to sell their stock and convert their currency into gold. Mississippi stock plunged, and so did the value of the currency.

The Royal Bank, the Mississippi Company—the entire edifice of deceit—heaved. In order to slow the crash, the government reportedly rounded up over six thousand Parisian derelicts, gave them shovels to put on their shoulders, and paraded them through the streets, meanwhile putting out the word that they'd been drafted to work in the gold mines of New Orleans.[27] The trick didn't fool anyone. So many people were trying to buy gold and silver to ship it safely abroad that the council made it illegal to own more than a few coins. One stockbroker secretly purchased as much silver and gold as he could, put it in a wagon, covered it with manure, disguised himself as a peasant, and drove the wagon to Amsterdam.[28]

In no time, the regent's new paper money collapsed, and the Royal Bank stopped making payments in specie. Mississippi Company stock was worthless. The government convened tribunals to find and punish those responsible. Some minor functionaries were sentenced to death, then had their sentences commuted to life imprisonment in the Bastille. Higher authorities generally escaped clear. Law fled abroad, and returned to the casinos, pursued by creditors. He died in poverty. He had always believed in his own plan, and to prove it, he had invested all his wealth in France. When he fled, the government confiscated everything he owned.

Law's failure profoundly retarded the development of modern financial institutions in France. "French experience with John Law was such that there was hesitation in even pronouncing the word 'bank' for 150 years thereafter—a classic case of collective financial memory," economic historian Charles Kindleberger notes.[29] Yet Law's ideas did not die. During the American War of Independence, Spain established a national bank in many respects similar to Law's first enterprise in France. After World War I, as Germany struggled with hyperinflation, a bank was established to issue currency based on the value of German land, echoing Law's original proposal to the Scottish Parliament in 1700. But not until the latter half of the twentieth century would the world again see universally accepted paper currency backed not by silver or gold or anything else except the confidence of the people who use it: so-called fiat money.

As Law's ideas have survived, so have the problems they cause. The central problem is that of determining what money is really worth when there is no apparent limit to how much of it a state may create. Economist Michael Bordo writes, "In a closed-economy environment, once the monetary authority has announced a given rate of monetary growth, which the public expects it to validate, the authority then has an incentive to create a monetary surprise to either reduce unemployment or capture seignorage revenue. The public, with rational expectations, will come to anticipate the authority's perfidy, leading to an inflationary equilibrium."[30] In other words, governments have an incentive to lie about what their money is worth, and rational people don't believe what governments say. This, in a nutshell, is the reason why private markets have developed means to protect themselves against the deceptions of states.

The Birth of the Gold Standard

One of the strongest systems for protecting the value of money was the classical gold standard that developed in England during the nineteenth century. A direct descendant of John Locke's philosophy, it put a strong fence around the king to prevent him from cheating his creditors by manipulation of the money supply. The gold standard signaled a shift in power from the throne to the merchants and financiers.

The philosophical upheavals of the Enlightenment had changed the way people thought about money and power. The divine right of kings was passé; science and reason were all the vogue. In medieval times, no one had pretended that life was reasonable. People accepted easily the notion of an inscrutable mystery about the ways of God. Now, though, reason seized the imagination of the age. Equipped with the filter of reason, new thinkers aimed to strain out the debris that had clogged the clear primal springs of human happiness. The notion that the universe worked according to basic laws that could be discovered by analysis, understood by reason, and put to work for the greater happiness of mankind swept through Europe like the Black Death. Reason ascended in a mad rush to the highest altars of France. Paradoxically, it sometimes seemed that there could be no madness madder than reason.

During the French Revolution, "Festivals of Reason" were held in cathedrals throughout the country to show just how thoroughly reason had supplanted faith. An actress dressed in tricolor led a procession into the cathedral of Notre Dame, which had been converted into a temple of reason. In the nave, a model of the Parthenon had been placed atop a stage-set mountain made of linen and paper. Some say that the mountain was also decorated with busts of Voltaire, Rousseau, and Benjamin Franklin. The actress bowed to the flame of reason and sat down upon a bench decorated with flowers. Elsewhere in France, the festivals may have been considerably more ribald.[31]

The British were less theatrical, but no less enamored of reason. In 1776, Adam Smith's *Wealth of Nations* had inspired a quasi science, quasi enthusiasm called political economy. In its earliest years, political economy was a fascination of well-to-do eccentrics who sought to discover underlying laws that governed the creation and distribution of wealth. Jeremy Bentham, a hedonist of the utilitarian stripe, marked out the intellectual playing field for this great contest of hypotheses and proofs. We now call it economics. As a hedonist, Bentham had a simple morality: if pleasure, then good, and if pain, then bad. Bentham thought that avoiding pain and seeking pleasure were the most excellent purpose for civilization. He laid down the principle that the task of legislators and even individuals is to produce the greatest pleasure for the greatest number. Taking a cue from Newton, who had invented calculus to aid him in physics, Bentham invented a "hedonistic calculus" to measure pain and pleasure in strict quantitative terms. One can distinguish here the germ of the principle that even today guides most economic policymaking.

When Bentham died, he leaped into immortality without quite leaving the pleasures of good fellowship behind. In accordance with the terms of a bequest he had made to his alma mater, his body was decapitated, decorated with a wax image of his head, preserved by the mummifier's art, dressed in his clothes, and brought out annually to attend meetings at the University College, London. If Bentham had used hedonistic calculus to calculate the present value of the anticipated pleasure the annual sight of him would elicit from most of his heirs, and offset it against the calculated value of the discomfort of those who might balk at conducting business under the glassy eye of a withering mummy, would he have made the same decision? Would his heirs have preferred something more French perhaps? We do not know.

Notwithstanding his eccentricity, Bentham's influence on the development of economics was profound. He was John Stuart Mill's teacher, and John Stuart Mill was David Ricardo's teacher, and Ricardo begat or helped beget every economist from Karl Marx to Milton Friedman and beyond.

Ricardo was a Sephardic Jew who married a Quaker lass and was disowned by his family. He went on to make a fortune as a stockbroker in the London exchange. After he had purchased an estate, and achieved the more respectable status of landowner, he began to study the new faith of political economy. John Stuart Mill taught him to write theoretical expositions. Malthus, whose dark prognostications about population growth and the inevitability of mass starvation gave the sobriquet "dismal science" to economics, was a friend and correspondent. Ricardo, under Mill's urging, took his policies to Parliament by getting himself elected as the member from an Irish "rotten borough" with only twelve electors.

Ricardo, like the other early political economists, was convinced that basic natural laws governed the growth of wealth. By discovering those laws and acting in accordance with them, nations could achieve prosperity. Ricardo would make his enduring mark by figuring out how money ought to work.

Ricardo's effort to put things right with money came about because of the Napoleonic Wars. Britain had been on a gold standard since Sir Isaac Newton defined the gold value of the pound in the great recoinage of the early eighteenth century. But in 1797, as war with France got under way, the Bank of England had to stop the practice of giving out gold in exchange for paper banknotes. Most people, even those who trusted the bank, put more confidence in gold coins than in paper bills. In fact, they trusted the paper only because they knew they could exchange it for gold whenever they wanted. A war was a powerful motive to do just that. But if enough people turned in paper notes for gold coins and buried the gold, stuffed it in a mattress, or even shipped it out of the country, there would be problems. In order to fight Napoléon, the British government needed gold to buy military supplies and bribe allies. Foreigners had little use for British banknotes.

The Bank of England did not simply refuse to exchange specie for gold; it abandoned the discipline of maintaining a strict relationship between notes in circulation and gold in the vaults. It lost no time in printing much more money than it could have issued had it been bound by the gold standard. England had in effect gone off gold and onto paper, much as France had done under John Law's tutelage almost a century before.

This excessive money creation by the British banks, supplemented by new capital sent from France to England for safekeeping during and after the Revolution, proceeded to finance the Industrial Revolution. War created a market for all manner of industrial products and agricultural supplies. In the era of easy money, it was easy for entrepreneurs to raise cash for new ventures. Industry boomed, and vulgar parvenus began to rub elbows with the quality folk, much to the latter's distaste. Speculation ran riot. Toward the end of the war, when the old Portuguese monopoly on trade in Brazil fell, British industrialists expected a market of Golconda-like wealth. Instead of waiting to receive sound information, the British manufacturers and merchants shipped goods to Rio de Janeiro on spec. So many goods were shipped that the warehouses could not contain them, and they were stored on the beaches, in the open. "Elegant services of cut-glass and china were offered to persons whose most splendid drinking vessels consisted of a horn, or the shell of a coconut," writes one observer.[32]

Yet to put it mildly, the excessive printing of money was not strictly in accord with the best principles of political economy. The French economy had also done well during the days of John Law, only to crash when the public realized that the money wasn't really backed by anything more substantial than their willingness to accept it. There was already a symptom of danger in England: the price of gold was rising.

By careful analysis of prices in England and abroad, Ricardo determined that the rise in gold prices had resulted from the vast number of banknotes in circulation. After a bruising debate in Parliament, the government decided that the notes of the Bank of England should once again be redeemable in gold.

This meant reversing the money creation of previous years. It meant money destruction, getting rid of all the excess money that was sloshing through the economy and driving up prices. It meant making it harder for entrepreneurs to raise cash, harder to sell products. The destruction of money coincided with a natural falloff in markets because armies were being disbanded and unemployed soldiers were pouring back into England. There wasn't much market for uniforms, boots, guns, bullets, ships, and all the other hardware of conquest. But there wasn't much chance of people beating their swords into plowshares, because it took money to do that, and money was being destroyed, not created. Corn prices plunged, and factories ground to a halt. A massive depression occurred.

The political economists had won their first major victory, and they held their ground. Despite the misery among farmers and workers, and powerful political agitation to repeal it, the government stuck to the gold standard. Ricardo said that the decision was "a triumph of science, and truth, over prejudice, and error."[33]

Eventually, the gold standard would become an international standard. By 1880, all the major countries of the world had adopted this rough discipline. The gold standard worked for more than thirty years between 1880 and World War I to keep the value of money more or less stable. In most places, the control of the money supply eventually became a responsibility of the central banks. The fraternity of central bankers was international, and central bankers often cooperated in their common task—for example, by lending each other gold in times of crisis.

The gold standard was a vast machine to regulate international trade and investment. The control panel was in London, where most central banks kept some of their gold reserves and where the pound sterling was "as good as gold." A country whose economy picked up and started to soar would soon be importing more from abroad—luxury goods, machines, whatever. Since international payments were settled in gold, gold flowed out to pay for the imports. But since the money supply was backed by gold, when gold flowed out, the central bank had to reduce the supply of money. When central banks choked back on the money supply, interest rates rose, so loans were harder to get and pay for. With money tight, businesses couldn't get financing and couldn't grow. They laid off workers and pared back operations. Because they weren't working anymore, people didn't have much money, so they bought less of everything, including imports. More businesses closed. Eventually, there wasn't a boom anymore—there was a bust. Prices fell because businesses and farmers would sell for almost any price just to keep afloat. Buyers in other countries found those bargain prices very attractive and started to buy all kinds of agricultural and manufactured products. They paid in gold. The more they bought, the more gold the country received. Since more gold was flowing in, the central bank could create more money. Interest rates fell; businesses could borrow, hire more people, expand; and before long, another boom was under way. That, more or less, was the gold standard. Boom and bust, over and over again.

But the exchange rate of the currency was stable, because the currency was tied to gold. The gold standard prevented inflation. Investors who loaned money out could expect to be paid back as much as they had loaned, plus interest. This made investing a lot safer. In most countries, the relationship of money to gold was written into law, and sometimes into the national constitution itself. The old problem of kings manipulating currencies, taxing their countries surreptitiously through inflation, was for the most part solved.

The gold standard as it worked between 1880 and 1914 represented an ideal state of monetary stability that would never again be duplicated. All of the systems that came afterward—Bretton Woods, floating exchange rates, the Snake,* the European Exchange Rate Mechanism—would attempt to duplicate its success, but all would fail.

Why?

Largely because the gold standard worked only as long as a large part of the population had no effective voice in politics. The burden of adjusting to changes in the economic cycle fell on the necks of labor. A vague awareness of this fact shows up in the novel *Oliver Twist*, in Dickens's comments about political economists: "I wish some well-fed Philosopher, whose meat and drink turn to gall within him, whose blood is ice, whose heart is iron; could have seen Oliver Twist clutching at the dainty viands that the dog had neglected. . . . There is only one thing I should like better; and that would be to see the Philosopher making the same sort of meal himself, with the same relish."[34]

In general, however, the notion that people would find themselves out of work not through any fault of their own but because of the way gold flowed in and out of the carefully designed economic machine in which they lived did not have a very wide acceptance:

> Unemployment emerged as a coherent social and economic problem only around the turn of the century. In Victorian Britain, social commentators referred not to unemployment but to pauperism, vagrancy and destitution. In the United States, such persons were referred to as out of work, idle, or loafing but rarely as unemployed. In France and Sweden the authorities referred not to unemployment but to vagrancy and vagabondism. These terms betray a tendency to ascribe unemployment to individual failings and a lack of comprehension of how aggregate fluctuations, referred to by contemporaries as the "trade cycle," affected employment prospects.[35]

Even when that reality became clear, those who paid in hunger for the maintenance of the gold standard usually lacked power to change it. In Europe, where the gold standard was strongest, the working class

---

* This colorful term refers to a 1972 agreement in which the countries in the European Economic Community committed to maintain fluctuation margins of 2.25 percent among their currencies.

did not vote, and farmers received tariffs and other favors to protect them from the blunt force of the gold standard. In the United States, by contrast, the gold standard was nearly overturned by populist forces. William Jennings Bryan's "Cross of Gold" speech is the best-remembered relic of the hard-fought battle over America's monetary standard.

The Prairie Populist and his motley coterie of farmers, workers, silver mining interests, and others sent shock waves through the international financial system. It was the "little guy" who cheered when Bryan thundered, "You shall not press down upon the brow of labour this crown of thorns, you shall not crucify mankind upon a cross of gold!" The gold standard barely survived the assault, and lasted only two decades more.

World War I finally broke the golden rule, putting an end not only to the gold standard and to the international cooperation that had lasted fifty years but also to the political structures that had made them possible. An important feature of the gold standard had been the freedom to convert paper money into gold at will. But who in his right mind would hold on to the paper notes of a war-ravaged country when he could exchange them for gold? In order to prevent the total loss of their gold reserves, just as England had done in its war with France over a century before, warring countries pulled the teeth of the gold standard. Although they maintained the public fiction that their paper was backed by gold, in fact they forbade people to exchange paper money for metal. The prohibition on conversion was straightforward in Russia, Germany, and France. In Britain, although the legal right to export gold was not tampered with, its exercise was made inconvenient if not impossible by patriotic appeals and bureaucratic red tape. Once again, governments resorted to the inflation tax to help finance their wars, printing more money than they had gold to back. In most cases, they also borrowed heavily by selling bonds to those well-off enough to afford them and patriotic enough or gullible enough to believe that the bonds would eventually be repaid with sound money.

Meanwhile, the smoke of Moscow's revolution drifted through the parliaments and palaces of Europe, carrying into those chambers the threat that the oppressed, poor, and restive masses would refuse to die in a capitalist war for the capitalist states that neither represented nor protected them. So, during and after World War I, those without property or wealth were granted the right to vote. Peasants and workers were no longer voiceless. They could not be ignored. They soon made it clear that they would not accept the brunt of future economic adjustments, no matter what kind of economic machine might be built after the war. As democracy spread, the gold standard became more and more unlikely to survive.[36]

For example, after the Treaty of Versailles, the Right and Left in Germany battled over who would pay the crushing reparations demanded by the Allies. The Right proposed that social spending be cut and suggested that workers ought to put in more hours to make coal, steel, and other products so that the reparations might be paid in kind. The Left suggested a tax on property, a tax on capital, a tax on whatever, so long as labor did not pay it. In the stalemate, the government's printing presses kept running, printing the money that would before long, according to legend, be carried in wheelbarrow loads to purchase a loaf of bread.

In France too, Right and Left fought over the same issues. Initially, the Center Right imposed sales taxes to balance the budget. Succeeding governments of the Left tried to replace these with taxes on property and wealth. The rich and the better-off scooted their assets across the borders. Meanwhile, the money presses continued to run. In June and July of 1926, annualized inflation rates hit 350 percent.[37]

International monetary cooperation had been a casualty of the war. Nations that had cooperated closely under the old gold standard now competed fiercely to become the European financial capital. Before World War I, there had been no doubt about British preeminence. London had been the center of global finance, and the Bank of England the single most important financial institution in the world. After the war, the situation was not so clear. Winston Churchill presided over an effort to restore the old eminence by reversing the depreciation of the British pound. Following in the steps of those who had restored the pound to its old value after the Napoleonic Wars, Churchill sought to assure the world that Britain's word and notes were as good as gold. The sacred, prewar gold price of £3 17s. 10.5d. per ounce would be restored, and once again the pound would be freely convertible into gold. Adjustment would be made as under the old, prewar regime, by choking back the money supply, putting the onus mostly on labor and on debtors.

In France, after the brush with hyperinflation in 1926, the authorities raised interest rates, drawing in capital from England. They were so successful that speculators expected France to follow Britain's lead and restore the franc to its old, prewar gold value. It looked like a one-way bet for speculators. They could sell British pounds for French francs to buy high-interest French securities. If the franc strengthened, they would win on both the interest rates and the currency appreciation. A powerful contingent in the French government, including the prime minister, supported restoration of the prewar franc.

Central Banks at Center Stage

But Emile Moreau, tough-minded chairman of the Bank of France, did not. "It was a very difficult game to play," Moreau wrote in his diary. "After all, arrayed against me were the most noble sentiments in the country. Therein was the true drama. To those who, together with the prime minister, were saying to me: 'The state must meet its commitments, the middle class must not be impoverished,' I was obliged to reply: 'It is not possible; we must stabilize. However worthy of reverence the past may be, we must think of the future of France.'" Moreau thought it best to accept that the war had damaged the franc, to stabilize the currency's value at a level lower than the prewar value, and to get on with the business of rebuilding the nation's financial credibility. "The Bank of France and France itself will have to regain their prewar strength and prestige in the financial sphere, that strength and prestige which weighed so considerably on the scales of victory in 1918," he wrote.[38]

In order to force the Bank of England to raise interest rates, and stem the flow of speculative capital to the French franc, Moreau took a bold step: he demanded that Britain convert some £30 million of sterling into gold. Britain couldn't afford such an outflow of gold. The British economy was already in a precarious condition, struggling to readjust to a price of £3 17s. 10.5d. per ounce of gold. At this point, further choking of the money supply could have pushed Britain off the gold standard altogether.

Through secret meetings and hurried correspondence, Federal Reserve chief Strong, Bank of England chairman Norman, and Mr. Moreau of the Bank of France worked out a compromise that saved the face of the postwar gold standard. The United States agreed to sell some gold to France, the French agreed to moderate their demands, and the British agreed to tighten up on domestic credit in order to stem the flow of capital to France. Moreau thereby stabilized the franc.

More importantly, the central banks had emerged as perhaps the most powerful institutions of the 1920s. Among themselves, the central bankers did not conceal their impatience and disgust with the messy accommodations of the political process. Moreau wrote tellingly of Bank of England chief Montagu Norman's ambition to reshape the financial and economic structure of the world:

> Politicians and political institutions seem to him to be unable to cope with this organization with the necessary degree of competence and continuity. He would therefore like to see this task undertaken by the central banks, simultaneously independent of governments and private financiers. This is the reason for his campaign favoring central banks totally autonomous from the state and ruling over their financial markets. Such banks would be able to derive their power from agreement among themselves. They would succeed in removing from the political arena the issues essential for the development of the prosperity of nations: monetary security, credit allocation, and price movements. They would then be capable of preventing the political infighting detrimental to the wealth of nations and to their economic progress. Even though such views are rather doctrinaire, undoubtedly somewhat utopian, perhaps even Machiavellian, they are certainly possible![39]

In this era, central banks were certainly "above politics." Milton Friedman would write, in 1962, "Though of course stated in obviously benevolent terms of doing the 'right thing' and avoiding distrust and uncertainty, the implicit doctrine is clearly thoroughly dictatorial and totalitarian."[40]

The central bankers had one overriding objective, that of monetary stability. They were willing to sacrifice almost everything else in order to achieve that stability. However, their very pursuit of stability turned out to be one of the most destabilizing forces in the twentieth century.

In the event, central bankers would not achieve Montagu Norman's objective of total power. In the United States, the Federal Reserve attempted in the late 1920s to put a stop to what it considered runaway speculation on the stock exchange by choking back on the supply of money to the economy. That would make loans more difficult to get, and since most stock was being bought on margin, with loans from brokerage houses, it would make it harder to buy and sell stock. Ample gold was flowing into the United States, and under the classical gold standard, the Fed could easily have created more money. But that would have made it even easier for people to buy stock. So, instead of creating more money, as the classical gold standard demanded, the Fed actually reduced the money supply. This meant that the international dimension of the gold standard, the flow of commodities and gold from country to country that provided the classical balancing mechanism, could not work. The Fed succeeded in putting a stop to speculation. In 1929, the greatest stock market crash in U.S. history occurred. One result of these efforts was the Great Depression, together with a complete collapse of international economic cooperation.

So, instead of cooperating in a carefully drawn program of worldwide economic organization, central bankers turned their national currencies into trade war artillery. One after another, central bankers depreciated their currencies in order to gain trade advantages. A currency depreciation gives an across-the-board boost to all of a country's exports. If the franc depreciates, then anything made in France is cheaper in terms of British pounds or American dollars. That means more demand for French products, more work for French factories, and more jobs for French workers. It also means less of all those things for the British and Americans.

In their quest for the frighteningly ideal state of gold-standard stability during the 1920s, central bankers and financial ministers plunged the world into the dark misery of the 1930s. This is not the place to trace all of the causes of and contributing factors to the Great Depression. It is a matter of historical fact that the careful plans of the central bankers degenerated into a worldwide trade and economic brawl. Every country tried to match and then exceed the currency depreciations of its competitors. Tariffs and other trade restrictions went up to protect home markets against incursions of cheaper products from abroad. In Germany, Hjalmar Schacht designed a diabolically ingenious system of capital controls to keep people, especially Jews, from spiriting their assets out of the country.

Yet notwithstanding the bitter results of the gold standard and the failure of the plans of central banks, the ideal of a rationally designed, automatic, enforceable international financial machine did not go away.

Paradoxically it got even more appealing.

Bretton Woods

In 1944, in the shadow of a New Hampshire promontory called, appropriately, Mount Deception, seven hundred representatives of forty-four nations convened. Their purpose was to solve the economic problems of the human race. They were confident that reason, science, and good common sense could overcome the centuries-old conflicts that divided them. As U.S. Treasury secretary Morgenthau opened the conference, he said, "The disruption of foreign exchanges can be prevented, and the collapse of monetary systems can be avoided, and a sound currency basis for the balanced growth of international trade can be provided, if we are forehanded enough to plan ahead of time—and to plan together. It is the consensus of these technical experts that the solution lies in a permanent institution for consultation and cooperation on international monetary, finance and economic problems."[41]

Since that date, scores of dissertations, books, monographs, and articles have been written about this almost alchemical scheme to organize rationally the irrational cravings of men and nations. They usually include the standard remark that the delegates met in a small New Hampshire village called Bretton Woods, and that is why the postwar monetary structure was called the Bretton Woods system. But the devil is in the details, after all: there is no New Hampshire village called Bretton Woods.

That is to say, Bretton Woods does not exist the way a village exists, and it never has. There are no streets in Bretton Woods, no houses, no dogs, no village green, no quaint shops, no stray cats or cattle ambling aimlessly through tree-lined lanes. There never were. The village of Bretton Woods was an invention of a hotel promoter of the Gilded Age. It is no more than a postmark that occasionally rises to the status of a spot on the maps of the less discriminating cartographers.

Bretton Woods, a village without people, a paperwork village, was thus arguably the perfect kind of village in which to smash the champagne bottle across the bow of a new ship of economic state. There is nothing irrational about it, nothing emotional, no political rivalries or deep historical antipathies, no greed, no selfless virtue, nothing remotely human. In 1941, the entire population of Bretton Woods consisted of the economists and officials who had convened to endorse the plans of John Maynard Keynes and Harry White.

If any of these economists noticed the general scarcity of the ordinary run of humanity in the neighborhood, no record or remark to that effect survives. As far as they were concerned, they were meeting in a beautiful hotel in the village of Bretton Woods, and they had important work to do designing a scientific system in accordance with the best economic thought of the day. Among the dwindling number of survivors of that conference, faith in the perfection of their work burns strong. It was, if anything, too good for the world. "The Fund didn't really have any technical defects," says Edward Bernstein, chief technical advisor to the U.S. delegation, now at the Brookings Institution. "In fact, there would have been no problem if the world were rational."[42] *The Fund* refers to the International Monetary Fund, one of the two massive and apparently immortal institutions created by the Bretton Woods conferees. The other was the International Bank for Reconstruction and Development, popularly known as the World Bank. Both have long survived their original purpose and the eclipse of their intended work. If thought were stone, the Bretton Woods system would endure for centuries as a monument to the exhausted aspirations of an age, its elaborate design elements checking the thrust of wild ambitions much as flying buttresses channeled the weight of Gothic stone. But there was a less ancient and more apt architectural corollary of the plan.

The Mount Washington Hotel, site of the meetings, is itself a kind of metaphor for the state of the world's financial system, a sort of Portrait of Dorian Gray for the international economy. It was built in 1902, the peak of the Gilded Age, an eclectic aggregation of architectural whimsies that the hotel's own newspaper chose to describe as Spanish Renaissance.[43] The man who built it had aimed to create the grandest of grand hotels. He named it for the highest mountain in the neighborhood, rather than Mount Deception, at whose foot it sprawls. A golf course, clay tennis courts, wicker chaise lounges on rambling porticoes, bridle paths, heated swimming pools, and sundry restaurants allowed the new rich—there wasn't any other kind of rich in America then—to head for the White Mountain wilderness and rough it in style. The hotel was entirely self-contained. It relied on its own electric generators, printed its own menus and papers on its own hydraulic presses, and even had its own post office. During the season, guests could mail letters that would be postmarked Bretton Woods, an old name for a nearby stretch of hemlock, larch, maple, and pine forest. Everyone who was anyone stayed at the Mount Washington, even Thomas Edison and Woodrow Wilson. Business fell off a bit during World War I, of course, but the 1920s roared. Then came the crash. By the end of the 1930s, the roof had literally fallen in. Then the U.S. government booked the whole spread and fixed it up at taxpayer expense as a site for the great economic conference. Afterward, the Mount Washington drifted from one owner to another, sort of holding together but never again reaching the glory of the Gilded Age—just like the Bretton Woods system. The present owners are a group of New Hampshire locals who bought the property at auction from the Federal Deposit Insurance Corporation in 1991. It is only the most recent in a long string of coincidences that the Mount Washington Hotel was a casualty of the savings and loan crisis.

The great monetary conference survives here as a marketing ploy. In the lobby, one small room is set off by velvet ropes: the Gold Room. New, gold-colored carpet matches the gold upholstery of the straight-backed, uncomfortable chairs. This is where the delegates actually signed the articles of agreement. Upstairs, a brass plaque affixed to each room identifies the delegate who occupied it during the 1944 conference. So a contemporary visitor may sleep, on queen-size beds, in the same room where John Maynard Keynes slumbered. Like Keynesianism, the room has suffered from the passage of time. Pigeons rustle in the chimney, sending crumbs of old soot down on a cold heap of birch logs in the fireplace. There is hidden irony in a contemporary press account of the conference, for it aptly describes the fate of the great monetary system created there: "In the upper ranges, rooms got mixed up, offices for delegates had to be hastily improvised, and there was a general feeling of ineffective good-will."[44]

Despite the talk of international cooperation and rational planning, the Bretton Woods Conference was a scramble among representatives trying to grab as much money as they could. They had not been invited here to give their considered opinions about the structure of the postwar financial system. The plan presented to the delegates was pretty much a take-it-or-leave-it proposition. Although the great international monetary conference took place in 1944, meetings had been going on between the United States and Great Britain since 1941.

Harry White, of the U.S. Department of the Treasury, had first sketched the outlines of the plan, and presented it to a conference in Rio de Janeiro as part of a program for a hemispheric union of North and South America. White's plan called for the creation of a sort of international central bank. Each country was to put in a contribution of gold to capitalize the bank, and also a contribution of currency. Each country would declare a fixed value for its currency. Countries would have the right to borrow from the bank when temporary balance-of-payments crises threatened the stability of their currencies.

John Maynard Keynes then offered an alternative plan. The Keynes plan differed from the White plan in several key areas. Whereas the White plan limited the amount of money the United States would have to put in the fund, the Keynes plan called for almost unlimited contributions by the United States. Keynes's plan would have begun with the United States potentially liable to contribute $26 billion.[45] Whereas the White plan called for all countries to contribute gold to the common pool, the Keynes plan did not, because the British did not want to surrender any gold. The White plan required borrowers from the fund to exercise some discipline, get their economic house in order, and repay the debt someday. "The main point was we wanted conditions attached to the use of the Fund's resources by the deficit countries," Bernstein said. "We weren't going to give countries money and say, 'You can do as you please with it.' "[46] The Keynes plan, on the other hand, was not concerned with actually paying back loans. "Their deficits could run on and on, financed by credit from the Fund," Bernstein recalls. In fact, instead of disciplining those who borrowed from the Fund, Keynes proposed to discipline any country that didn't need to borrow from the Fund. He had the United States chiefly in mind. The United States would have paid a fine to the Fund if its finances were too sound. Strange as that sounds, it was not utterly irrational. Keynes wanted to prevent the United States from deflating the entire global monetary system, as it had done in the late 1920s when the Federal Reserve reduced the money supply.

The two plans did have quite a few elements in common. The most important was the Olympian assumption that the results of government planning would be much more successful and attractive than anything private markets could produce. Governments would declare the value of their currencies, then cooperate to defend those established values, regardless of whether the values made sense to anyone outside the charmed circle of economic cognoscenti.

For example, if Britain decided that stimulating the economy in the short term was necessary, it might try to drop interest rates. If other countries did not drop their rates too, investors would probably prefer to invest where returns were best, take their capital out of the low-interest-rate country, and buy securities issued in the higher-interest-rate currencies. But that would make it more difficult, if not altogether impossible, for Britain to maintain the exchange rate it had declared. As people sold their pounds to buy dollars, francs, or marks in order to invest abroad, the market price of sterling would fall. The only institution willing to buy and sell pounds at the higher, official exchange rate would be the Bank of England. Eventually, the Bank of England would run out of reserves. This is almost precisely the scenario that took place in 1992, when Great Britain was forced out of the European Exchange Rate Mechanism, a successor to Bretton Woods.

In order to prevent private capital movements from upsetting government programs, the compromise plan that emerged from the negotiations between Keynes and White allowed countries to impose all sorts of controls on capital movements. They were quite willing to sacrifice individual freedom in order to achieve economic objectives. "Keynes says at one point in one of his papers, 'We may have to go as far as opening the mail,' " recalls Allan Meltzer, an economics professor at Carnegie Mellon University.[47] White had scarcely more sympathy for private interests. A strong supporter of the Soviet Union, he would eventually be accused of having been a spy for Moscow.[48] But U.S. Treasury secretary Morgenthau expressed most succinctly the sense of sacred state power and profane private interests when he summarized the Bretton Woods system as one that would "drive the usurious moneylenders from the temple of international finance."[49]

Once again, the world had started down the course first mapped and trod by John Law. Once again, states would seek to prevent anyone from speculating against them, as Law had prevented Cantillon with a threat of the Bastille. For a time, the Bretton Woods system seemed to be a success—just as John Law's system had, for a time, seemed to be a success. However, the states could not deceive people forever. People found ways around the rules, and eventually the markets overwhelmed the international economic empire like vandals sacking Rome.

INTERREGNUM

THE ATTACK ON THE EUROPEAN MONETARY SYSTEM, PART I

On the tarmac of O'Hare field in Chicago, pinned down by a rainstorm, two young Pittsburgh bankers sat and waited for their plane to move. The tall one, Stan, turned as if to speak to his companion but instead stared intently at the window. His fellow traveler in the window seat could not understand why. After all, it was almost impossible to see through the storm. The driving wind pounded, rain spattered against the pane, the drops hung for an indeterminate moment, then trickled randomly down. That was all. After a minute or two, Stan leaned over and said, "I'll bet you a thousand dollars I can tell you which raindrop will go down the window next."

Twelve years later, Stanley Druckenmiller was chief of investments for the most notorious speculator in the world. The $1,000 bet had become a $10 billion wager, and the object was to predict not which raindrops would slide down a window, but which currencies would tumble out of the European Monetary System's Exchange Rate Mechanism (ERM). All the world's newspapers and many of the world's central bankers would later say that George Soros was the man who single-handedly forced Great Britain and Italy out of Europe's monetary system. Yet like much popular lore about George Soros, this is at best a half-truth. For Stanley Druckenmiller designed the series of bets that paid his employer a jackpot win of over $1 billion in clear profit and made George Soros—not the secretive Druckenmiller—a famous financial oracle.

At a cocktail party, Soros observed that he had never been more anonymous than after the ERM collapse made his name a household word.[1] British tabloids tagged him "The Man Who Broke the Bank of England." He played the publicity game artfully. Sometimes he even announced his trading strategy to the press.

Soros attracted attention in part because he was the only hedge fund manager willing to say much of anything to reporters. There may be over a thousand hedge funds. No one is sure of the exact number, because they are not regulated. At least a dozen hedge fund managers, like Soros, manage more than $1 billion each. Many of them trade currencies, and made handsome profits when the EMS went down, but only George Soros was willing to be publicly identified as the nemesis of the central banks and the guru of international finance. The others would rather not be noticed.

Soon rumors of a new Soros coup would fly whenever currency rates or gold prices shifted. Reporters would note his every stock purchase and even analyze his real estate dealings, although Soros had never been known to have a knack for real estate.

His public image has swollen grotesquely. To the casual student of the plutocracy, George Soros floats above lesser financiers like a balloon in the Macy's Thanksgiving Day Parade. *Business Week* tagged him "The Man Who Moves Markets." It is easy to see why he considered such fame to be as good a camouflage as anonymity. Because he was blamed or credited with almost everything, he can act in real secrecy. No one would be able to separate out the one needle of truth about his actions from the haystack of false rumors.

Skeptics wondered whether Soros himself might be sending false signals. Johann Wilhelm Gaddum, a Bundesbank board member, told a German television interviewer: "One reads what he says with interest. But the particular phenomenon is that he is one of the few representatives of this sector who announce in advance what they intend to do. This always sounds a bit suspicious because the normal speculator earns money by doing exactly the opposite of what everybody else does."[2]

Ironically, though, after the fall of the Berlin Wall in 1989, Soros had spent most of his time carving out a role as a power player on the world stage, scattering cash throughout Eastern Europe, funding universities, underwriting projects, and meeting with presidents and prime ministers in places far from the market action.

He couldn't possibly make the nitty-gritty investment decisions for his flagship Quantum fund.

It was not Soros but Druckenmiller who masterminded the great "Soros coup" in 1992.

While George Soros handled the spending of money, Stanley Druckenmiller attended to the making of it.

Stan had come a long way. In Pittsburgh, there are still a few people who knew him when. Long before Druckenmiller's bets intimidated Rome, London, and Paris, he had bluffed his way around the provincial movers and shakers of Iron City. A still-awestruck local banker remembers him as "a big goddamn gambler." Once during a meeting, when someone challenged him on a point of fact, Stan offered to put his money where his mouth was, with a $5,000 wager that he was right. No one took the bet. Stan was right often enough to make it dangerous.[3]

He didn't fit the mold of a Pittsburgh banker at all. Having dropped out of graduate school at the University of Michigan without a degree, he began his business career by failing the training program for loan officers at Pittsburgh National Bank.[4] Then he got a lucky break. The brilliantly eccentric Greek—another outsider—who headed the bank's investment research unit had spotted his potential and brought Stan upstairs as a stock analyst.

He was soon initiated into the exotic folkways of Pittsburgh's commercial elite. During the annual deer season, the men of Pittsburgh still escape to the woods for Deer Camp, a long week of whiskey, cards, guns, and sometimes even game. To outfit Stan for his first trip to Deer Camp, the boys in the trust department took him to a local sporting goods store. His head was so big that they had to buy the largest size hunting cap in the store and slit it up the back to open it up enough for him to wear it comfortably. He bought a gun that no one ever remembers him shooting, and spent most of his camp time around the poker table.[5]

Golf was his real game, though. Stan played so well that the bank's top man wanted Druckenmiller on his team when he played against the brass of Westinghouse and other big companies in the territory. No doubt Druckenmiller could have become a local chamber of commerce star on the strength of his golf game alone, even if he hadn't had an amazing knack for winning big market bets.

He says himself that it was brashness and luck rather than brains that made him a star.[6] For example, when the shah fell from Iran's Peacock Throne, Stan put 70 percent of the bank's investment assets in oil stocks, the rest in defense companies. It was a very risky bet, but it paid off hugely. The bank's funds have never done so well as when Stan managed them, his old colleagues say.

Eventually, he became a local phenomenon, and in 1980 a broker offered him $10,000 a month just to talk with him about the market. Druckenmiller quit the bank and started his own company. He nearly went broke once, in 1982, when his main client failed, but he was able to talk someone into paying him $150,000 for a quarter of the company. He still had the knack. Within a year, tiny Duquesne Capital had $40 million under management. In 1985, a big shot from New York introduced Stan to the people at Dreyfus, and he started managing real money. By the time he left Dreyfus to join Soros, he was running seven funds.

He joined George Soros in 1988, although his friends all advised him not to. Soros had a reputation as a difficult man to work for. Druckenmiller soon discovered for himself just how difficult. When he met with Soros at his home, the old man's son answered the door laughing. Soros had called Druckenmiller his successor. The old man had been looking long and hard for a successor. So far, ten successors had come and gone. To be called the successor was to be marked as a man without a future in the firm. At headquarters, Stan got used to hearing laughter.[7]

The man he was to succeed, George Soros, had been born in Budapest in 1930. His father was an attorney who had survived the Russian civil war and fled to Hungary. The family was well-off. When George was nine years old, a Jewish organization gave him a stack of notices to deliver. The Jewish organizations had been enlisted to help round up Jews for the Final Solution. The notices directed each recipient to bring a blanket and food for twenty-four hours. His father recognized immediately that the recipients of these notices would be deported, at best, and directed young George to tell them so when he delivered the notices. Then George was sent to live with a gentile family and thus survived the war. The incident gave him a permanent aversion to financing Jewish organizations.[8]

After the war, he went to London and worked for a while as a waiter, eating leftover food to save money. He completed a course of study at the London School of Economics and eventually found work at the stock exchange. By 1956, George Soros was in New York. In 1969, he founded his own firm.

It cost $41.25 to buy a share of the Soros fund in 1969. By 1992, the same share was worth $21,543.55.[9] People who know him say that his investment style is like no other. One friend remembers running into Soros on the street, just after the Mount St. Helen's volcano had erupted in the remote northern wilderness of Washington State. Soros was trying to figure out how the markets would respond. Not only were Soros's investment decisions driven by factors no one else even considered, but he even developed his own philosophy of history, albeit an almost incomprehensible one, to help give his investment program some sense of structure.

Yet the only constant about George Soros is a willingness to take big risks. In 1981, he lost a great deal of money on a wrong call about the stock market. In 1987, though he had predicted the U.S. stock market crash, he lost heavily again. Why? He had expected Japan to do even worse than the United States and bet against the Tokyo market. When the Japanese government stepped in to rescue the country's financial system that year, Soros's investment strategy failed. In 1994, the Soros funds took another $600 million in losses when interest rates hopped unexpectedly.

He was not destroyed, as other investors caught in similar reversals have been, because he backed away fast when he saw that his strategy wasn't working. If Soros is chiefly renowned for taking big risks, he is known secondly for his absolute willingness to retreat quickly when his bets turn out wrong. The real secret of Soros's success may simply be that he rigorously follows the oldest rule of trading: cut losses, and let profits run.

That's a rule Stanley Druckenmiller apparently learned well. Druckenmiller has said, "It takes courage to be a pig."[10] In 1992, he and Soros were not the first to notice the weak position of Great Britain and Italy in the European Monetary System. They were merely the boldest bettors. They put their investors' money, and a lot more borrowed money, on several propositions that were already widely known and accepted among economists.

The European Monetary System was a cornerstone of the new united Europe that had been taking shape in bureaucratic position papers for most of the postwar generation. According to the grand plan for European unity, instead of fighting each other, the countries of Europe should unite harmoniously in a community where people could trade, travel, or invest freely regardless of national borders. There would be no more trade wars, no more selfish nationalisms. The plan was eminently rational. Unfortunately, the world was not.

The year 1992 was to have been the capstone year for European unification, the victory of reason over self-interest, the triumph of the long-term good of all over the short-term advantage of a few. Instead, 1992 was the year in which self-interest and short-term advantage shattered the illusion that the bureaucrats had so carefully nurtured.

What went wrong? George Soros, Stanley Druckenmiller, and thousands of other traders at hedge funds, banks, corporations, insurance companies, mutual funds, and pension funds pulled the financial foundation out from under the new Europe.

Astonished by the force of the blow, European regulators blamed the speculators. The speculators were annoyed by this impertinence. Said one, "The thing you have to remember about bureaucrats and governments is that what they'd really like is for everyone to go away and just let them do whatever the hell they like and be answerable to no one and sit on a big pedestal and announce to the little people below what's happening in the world. When the people in the world sit up and say that's nonsense, you guys are wrecking the economy, they get upset. Then they start blaming speculators and program traders and all these things. People are questioning their actions, and they don't like it. They'd rather pursue their nonsensical goals unfettered."[11]

Bureaucrats may have indeed believed what they were saying to each other and to the public about a new, improved Europe. But there had really been only two questions for speculators: when would the European Monetary System fall apart, and how much should they bet?

THE GOLDEN VANITY

The challenge of designing a sound international monetary system went beyond the merely technical. In fact, its solution depended on the answer to one of the weightiest philosophical questions ever raised: can human beings build a harmonious state?

This problem had occupied great Western thinkers for around two millennia. The ancients had identified a solution, but it was demanding. According to St. Augustine, a society could be harmonious only if the people who composed it were just. Order was the fruit of virtue. If the society was composed of selfish, immoral individuals, justice and order were impossible. Before there could be a just society, there had to be a society of saints—a city of God.

When the ancients had said that only a society of saints could be just, they were saying both that God had made man free and that human freedom is immensely powerful—so powerful that unless everyone freely chooses to be a saint, social harmony cannot be. Freedom was part of the very nature of humanity; it couldn't be ignored, and it had to be used rightly. By and large, the planners who gathered at Bretton Woods had scant faith in Augustine's God. Between Augustine and Bretton Woods, after all, there had been the Enlightenment and the birth of faith in reason.

Thus, the philosopher Immanuel Kant wrote, "Hard as it may sound, the problem of establishing the state is soluble even for a nation of devils, provided they have sense."[1] In other words, even if everyone in the society was thoroughly and deliberately selfish, it would still be possible to ensure the common good, provided that the designers of the system thought things through carefully. It was a short progression from here to the notion that appropriate institutional structures could subdue and harness the power of human freedom and direct it on a constructive course, regardless of the moral condition of the humans who were being directed. This was the faith that gave hope to technocrats.

The objective of the Bretton Woods Conference was to establish international economic institutions that would deliver universal prosperity through free trade, full employment, and exchange rate stability. In order to work, the institutions had to overcome jealousies, tensions, and contradictions that ranged from the petty and personal to the national and historic. Kant had written hyperbole, but by the time the Bretton Woods Conference convened in the midst of World War II, a nation of devils did not seem too far-fetched a description of the actual state of the world.

The greatest of the planners who gathered at the Mount Washington Hotel during the war-darkened summer of 1944, the inspiration for all of them, was John Maynard Keynes. A member of the aesthetic Bloomsbury Group, Keynes was also a practical civil servant in the British Treasury and a successful investor. He was, moreover, a late-flowering genius who exemplified an age that refined means even while it lost sight of ends. Keynes saw that his civilization depended on economic order, and when an old order had broken down he saw it as the task of a government of experts to create and maintain a new one.

Keynes's ethics and philosophy were the foundation of his economics. He was a disciple of the philosopher G. E. Moore, who held that it was impossible to really define "good," that right or wrong depended on circumstances, and that friendship and beauty were the only things worth living for.[2] For the Bloomsberries, as they called themselves, falling in love was the summit of human existence. They fell in love frequently and sterilely. "In the long run, we are all dead" is perhaps the single most frequently quoted remark of Keynes, and several commentators have seen a connection between the short-run Keynesian economic solutions and his "childless vision."[3]

"Keynes rarely used the word, but he thought of himself as part of the 'clerisy'—a secular priesthood, setting standards of value and behaviour, practising the arts of leadership and mutual accommodation."[4] Keynes was neither egalitarian nor democrat. He sought not social justice but sound management. He was a technocrat, the first of the breed, and he wanted to preserve a society that allowed aesthetes like himself and his fellow Bloomsberries to enjoy the good life as defined by Moore. Yet he did more than anyone else to legitimize government economic action for relief of the poor and devised an international monetary system that removed the burden of the gold standard from the necks of labor.

A visionary of protean intellectual flexibility, as befits one who believed that circumstances determine the value of any action, Keynes had thundered forth his first jeremiad upon President Wilson's failure to secure an effective peace settlement after World War I. In *The Economic Consequences of the Peace*, he soared from the drama of myth to the humdrum of balance-of-payments analysis, damning the makers of a Carthaginian peace that had burdened Germany with impossible reparations and set the stage for future disasters. It was not the injustice of the settlement but its impracticability that most agitated Keynes. Similarly, in his 1925 pamphlet *The Economic Consequences of Mr. Churchill*, he foretold with caustic prescience the consequences of reestablishing the gold value of the pound at its prewar value, particularly the effect upon the working classes. Yet his personal relations with the working classes were limited to employing servants and occasionally picking up working-class boys in London for sex.

In the sexually charged atmosphere of Bloomsbury, it was probably inevitable that economics, too, would be discussed in sexual terms. Freud had written that a baby's attention to its feces is sublimated to gold and money. The idea fascinated Keynes, and he referred to the anal-sadistic character of the gold standard in his writings on monetary reform.[5] Lytton Strachey, a fellow Bloomsbury Group aesthete, wrote of Keynes, "The only subjects in which he takes any interest are what he calls 'fie-nance' and lechery—and they certainly do seem to make a nice combination. . . . He brings off his copulations and speculations with the same calculating odiousness, he has a boy with the same mean pleasure with which he sells at the top of the market, and can hardly tell the difference between pocketing fifteen per cent and kissing Duncan."[6] Harsh words—but Keynes himself had written to his lover the painter Duncan Grant, "Nothing except copulation is so enthralling," while compiling an index of economic statistics.[7]

In 1944, Keynes was near the end of his life, a grey eminence in the "dismal science" who had nailed to the cathedral door of economic orthodoxy a boldly inconsistent program for reformation. Both the American and the British planners at the Bretton Woods Conference believed that the world's biggest problem was incompetence, not evil. Keynesian economics taught that knowledgable regulators could save the world by managing it well. Yet Keynes found little to praise in his colleagues in government or academia. This paradox had been widely remarked on two decades prior to the Bretton Woods Conference, when Keynes had first published his suggestions for monetary reform in Great Britain. "For one who often finds the living occupants of our most reputable national institutions so lacking in true qualifications for their task, he shows a surprising confidence in the effectiveness of human agency for giving theory a perfect touch in practice," one commentator had written.[8]

The history of Bretton Woods put on trial the philosophical heritage of the Enlightenment and the very notion that human society could be managed by experts. Subsequent attempts to manage international economic affairs have often been modeled on Bretton Woods, and although Bretton Woods and its successors have all been swept away by the power of the market, hope springs eternal. Some persist in the belief that a new Bretton Woods system designed to eliminate the flaws of the previous model could yet bring the world into the Keynesian promised land of full employment, price stability, and free trade. So the course of this great, failed experiment deserves close attention.

There were signs of trouble from the very start.

At the personal level, pride and envy fired a mad rivalry between Maynard Keynes and Harry White. An observer at the conference wrote, "What absolute Bedlam these discussions are! Keynes and White sit next [to] each other, each flanked by a long row of his own supporters. Without any agenda or any prepared idea of what is going to be discussed, they go for each other in a strident duet of discord which after a crescendo of abuse on either side leads up to a chaotic adjournment of the meeting."[9]

Keynesian thought had already transformed economic science and profoundly influenced American economic policy. Roosevelt's New Deal was nothing if not Keynesian, and like most of his contemporaries,

White considered Keynes to be the greatest living economist.[10] However, White's character was anything but deferential. One historian describes him as "aggressive, irascible, and with a remorseless drive for power."[11]

White had come to Washington in the 1930s, the graduate of an undistinguished midwestern college, but through force of intellectual acuity and sheer plodding hard work, he impressed Secretary Morgenthau. He rose fast and ultimately took charge of all planning for postwar financial policy. Now he was negotiating directly with Keynes. White had the stronger hand, because he represented the stronger party, but he did not play it graciously: "He could be wrathful and rude. His earnestness carried him forward in a torrent of words, which sometimes outstripped his grammatical powers."[12] Keynes stoked the animosity by turning his eloquently polished sarcasm in White's direction.

Keynes did not reserve his venom for White, though. In fact, he poured it even more abundantly upon White's subordinate, Edward Bernstein. In 1943, before the conference, Keynes visited the United States for meetings to resolve differences between the White and Keynes plans. Keynes said that the British were prepared to accept the substance of what White proposed, but insisted that he wanted to rewrite it himself. Bernstein recalls, "I asked, 'If you are prepared to accept the plan, what's the need to rewrite it?' Keynes answered, 'Because your plan is written in Cherokee.' I am sure it wasn't written in as elegant a style as the Keynes Plan, but the Treasury was more concerned with substance than with style. So I said, 'The reason it's in Cherokee is because we need the support of the braves of Wall Street and this is the language they understand.' Keynes became nasty to me at this meeting. He said it was just ignorance of me not to recognize how much better it would be if the White Plan were rewritten in his terms."[13]

Keynes made up his mind that Bernstein, who had dared to oppose him on this matter, was an enemy. Keynes let his poison flow in a memorandum he wrote after this exchange: "Both the currency scheme and the investment scheme are, I think, largely the fruit of the brain not of Harry but of his little attaché, Bernstein. It is with him rather than Harry that the pride of authorship lies. And when we seduce Harry from the true faith, little Bernstein wins him back again in the course of the night. Bernstein is a regular little rabbi, a reader out of the Talmud, to Harry's grand political high rabbidom. . . . The chap knows every rat run in his little ghetto, but it is difficult to persuade him to come out for a walk with us on the highways of the world."[14]

Only personal pride and personal jealousy could generate such vin-
dictive sarcasm. Yet the personal sins were in the service of national
pride and national jealousy. It had been clear for decades, and was now
indisputable, that the United States had supplanted Great Britain as
the world's foremost economic power. By the end of World War II, two-
thirds of the world's gold reserves were held by the United States.[15]
Moreover, the United States was the only country whose productive
capacity had been untouched by Axis bombs. Underlying Keynes's
acerbity was the realization that ultimately the Americans could do
whatever they pleased, whether or not he or anyone else in the world,
but especially in Britain, agreed. The British were already heavily in
debt to the United States as a result of wartime Lend-Lease arrangements and, moreover, would soon be returning to the U.S. Congress,
hat in hand, to ask for another loan.

To make matters worse for the policymakers, in certain critical areas
the international economic objectives of the United States contradicted
those of Great Britain. The Americans, especially those of the State Department, wanted free trade. Roosevelt's secretary of state, Cordell
Hull, believed that the British, German, and Japanese trading blocs established during the 1930s had caused World War II. "If goods can't
cross borders, soldiers will" was the foundation of Hull's economic
thought. So confident was he in the benefits of free trade that in 1939
his aides had proposed that a trade agreement with Hitler could prevent war with Germany.[16]

The British, by contrast, sought to protect the "imperial preference"
system of trade protections, under which trade with Commonwealth
countries was officially blessed by tariff incentives. Conservative British
patriots pined for the glorious days of empire, and for them the Commonwealth was an important symbol. It showed the world that the
sun had not yet set on the empire. After the war, the Conservative ranks
were, oddly enough, augmented by socialists. They saw in imperial
preference a structure that would protect Britain from low-cost foreign
competition and thus make it easier to pursue full-employment
policies.

On this point, Keynes found himself on the side of the Americans.
He ridiculed the strategy behind imperial preference as an attempt to
"build up a separate economic bloc which excludes Canada and consists of countries to which we already owe more than we can pay, on
the basis of their agreeing to lend us money they have not got and buy

only from us and one another goods we are unable to supply."[17] However, the imperial preference continued to have a strong appeal in Britain. In 1941, the *Times* editorialized, "We must . . . reconcile ourselves once and for all to the view that the days of 'laissez-faire' and unlimited division of labour are over; that every country—including Great Britain—plans and organises its production in the light of social and military needs, and that the regulation of this production by such 'trade barriers' as tariffs, quotas and subsidies is a necessary and integral part of this policy."[18]

Britain also had a strong interest in ensuring that the pound sterling continue to be regarded as an international reserve currency. During the war, many of the Commonwealth nations had accepted sterling or sterling debt in payment for supplies and services. They had accumulated so much sterling in their accounts in the Bank of England that to exchange it for dollars would have more than exhausted the British reserves. Britain's interest in maintaining confidence in the pound was not shared by the United States, some of whose officials recommended that Britain deal with the overhang of sterling obligations simply by repudiating them. That would have destroyed British financial credibility and any confidence in sterling as a reserve currency.

The system placed on the table before the delegates assembled at the Mount Washington Hotel in New Hampshire in 1944 was a tortuous compromise. Although it nodded in the direction of Britain, it was essentially a compromise on American terms. However, that does not mean it was a compromise endorsed by most Americans. The Bretton Woods system was created by a small band of economists who agreed on basic principles. The most important basic principle was their faith in their own ability to plan a better world along rational and broadly Keynesian lines. Out of the Bretton Woods Conference and subsequent meetings among the experts emerged three major institutions of the international postwar economic organization: the International Monetary Fund, the World Bank, and the General Agreement on Tariffs and Trade. Yet some differences would never be fully resolved. Despite the appearance of an agreement at Bretton Woods, the United States and Britain remained far apart on some key issues.

The articles of the International Monetary Fund (IMF) were a blueprint for an entirely new international monetary machine. It aimed to square the circle: to accommodate the classic liberal ideal of free trade with the socialist ideal of full employment and to combine the boomtown prosperity of John Law's monetary policies with the monetary stability of the gold standard.

John Law had promised to make gold out of paper, and so did the IMF. The fund's treasury was stocked by subscriptions from each member, 25 percent in gold and 75 percent in the member's own currency. Most of the fund's resources were therefore paper, yet they provided backup reserves to members whose domestic economic policies might otherwise have caused their currencies to depreciate. Members could stimulate their economies by deficit spending without suffering the usual consequences of capital flight and currency depreciation. Capital controls would prevent capital from fleeing, and borrowings from the fund would bolster reserves and help support the currency's value.

Initially, Keynes had planned for a fund of about $26 billion, $23 billion of which would have been contributed by the United States. The United States was unwilling to take on such a large commitment and whittled this down to a fund of only $8.8 billion, with U.S. liability limited to a little over $3 billion.

Countries had the right to borrow from this fund according to the quota they had been allocated. As far as Keynes was concerned, a country's IMF quota was to be automatically available whenever the country needed it. Speaking before Parliament, he referred to Britain's quota as being part of its foreign exchange reserves. Some language in the agreements seemed to support this view, but the Americans did not agree with Keynes's interpretation. They wanted tighter controls on when, how, and why countries could access their IMF quotas, and they eventually got them.

These were minor issues compared to the disagreements over trade. Americans considered the British protectionist system to be nothing less than economic warfare. Congress had no stomach for aiding a country that discriminated against American business. The U.S. Congress approved the Bretton Woods agreements only after a massive PR campaign succeeded in framing the issue as a choice between the international cooperation symbolized by Bretton Woods and another war. In the course of persuading Congress to ratify Bretton Woods, administration officials also assured Congress that there were no plans to send to Europe any American aid beyond what the United States contributed to the Bretton Woods system.

The U.S. negotiators considered Bretton Woods to be a step along the path toward a free-trade world. Monetary policies have a direct effect on international trade. During the 1930s, a cycle of so-called competitive depreciations by major trading countries constituted a predatory trade practice as undesirable in retrospect as the high tariff walls most countries erected at the same time.

A currency depreciation is essentially an across-the-board discount on all of the products a country exports, because it makes all of those products cheaper in terms of foreign currency. What's more, it simultaneously increases the price of products that are imported from other countries. So it provides a two-edged trade advantage—it makes the country's products cheaper to foreign customers, and it makes foreign products more expensive to domestic customers. It has the same effect as putting a tax on foreign products while simultaneously subsidizing domestic producers. In the years before World War II, the countries of Europe managed to ensnare themselves in a vicious circle of competitive depreciation that led to trade protectionism and helped set the stage for violent conflict.

Mindful of competitive depreciations and other monetary policies that could constrain free trade, the Bretton Woods planners thought it best to take the power to set currency values out of the hands of countries that had so obviously abused it. They decided that the IMF should have sovereignty over the world's money. The IMF, not the countries that issued money or the people who used it, would define reasonable values for each of the major currencies. The IMF stated these values in terms of either gold or dollars. A Mexican exporter who shipped products to France might receive francs in payment. When he brought the francs to Mexico, he could exchange them for pesos. He had received X dollars' worth of francs, and he exchanged them for X dollars' worth of pesos. When the Mexican central bank settled its accounts with the French central bank, it received X dollars in return for the francs, or an equivalent quantity of gold.

The IMF articles required that currencies be convertible for trade transactions.* Planners also forbade countries to have multiple cur-

---

* However, there was no obligation to make currencies convertible for capital transactions— buying or selling stocks and bonds, for example, or buying and selling currencies themselves for speculative purposes. The IMF planners wanted trade to move freely, but they didn't want big, destabilizing flows of capital. Thus, there were to be no restrictions on the movement of currencies for the purpose of trade, but regulations prevented investors from moving their money in and out of different currencies to take advantage of higher interest rates or to protect themselves against possible devaluations.

rency exchange rates that could be used to discriminate in favor of some and against other trading partners.

The planners almost grudgingly allowed *some* flexibility in rates. They recognized that ultimately, currency values would have to reflect differences in costs, prices, productivity, and other factors that might well be expected to change as the world recovered from the destruction of war. But countries were not free to set their own currency values as they pleased. The IMF had the authority to approve any proposed changes in exchange rates by members. The IMF's authority was given teeth as well. It had the power to set conditions that governed borrowing by members, and it could use that power to punish violators by declaring them temporarily ineligible to use the fund's resources or, in extreme cases, to expel them altogether. Since the ability of members to borrow from the fund was one of the main advantages it offered them, the planners considered that the power to suspend borrowing privileges would be a strong disincentive to breaking the rules.

This international monetary machine had been designed by the best economic minds of the age, in accordance with the most rigorous strictures of their science. The IMF blueprint was a flawless example of rational institution building but at the same time seemed a product of the economic corollary of *ars gratia artis*.

That is, the Bretton Woods exercise shared a spirit of abstraction that had already swept through arts and letters. In the astonishing exactitude of its geometry, the IMF resembles a painting by the Dutch painter Piet Mondrian, whose style banished all curves; all colors except red, yellow, and blue; and all angles except right angles.

Alas, a comparison is even more apt to Marcel Duchamp's *The Bride Stripped Bare by Her Bachelors, Even (Large Glass)*, painted in 1915. Duchamp's parody had anticipated the postwar economists by almost three decades. It consisted of two delicately balanced surrealist machines painted on cracked plate glass, their meaning described at length in an accompanying booklet. Careful study was repaid with the discovery that the machines could not possibly work.

The Bretton Woods designers began with a cracked world and painted on it their own hyperrational construction, abstracted from the messy unreasonableness of ordinary living. Unlike the clowning Duchamp, though, they really wanted their machine to work. Their plan had no technical flaws. Unfortunately, the world had many.

So the Bretton Woods designs satisfied the economic connoisseur's desire to contemplate perfection, but they were ultimately unworkable. Perhaps the philistine world simply lacked the good judgment to understand what was obvious to the cognoscenti. Or perhaps, after almost two thousand years, there was something to Augustine's notion that a perfect system could be realized only by perfect souls. Or perhaps it would have been impossible for the planners to design a system for the real world, since the real world in which the system had to work would be a future world whose conflicts, complexities, and contradictions were not yet revealed.

The first collision of theory with reality occurred when the ink was scarcely dry on the agreements. Britain's Parliament held back from approving it, suspecting that the liberal trade and monetary arrangements of the Bretton Woods system would toll the knell of the imperial preference and scuttle socialist plans for full employment. Keynes put the best spin on the agreements. He claimed that there would be a long transition period in which Britain could continue to maintain its protectionist system, and he also stated frankly that the Bretton Woods system did not allow interference in the domestic policies of member states. This was not at all what the United States understood the system to allow.

Parliament had not yet approved the Bretton Woods agreements when Keynes returned to the United States in September 1945, to try to obtain a $6 billion grant for Britain. The British believed that, having sacrificed greatly in the common cause, they had a right to expect the United States to underwrite their recovery. Americans, however, had tired of international affairs. Keynes's style didn't help. He negotiated with his hand out and his nose in the air; insulted the new secretary of the treasury, Fred Vinson; and ignored the advice of British diplomats more knowledgeable than he about the political climate in Washington. He consequently not only managed to get less money than Britain needed but received it in the form of an interest-bearing loan rather than an outright grant.

What's more, the loan was linked none too subtly to approval of the Bretton Woods agreements in a manner that smacked of blackmail. If Britain's Parliament had not accepted Bretton Woods, three other Commonwealth countries (Australia, New Zealand, and India) probably also would have bowed out. In that case, neither the World Bank nor the IMF could have proceeded. So the financial agreements submitted to Parliament only three weeks before the deadline for British ratification of the Bretton Woods system included the loan, Bretton Woods, Lend-Lease settlements, and commercial policy proposals from the United States. The debate was intense, but the outcome predictable. The Bretton Woods agreements were approved.

Other differences between theory and reality had also begun to appear. The most obvious example was in the role of the Soviet Union. In 1943, when the White plan was first published, Moscow had been brought into the information loop. Soviet ambassador Andrei Gromyko came to the Treasury Department to introduce the Russian delegates who would attend the meetings on the new monetary system. Edward Bernstein recalls, "He told White, 'They are the ones who will be our observers at these discussions. They'll ask you questions.' Then, as we were finishing, he turned to his Russians and said, 'Remember! You are observers. You are not to give any opinion of any kind.' "[19]

Moscow did give opinions, though, and the Soviets were active participants in the negotiations. At an early press conference, White happened to give off-the-cuff estimates of how much quota each fund member would enjoy and managed to set a trap for the United States by suggesting that the Soviet quota—the amount that the USSR could borrow from the fund—would be about $1 billion. Later, as the actual dimensions of the fund became clearer, he offered the Soviets a lesser quota of only $800 million. The Soviets filed a formal protest with the U.S. secretary of the treasury claiming that White had misled them, and their quota was raised to $1.2 billion, only $100 million less than that of Great Britain and its dependencies. The Soviets also demanded exemption from the IMF's authority to approve exchange rate changes, and this exemption was written into the fund agreement. They further demanded exemption from the requirement to subscribe 25 percent of their quota in gold, but this exemption was not granted.[20]

The Soviets did sign the agreements establishing the IMF and the World Bank but never ratified them. Edward Bernstein believes that the refusal was related to the fact that the United States turned down a Soviet request for a $10 billion loan for postwar reconstruction. Whatever the reason, the Soviets refused to play their scripted role.[21]

That was the most immediate divergence of plan from reality, but hardly the only one. After the war, as the nightmarish lineaments of Europe's ruins emerged from behind the smoke and clouds, Harry White described the broken dream of the postwar economic planners in terms that have some of the poignancy of childhood memories: "It was expected that the early post-war world would witness a degree of unity and good-will in international political relationships among the victorious allies never before reached in peace-time. It was expected that the world would move rapidly . . . toward 'One World.' . . . No influential persons, as far as I can remember, expressed the expectation or the fear that international relations would worsen during these years."[22]

No one foresaw that military spending would continue through the cold war after peace treaties had ended the hot war. Nor was it understood at the time of the Bretton Woods Conference just how extreme was the destitution of most of Europe. Most countries had almost no international reserves, their export industries were in bad shape, they had considerable demands for imports of raw materials to get back on their feet, and they were consequently neither willing nor able to make their currencies convertible in accord with the IMF articles of agreement.

Americans had been led to believe that no funding beyond the IMF contribution would be necessary to meet the needs for reconstruction in Britain, and that the fund would also fulfill most aid requirements elsewhere. However, in 1947, the U.S. secretary of state, George C. Marshall, announced an unprecedented program of foreign economic assistance. During the four years from 1948 to 1952, the United States provided $11.6 billion in grants and $1.8 billion in loans to Europe.[23] Accompanying the grants and loans were U.S. advisors who directed the funds and instructed European recipients on the economic reforms they should implement. Unquestionably, the Marshall Plan spoke with a louder voice than the IMF and commanded more attention from European economic ministers. The Marshall Plan replaced the multilateral economic police force of the IMF with a unilateral American one. Americans used the Marshall Plan to encourage adoption of economic policies favored by the United States. So the enforcement powers of the IMF, such as the ability to control access to the fund by countries seeking to borrow, became less important to borrowers than the Bretton Woods planners had expected they would be. In fact, members found that they could violate the IMF articles without paying a real price.

France was the most notable example. In 1948, the French proposed to devalue their currency by about 25 percent against the dollar, without changing its relationship to the pound and the other European currencies. The French franc would have then had two exchange rates, and French traders would have had a golden opportunity to exploit the difference between the two. For example, a French cloth manufacturer could buy wool in Australia, paying with sterling, which was an acceptable international reserve currency. He could then ship the wool to France, turn it into cloth, then sell the woolen cloth in the United States, receiving dollars. There was a built-in profit of 25 percent on the wool just because of the difference in the two exchange rates. It would cost the manufacturer 25 percent fewer francs to buy the wool than he received when he sold the wool for dollars.[24]

The IMF refused to approve the French proposal, but that didn't keep the French from implementing it. As a punishment, the IMF made the French ineligible to borrow from the fund until 1952. However, the penalty was no more than an embarrassing slap on the wrist. It had no value as a deterrent, because there was plenty of money available to France from the Marshall Plan.

France's devaluation was followed by a British devaluation in 1949. Again, the IMF was taken somewhat lightly. The IMF did not dispute the fact that the pound needed to be devalued, but it is doubtful whether IMF objections would have mattered in any event. Britain notified the IMF about the devaluation twenty-four hours before it took place, and devalued the pound more than the IMF economists thought was either necessary or desirable.

More importantly, the British devaluation both demonstrated that free markets had not been tamed by the planners and debunked Secretary Morgenthau's boast that the usurious bankers had been driven from the temple of international finance. Under the IMF approach to currency management, devaluation was a last-ditch measure, permissible only when it was absolutely necessary. Britain's financial woes were clear to any astute observer, and as the inevitable day of reckoning approached, the markets took what measures they could to protect themselves against damage. Foreign buyers of British goods postponed their purchases and delayed their payments because British goods would be much cheaper after the devaluation. British importers of foreign goods, by contrast, sped up their purchases and payments because foreign products would cost more British pounds after the devaluation. This practice, called "leading and lagging," brought Britain's reserve position under pressure and helped accelerate the decision to devalue. The authorities could not resist the force of the markets. A scant two weeks before they devalued the pound, British financial officials denied that they would take that step. However, those who knew anything at all knew better than to take the officials at their word. The incident proved that markets had not been tamed.

Then, in 1950, Canada decided that it was better to endure the curse of the markets than to accept the cure of the IMF. In fact, the country's leaders determined that one of the basic justifications for the IMF—exchange rate stability—posed risks that the society was unwilling to take and floated the Canadian dollar. Canada's decision brings to mind Gracian's aphorism: "The wise man does at once what the fool does finally."[25] Two decades later, the rest of the world would follow its lead. However, at the time, the decision seemed radical and fraught with peril. Based on an analysis of the country's reserve position and cost structure by IMF and Canadian economists, the value of the Canadian dollar had been fixed at about U.S. $.90. During 1950, as the U.S. economy boomed, dollars poured into Canada. Americans were buying cheap Canadian products and investing heavily in the country. Soon it was clear that the exchange rate was too low. Under a floating rate system, supply and demand would have set the value of the Canadian dollar higher. But under the IMF regime, in order to devalue or revalue currencies, countries had to go through a time-consuming process that involved review of the economic fundamentals by IMF technicians, who then set an appropriate rate. Canada not only wanted to move quickly but also feared that the planners might err. Canadian producers could have been stuck with a too-high exchange rate that would make their exports uncompetitive and eventually lead to economic stagnation. So instead of putting its fate in the hands of theoreticians, Canada decided to trust the markets.

In September 1950, Canada decoupled its dollar from the fixed-rate system, allowing it to float freely on the international currency markets. Dire consequences were predicted by those who favored fixed rates—capital flight, destabilizing currency swings, and so forth. In fact, Canada's exchange rate quickly reached an appropriate level, thanks to the interplay of market forces. Like the little boy who pointed at the bare emperor, Canada's action told an uncomfortable truth about fixed currency rates and the elaborate institution that had been designed to enforce them. At the time, in response to vehement IMF criticism, Canada claimed that the float would be only temporary. In fact, "temporary" meant over a decade; the Canadian dollar floated from 1950 until 1961. Canada's successful economic progress under a floating rate regime later became an exemplar for economists who doubted that Keynesian planning mechanisms could work well in the long run.

The Bretton Woods system had really been designed to solve the problem of the 1930s, and the biggest concern of the economists who administered it was to prevent a recurrence of global deflation and depression. In order to buy the equipment and supplies they needed to reconstruct their economies, European countries had to do business with America, which was in effect the only store in town. This meant they needed dollars. Because the United States was the only economy that had survived the war intact, American industry dominated world markets. Since European industries were in no position to compete against U.S. suppliers either in their home markets or in export markets, they had no way to earn the dollars they needed. In 1950, partly in order to confront the so-called dollar shortage, the countries of Europe formed the European Payments Union (EPU), a mechanism that allowed them to settle their mutual payment obligations without recourse to the IMF. The EPU decreased the need for dollars by allowing participating countries to simply settle their net obligations, rather than make multiple dollar payments.

Another measure is nothing less than astonishing to contemporary readers. U.S. advisors actually directed European countries to put in place a wide range of trade protectionist measures that discriminated against U.S. products. The purpose of these fateful measures was to reduce the Europeans' need for dollars by encouraging the growth of domestic industries.[26]

Although the EPU helped, it did not solve the problem of the "dollar shortage." In fact, the design of the world financial system had a serious flaw. Because all currencies were pegged to the dollar, the United States had become the central banker of the entire world. If America were to balance its books and spend no more than it received, there would be no outflow of dollars to the rest of the world. But if there was no outflow of dollars to the rest of the world, other countries could not grow any faster than the supply of gold. Under the gold standard, countries could print only as much money as their gold reserves had permitted. Now they could print only as much money as their dollar reserves—including their quotas at the IMF—permitted. The result of all this was that the world depended on the United States running a deficit. Barring deflation, the world could have economic growth only if the United States sent out more dollars than it took in.

Only then would central bankers in Europe be able to expand their own money supplies and stimulate their economies.

The United States ran its first deficits in 1950. These were not trade deficits; America still exported more than it imported. However, military spending, foreign aid, tourism, and private investment by American corporations all sent dollars into the coffers of European central banks and generated balance-of-payments deficits throughout the 1950s. Under the circumstances, official statistics did not at first call them deficits, preferring instead the more neutral phrase "net transfers of gold and dollars to the rest of the world."[27] Indeed, for most of this period, American policymakers and international economic officials not only did not fear deficits but actually encouraged measures to make the deficits larger. In 1953, Congress established a Commission on Foreign Economic Policy that recommended a series of measures to increase the flow of dollars abroad, such as tax incentives to encourage foreign investment.

Throughout the 1950s, as the U.S. deficits expanded, European economies grew. However, with prosperity came a certain audacious resentment of the dollar—understandable, since in fact, by 1959, the "dollar shortage" had been replaced by a "dollar glut."[28] In theory, the U.S. dollar could be exchanged for gold. In practice, the more the U.S. deficits expanded, the less likely it was that the United States would have enough gold to back all of its outstanding dollars. The dollars held by foreign central banks were like bank passbooks that entitled them to claim U.S. gold. The survival of this bank depended on confidence. Ironically, the structure of the Bretton Woods system virtually guaranteed that confidence would sooner or later run out.

In 1960, the economist Robert Triffin formally identified the Achilles' heel of the Bretton Woods system. In his honor, the weakness was named "Triffin's Dilemma." On the one horn of this dilemma hung the fact that the world depended on U.S. deficits in order to have money supply growth and economic expansion. On the other horn hung the fact that U.S. dollars were supposed to be convertible into gold at the $35 per ounce official price. In John Law's France, the prince de Conti had exposed the weakness of the bank by sending several wagonloads of notes and demanding gold payment for them. A similar fate lay in store for a world financial system should foreign holders of dollars make the very reasonable decision to hold gold instead of that American IOU called the dollar. The obvious solution to this problem was for the

United States to cut its deficits and stop spending more than it received, but if the United States wiped out its deficits, it would decrease world reserves. As a result, the money supply in Europe would decrease, and recessions or depressions would follow.

Triffin's Dilemma proved prophetic, in a way that Triffin himself had not expected. Like other economists of his day, he truly considered deflation to be the greatest danger to the world economy. He did not really expect inflation to sink the Bretton Woods system. In fact, he believed that the Triffin Dilemma could be avoided by turning the IMF into a real central bank with the power to create a new international reserve currency, instead of putting the dollar at the core of the entire global financial system.

However, the U.S. Department of the Treasury fought this proposal vigorously and successfully.

By 1960, the dollar's weakness was unquestionable. In London, the center of the international gold market, an ounce of gold could buy $40. Of course, the official price in the United States was $35. The difference reflected fears that the dollar would have to be devalued. The strong showing of Democrat John Kennedy against Republican Richard Nixon in the presidential campaign seemed to make the fears more plausible, since the Democrats did not have a reputation for making sacrifices in favor of financial interests. For this reason, shortly before the election Kennedy made a public statement that "if elected President, I shall not devalue the dollar from the present rate. Rather, I shall defend its present value and its soundness."[29] That statement, coupled with heavy sales of gold for dollars by the Bank of England, helped bring the market price back to $36, but it did not solve the underlying problem. Early in his presidency, Kennedy told advisors that there were two things he feared—nuclear war and the payments deficit.[30] Though he narrowly avoided nuclear war, he could not escape Triffin's Dilemma.

Elected with a razor-thin margin, Kennedy had to choose between policies that would strengthen the dollar and policies that would strengthen the domestic economy. Strengthening the dollar meant cutting the deficit. Cutting the deficit meant choking back on domestic economic growth. Yet domestic economic growth was already anemic.

A task force proposed measures to keep dollars from flowing abroad: discourage foreign investment by U.S. companies, slow the rise of wages and prices, change the farm price support system, and open foreign markets to U.S. exports. It also recommended that Triffin's proposal for an international central bank be taken up seriously. Reform of the monetary system was controversial, however. The secretary of the treasury was quoted as saying that the United States should continue to be the world's banker.[31]

Instead of introducing fundamental reforms, the United States procrastinated. President Kennedy gave a speech that recognized Triffin's Dilemma—the world's dependence on U.S. deficits and the need for the United States to get its deficits under control in order to prevent further erosion of confidence in the dollar. However, actions fell short of words. More resources were given to the Export-Import Bank, the American finance agency that makes loans to help foreign customers buy American products. Defense spending was reduced, very tentatively and very temporarily. Curiously, a 1962 order required the armed services to buy supplies and equipment in the United States when possible, even if they had to spend more to ship the stuff overseas than it would have cost to simply buy it there. Foreign aid was tied to the purchase of U.S. goods. Higher taxes on foreign earnings were proposed, to discourage foreign investment by U.S. corporations. Most of the measures were short-term. Some were counterproductive. None met the dimensions of the problem.

One regulation put in place during this period shows just how direly consequential the unintended consequences of government action can be. In 1963, an "interest equalization" tax was imposed on foreign borrowers of dollars. The reasoning behind the tax was unassailable. Europeans had been borrowing heavily in the U.S. capital markets, exacerbating the balance-of-payments deficit. The traditional way of addressing that problem would be to raise interest rates, so that borrowing dollars would be more expensive. Instead of flowing abroad to take advantage of profitable investment opportunities, dollars would have flowed into the United States to take advantage of high interest rates. However, the fragile state of the economy ruled out tight money policies, since high interest rates would have discouraged borrowing by domestic business borrowers, homebuyers, and others whose purchases were needed to stimulate growth. Also, the Europeans had not been drawn to the U.S. market simply because of attractive interest rates. Costs of borrowing in Europe were high not only because of interest rates but because the development of European capital markets had been stunted by controls and red tape. Treasury Department planners thus decided to raise the cost of borrowing in the United States, but only for foreign borrowers. Accordingly, instead of raising interest rates, they elected to impose a tax on foreign loans. The tax would add an additional one percentage point to the cost of new borrowings.[32]

The measure did succeed in keeping foreigners from borrowing in the U.S. markets. However, it did not put a stop to foreign borrowing of dollars *offshore*. Unnoticed by the American regulators, a vast offshore pool of dollars had collected and needed only the appropriate economic signal to become a powerful capital market. During the 1950s, the cold war had led the Russians and the Chinese to examine carefully the vulnerability of their financial arrangements. Both countries used dollars in international trade. However, to maintain a dollar deposit at an American bank would be to leave their treasure in the hands of their enemies. American authorities could easily instruct the American bank to freeze the deposits. So, during the Korean War, China placed some dollar deposits at the Banque Commericale pour l'Europe du Nord, under the cover name of the National Bank of Hungary. Later, the Soviet Union, for similar reasons, placed dollar deposits in European rather than American banks, to keep them beyond the reach of American regulators.[33]

In 1958, with the pound sterling under pressure, British authorities asked their merchant banks to cut back on the use of sterling to finance trade transactions that did not involve Britain directly. Instead of using sterling, they were to use dollars. The Russians, who were earning dollars from their oil sales but did not want to place the dollars in American banks, were an obvious source of dollars. Thus, a small market in dollars began to develop outside the United States, based on Russian oil money. The offshore market had some advantages over the U.S. market besides the advantage that deposits could not be easily frozen. For example American banks had to abide by reserve requirements. For every $100 deposited, they could lend out only $97, because 3 percent had to be kept on reserve. This meant that if interest rates were 10 percent, an American bank would have to charge a borrower more than 10 percent in order to cover the cost of reserves.[34]

Thus, it was potentially more economical to borrow dollars in Europe, where there was no reserve requirement, than to borrow them in the United States. Moreover, when the Treasury Department put into effect its interest equalization tax, the economic advantage became significant enough to draw business away from the United States. The result was the birth of the Euromarkets. Shortly after the interest equalization tax became effective, the Italian highway authority Autostrade borrowed $15 million, not from the U.S. market but from investors in Europe.[35] The Treasury Department's interest equalization tax had created a new problem: Europeans developed the technology to compete with the American financial system. The Eurodollar market became a major fact of international financial life, totally beyond the reach of U.S. regulation. In 1973, when American regulators froze the bank accounts of Libya, the American bank Bankers Trust refused to honor Libya's request for funds from its account at a Bankers Trust branch in London. After a long court battle, the high court in London ruled that deposits in the London branch were subject to British law and that Bankers Trust was wrong to honor the U.S. freeze.[36]

Eventually, even American companies that needed to borrow money found that London was an attractive alternative to New York. By 1989, Eurodollar borrowings were well in excess of $100 billion per year. Not all the borrowers have been European. Big-name American corporations like Coca-Cola, IBM, General Motors, and Sears have all had occasion to borrow in the Eurodollar markets rather than in the United States.

Obviously, attempts to solve the balance-of-payments problem through administrative controls didn't work. They didn't address the fundamental cause of the situation—to wit, that the United States was printing too many dollars to keep the gold price at $35 per ounce. Throughout the 1960s, while presidents and their counselors considered and sometimes implemented regulations, controls, and restrictions to reduce the balance-of-payments deficit, the Federal Reserve Board continued to print dollars. The horns of the Triffin Dilemma grew sharper. In order to forestall demands for gold, the U.S. Treasury and the Federal Reserve worked out a series of "swap agreements" with foreign central banks. These swap agreements allowed the United States to draw loans denominated in foreign currencies. Instead of paying obligations in gold, it could pay in the currency of the payee. This provided a sort of insurance against devaluation of the dollar, since the United States was borrowing and would have to repay foreign currencies regardless of their cost in dollars.[37] But these measures amounted to little more than temporizing. Eventually, most of the swap credits were refinanced as long-term debt.

Another interesting attempt to patch rather than fix the Bretton Woods system—interesting because it illustrates the impotence of rhetoric about international economic and financial cooperation in the face of national self-interest—was the "gold pool." Eight countries—Belgium, Britain, France, Germany, Italy, the Netherlands, Switzerland, and the United States—agreed to intervene in the London gold market, buying and selling gold to keep the price close to $35 per ounce. The free-market price for gold was an important indicator of the level of confidence in the U.S. dollar. As long as $35 could buy an ounce of gold both in the private and in the official market, there seemed to be no compelling reason for anyone to exchange dollars for gold. However, if the value of the dollar began to fall in the private market, as it did in 1960, when it took $40 to buy an ounce of gold, rational people would certainly want to exchange their dollars for gold before the dollar fell farther. Thus, a fall in the gold value of the dollar could precipitate the much-feared "run on the bank" that might deplete U.S. gold stocks and lead to the collapse of the Bretton Woods system.

The gold pool worked, in a manner of speaking. It stabilized the market price for gold at $35 per ounce. However, it did not stop the golden hemorrhage from Fort Knox.

European central banks had no intention of depleting their own gold reserves in order to keep the gold price of the dollar at $35 per ounce. So they honored the letter of their agreement while flouting its spirit. European central bankers first cashed in dollars for U.S. gold, then sold the gold on the London market. Thus, although the European central banks were among the biggest sellers of gold, they were also among the biggest buyers, and the very thing that the gold pool was created to prevent, a run on U.S. gold, was brought about. Between 1960 and 1967, the non-U.S. members of the G-10 (the ten biggest economic powers, known as the Group of Ten) bought 150 million ounces of gold, increasing by one-third the gold stocks they held at the end of 1960. Except for Britain and Canada, every member of this group added gold to its stocks. While Britain sold 38 million ounces, and the United States 164 million ounces, France bought more than 100 million ounces, accounting for two-thirds of the total acquisition by G-10 countries.[38] The gold pool was no more than a gilded circle in which central banks bought gold from the United States for dollars and then sold it to each other.

European economies had more than recovered from the devastation of the war. The United States, once preeminent, had lost gold, and with gold, power. The foundations of the Bretton Woods system, one of the West's most important institutions, had corroded. Yet the push that toppled the system came not from Moscow but from Paris. General de Gaulle aimed to make France supreme in Europe, and in order to achieve his goal, he had to beat back U.S. hegemony there. So, in the mid-1960s, he precipitated the inevitable crisis for Bretton Woods.

President Johnson was in office, and he had decided to step up American involvement in Vietnam. He needed money to do it. "The sinews of war, unlimited money," Cicero had written two millennia before. That verity had not changed. Instead of raising taxes to prosecute the war, President Johnson opted to finance it by running larger deficits. His decision put him squarely in the tradition of the medieval kings who had mixed base metals with gold in order to finance their caparisoned battle arrays. From a domestic political point of view, this decision made excellent sense. As a result of the increased deficit spending, the American economy boomed. Unemployment fell, while GNP grew at an astonishing 8.5 percent.[39]

However, increasing U.S. deficits also poured more dollars into the coffers of European central banks. There were already too many dollars to support the gold price, and now the printing presses were running overtime. Europeans accused the United States of "exporting inflation," since the increase in the dollar supply helped spur an increase in money supplies in Europe. In fact, a close look at the numbers shows that despite the U.S. deficits, world reserves were increasing on average by only about 2 percent per year. More important issues than economics were driving the debate.

French president de Gaulle used the monetary issue to press his drive against U.S. hegemony. At a press conference in 1965, a reporter asked him a question about the international financial system. The president took advantage of the occasion to call for a new monetary standard that did not bear the stamp of any one country in particular: "On what basis? Truly it is hard to imagine that it could be any standard other than gold, yes, gold, whose nature does not alter, which may be formed equally well into ingots, bars or coins, which has no nationality, and which has, eternally and universally, been regarded as the unalterable currency par excellence."[40] Thus did France fling a golden gauntlet at the feet of Uncle Sam. The challenge was not only to the Bretton Woods system but to the political and economic hegemony of Washington. De Gaulle sought not only a new monetary standard but recognition of the grandeur of France.

France had long had a special fondness for gold and the gold standard. Under the golden rule, after all, they who have the gold make the rule. As it happened, an undervalued franc had allowed France to capture much of Britain's gold during the interwar period, and the power relationship between Britain and France had tilted decidedly in favor of Paris. So gold had been good to France.

No wonder that, before the conference at the Mount Washington Hotel in 1944, France had designed its own detailed plan to restore the gold standard.[41] But neither Britain nor the United States considered the gold standard either desirable or workable. The whole point of Bretton Woods was to free the world from slavery to old economic ideas, to build new institutions that would provide liquidity, prosperity, and the blessings of deficit spending untrammeled by old golden fetters. France was at the time an occupied nation, and its plan was given scant attention. Gold's role in the postwar economy was minimized. Under the Bretton Woods plan, only the United States pegged its currency to gold, buying and selling at the official rate. All other nations held dollars and had to maintain the value of their currencies in dollars. The United States was exempt from the discipline that yoked most other countries, because there was no standard beyond itself, no discipline except to buy and sell gold for $35 per ounce. With most of the gold already in the United States, that was hardly onerous.

This dollar discipline chafed France, a country where slights are not worn well. Recall that in 1948, the IMF—dominated then as always by Americans—had punished France for introducing dual exchange rates. These rates gave French traders an opportunity to profit by as much as 25 percent simply by purchasing raw materials in sterling and selling them for dollars. As a penalty for introducing them, France was not allowed to use IMF resources for four years. However, when Italy introduced a similar exchange rate regime for the lira, it did not suffer the same punishment.

Another blow to French pride came with devaluation in the mid-1950s. During the early 1950s, the French economy surged, stimulated by deficit spending. By the middle of the decade, inflation and balance-of-payments problems were serious. In 1958, France proposed to devalue the franc by 29 percent. While the IMF approved the devaluation, it attached strong conditions, requiring France to implement various reforms. One historian of the period says that French officials were "humiliated," since Britain had not been subject to similar conditions when it had to draw on IMF resources after the Suez crisis.[42]

It was not merely in retaliation for these slights that French authorities put into motion what appears to be a long-term strategy to torpedo the Bretton Woods system by attacking the dollar. While France endured penalties and the humiliation of devaluation, the United States ran deficits with impunity. This privileged position of the United States under Bretton Woods affronted President de Gaulle and his key financial advisors, most notably Jacques Rueff. Rueff's role in French monetary affairs dated back to the 1920s, when he had advised Prime Minister Poincaré on how to stabilize the franc. In 1943, he had helped draw up the French plan for an international monetary system that was virtually ignored by Britain and the United States. In the spring of 1961, he published an article criticizing U.S. policy, especially the $18.1 billion U.S. deficit. He demanded that the United States pay off in gold all dollar assets held by central banks, even if this meant that the dollar price of gold had to be raised.[43]

That year, France steadily but rather quietly converted enough dollars to gold to more than double its gold reserves.[44] Later in 1961, France opposed an effort to deal with the problem of the dollar by simply expanding the borrowing authority of the IMF. The United States had a potential right to borrow $5.8 billion from the IMF, but the fund's holdings of major currencies amounted to only about $1.6 billion.[45] One solution was to allow the IMF to borrow the additional currencies. However, as a result of French pressure, the European powers attached stringent conditions to what became the General Agreement to Borrow, including the condition that the borrower could not vote on the question of whether or not a loan should be granted.

Meanwhile President de Gaulle siphoned gold from Fort Knox to Paris, by exchanging dollars for gold. By December 1964, gold accounted for 73 percent of the reserves of France.[46] In that year, French Finance Minister Valéry Giscard d'Estaing officially proposed reforming the international monetary system in the direction of a gold standard. He was resurrecting elements of the 1943 French plan, and like their predecessors before them, U.S. Treasury secretary Douglas Dillon and British chancellor of the exchecquer Reginald Maudling strongly opposed the proposal.

France pressed the offensive. During 1966 and 1967, French officials fenced publicly with Americans over the question of how to reform the international monetary system. In March 1967, the United States took the extraordinary step of requesting that nations holding dollars not exchange them for gold.

In June, France effectively withdrew from the Gold Pool, refusing to continue contributing to the effort to maintain the official price of gold at $35 per ounce. Gold formerly contributed to the pool by France now had to be contributed by the United States. However, this was kept secret by mutual consent—secret, that is, until France found it advantageous to stimulate market panic with a well-timed press leak.

The opportunity soon came. Great Britain was on the verge of devaluing the pound. France refused to join with the other major nations in an agreement not to devalue their currencies in response to a British devaluation. France's refusal was leaked to the press. Uncertainty drove more investors to gold. In November, sterling was devalued by 14.3 percent.[47] Another leak followed—this time, it was the explosive news that France had stopped contributing to the Gold Pool in June. The markets went into a frenzy. On November 27, President de Gaulle flung another gilded gauntlet down, saying, "It is possible that the problems resulting from the devaluation of the pound will lead to the reestablishment of the international monetary system founded on the immutability, impartiality, and universality which are the privileges of gold."[48]

At the beginning of 1968, the U.S. government slapped on controls to prevent the export of dollars. Triffin's Dilemma turned its other horn. The threat of deflation was serious enough that on March 15, the remaining members of the Gold Pool de-emphasized the importance of gold as a reserve asset by instituting a two-tier price system that committed them to maintain the $35 per ounce gold price only for official transactions between central banks. For all others, the market price would apply. The Gold Pool members also agreed not to sell gold to private parties and to refrain from exchanging their dollars for gold from the U.S. reserves. Finally, and most importantly, the Gold Pool decided not to allow new gold to enter the international monetary system. In essence, this decision demonetized gold. New gold might have many valuable uses, but the only gold that counted as reserves or international money was old gold. This decision went directly counter to the French effort to reestablish the gold standard.

Yet France stuck to its line. On numerous occasions, French officials, including the president, publicly demanded that as a condition of reforming the monetary system, the United States must balance its books. In March, after the Gold Pool had made its decision to demonetize gold, President de Gaulle declaimed that France would not participate in any effort to shore up the dollar short of a new monetary conference to replace Bretton Woods with a gold standard. On March 29, as the Group of Ten opened its ministerial meeting in Stockholm, the French representative called for an increase in the dollar price of gold—in effect, a devaluation of the dollar.

It seemed that France had pushed too hard. Common Market principles and European unity notwithstanding, the risk of a collapse of the international monetary system was too frightening to confront. Over French objections, the ministers voted to accept a plan creating a new international reserve asset called special drawing rights, which would be a sort of synthetic international supermoney used only by central banks.

The French offensive on the United States and Bretton Woods ended in the spring of 1968, amid tremendous domestic upheaval. In May 1968, students tore up the streets of Paris to build barricades. Workers seized factories, and a general strike shut down even the Bank of France.

France bled gold. Terrified citizens stuffed currency into suitcases and fled the country. New exchange controls made it illegal to send money abroad. France requested international monetary authorities to stop exchanging French currency. As a result, stores and gas stations on the French border stopped accepting francs, and the value of French money plunged. Soon France was caught in the very snare it had so long and so patiently laid for the United States. In May, French reserves fell by over $300 million. In June, France borrowed the maximum under its swap agreement with the U.S. Federal Reserve, in order to prevent the United States from exchanging francs for gold. In July, the Bank of France and the Federal Reserve agreed to increase the swap limit from $100 million to $700 million. France also tapped the IMF for $745 million, an action that required the approval of other countries under the restrictive General Agreement to Borrow (a process put in place, ironically enough, because of President de Gaulle's desire to discipline the United States). In June, renewed violence put the franc under pressure again, and France had to sell $400 million in gold to defend the currency. Later in the year, France sold $900 million more of its gold reserves. French reserves fell from $6.9 billion to under $4 billion as the speculative crisis forced the Bank of France not only to spend its own reserves but also to borrow from other central banks.[49]

In response to France's request to borrow, American officials tried to walk a thin line. Clearly, a devaluation of the franc would be necessary. The riots had cost France about 3 percent of its GNP. Steel production was down a third; car production, by more than half. France's trade deficit surged from $700 million in the first quarter of 1968 to over $2 billion in the first quarter of 1969. Yet the Americans worried that if France devalued the franc too much, it could gain such a great trade advantage that other countries would follow suit, launching a wave of competitive devaluations.[50]

There was, however, an alternative—German revaluation.

Germany's domestic economy was strong, and its balance of payments was more than comfortably in surplus. In fact, Germany had a unique problem—how to keep capital out of the country. For some time, the Bundesbank had kept interest rates low in order to discourage international investors from buying German bonds. However, the low interest rates caused the economy to boom, and inflation loomed as a threat. The German mark was thus unquestionably worth more than its official value. Yet the German authorities did not want to revalue the mark. Why? They feared that if they revalued, France might devalue anyway, just to capture a trade advantage over German producers. Instead of revaluing, the German government decided to impose a tax on exports and to ease taxes on imports. The tax measure was something like a revaluation, since it made exports more expensive and imports cheaper. Meanwhile. France agreed to cut its budget deficit. However, international cooperation could only go so far.

On November 20, 1968, the Group of Ten financial ministers and their central bank colleagues convened at the Ministry of Economics in Bonn. In a meeting characterized by Great Britain's Harold Wilson as "inspired lunacy," delegates locked horns. The German delegates announced to the world press that a French devaluation was imminent, thus giving the impression that the really important decisions about France were made somewhat farther East than Paris. What appeared to be a decision to devalue the franc, however, turned out later not to be. French president de Gaulle instead blamed France's financial plight on "odious speculation" and announced a series of budget cuts and capital controls that he maintained would solve France's problems without devaluation.[51]

The following April, President de Gaulle lost a referendum and resigned. In August, President Georges Pompidou took his Common Market partners by surprise with an 11.1 percent devaluation of the franc. Just as people had feared, the franc was now undervalued. French exports were cheap on world markets, imports expensive. The French economy more than recovered. Thanks to the devaluation, France was back on the road to a balance-of-payments surplus.

As a result of the crises of the late 1960s, a new light began to dawn in the consciousness of international monetary policymakers. The fixed-rate system of Bretton Woods was admirably suited to a bygone age when events moved at a slow pace and private markets were weak. However, the delegates at the Mount Washington Hotel had not anticipated capital movements as forceful as those that now occurred. The world moved faster now, and it needed a mechanism that would allow currencies to adjust flexibly and smoothly to sudden changes. For ten years, the efforts of international monetary policymakers had been directed at maintaining the adequacy of reserves—the so-called liquidity problem. However, beginning in 1967, a series of panics caused first a flight from the pound, then a flight from the franc, and then even a flight from the mark. Capital surged across borders uncontrollably—or rather, the kinds of controls necessary to restrict it were really only feasible on the Eastern side of the Iron Curtain.

By the end of 1968, a few tentative voices began to be raised in favor of more flexible exchange rates. The dollar was clearly not worth $35 an ounce on the open market. The United States could simply have devalued the dollar, of course, but since devaluation would give the United States a sudden trade advantage, there was a real possibility that other countries might try to match the devaluation by devaluing their own currencies. An alternative was for the strong European economies to revalue their currencies. Doing so would have meant giving the United States an advantage in trade, something the Europeans were unwilling to do.

From 1968 to 1971, international planners struggled to find a new formula that would allow currency exchange rates to be both fixed and flexible. Private capital flows were now much bigger than anyone had ever predicted, and the Eurodollar market had emerged as a significant force in the international flow of funds. No matter what regulators tried to do, markets seemed to be a step ahead of them.

By 1970, the flow of capital into Germany made a mockery of the declared par value of the mark. Demand for marks ought to have made the mark more expensive, but Germany was unwilling to revalue. The Bundesbank cut interest rates to discourage capital from flowing in. The cuts weren't deep enough, though. Capital continued to flow in.

By April 1971, the Germans were talking publicly about abandoning the fixed currency exchange rate system and simply letting the market determine what the price of currencies ought to be. The alternative was draconian capital controls, and Germans who had experienced capital controls under the Third Reich were not inclined to repeat the experience. In May, the finance ministers of the European Economic Community adopted a carefully worded resolution that endorsed the German decision to float the mark. The Dutch also floated the guilder. The Bretton Woods system of fixed par values was wounded.

Pressure on the dollar continued to mount during the summer of 1971. In August, President Nixon announced an economic plan to combat inflation. The plan included tax credits, import surcharges, federal spending cuts, and an announcement that the dollar could no longer be exchanged for gold. He blamed speculators for "waging an all-out war on the American dollar."[52]

The Bretton Woods system had been Keynes's monument. Appropriately enough, then, in the long run it too was dead. Designed to fight the deflation that had led to the Great Depression and contributed to World War II, it was done in by inflation. The problem was both inevitable and unpredictable. Born in a village without people, the great economic plan to coordinate the prosperity of nations failed because it had left human freedom out of its calculus.

POWER PITS

Bretton Woods fell with the force of a monetary Bastille. When the experiment failed, it proved that money was too powerful to be contained in the cage of reason. The British devaluation in 1947, the French devaluation in 1958, the steadily worsening dollar dilemma, and the various monetary crises of the 1960s were early indications of the limits of Bretton Woods; although governments could keep adjustments at bay for a time, eventually the markets forced them through. When they were finally made, they were usually extreme: 14.3 percent in the case of Britain in 1947, 29 percent in the case of France in 1958, and so on. Adjustments of this magnitude held out a promise of great profit and a threat of great loss. People with investments in a currency that was weakening had every incentive to move their money out before the devaluation hit. Through leading and lagging and other measures, including, in the case of France in 1968, simply stuffing suitcases with cash and driving across the border, people sometimes managed to circumvent capital controls. However, these techniques were cumbersome, and in some cases illegal.

Although big banks and corporations could work their way around capital and other controls by using such avenues as the Euromarkets, ordinary people felt the full brunt of the official bans on the movement of money. In the later years of the Bretton Woods system, as the

95

distance widened between what governments pronounced as the official value of their currency and its actual market value, the international monetary system had a more and more intrusive effect on personal economic freedom. Currency stability took precedence over personal freedoms, and border police enforced controls on how much of their own money travelers could take on a trip. In his 1969 comic novel *Travels with My Aunt,* Graham Greene captures the spirit of the last years of Bretton Woods. A little old lady is waiting with her nephew at Heathrow Airport for a flight that will take them to France:

> As we sat over two gins and tonics in the departure lounge a loudspeaker announced, "Passengers on flight three-seven-eight to Nice will proceed to customs for customs inspection."
>
> We were alone at our table and my aunt did not bother to lower her voice amid the din of passengers, glasses and loud-speakers. "That is what I wished to avoid," she said. "They have now taken to spot-checks on passengers leaving the country. They whittle away our liberties one by one. When I was a girl you could travel anywhere on the continent except Russia without a passport and you took what you liked in the way of money. Until recently they only asked what money you had, or at the very worst they wanted to see your wallet. If there's one thing I hate in any human being it is mistrust."[1]

Around the same time, American travelers in France found it impossible to cash traveler's checks denominated in dollars. International monetary politics and fear of a dollar devaluation discouraged French banks from increasing their dollar holdings. The system designed to ensure prosperity, exchange rate stability, and free trade had become progressively less prosperous, stable, and free. In 1967, as the foundations of Bretton Woods crumbled and government delegations met to talk about adjustments and new plans, a financial revolution began.

Quiet but momentous, it would eventually wrest from sovereign states a power that governments had jealously guarded since antiquity: the control of money and finance. The revolution replaced the ordered despotism of bureaucrats with the chaotic, Darwinian democracy of the trading pits. Since governments had proven unable to deliver financial law and order, markets took the law into their own hands.

Financial vigilantes developed elaborate systems for managing the risks of a world on the frontier of chaos. They had more in common with casino gamblers than most of them care to admit, yet they transformed the financial institutions and structures that had grown up in a more stable time. Risk was their raison d'être. They depended on uncertainty; indeed, they could not survive *without* disorder.

Like most revolutions, theirs started with a small, almost negligible slight. In November 1967, an anonymous Chicago banker refused to lend British pound sterling to a college professor who wanted to sell the currency short. The college professor, Milton Friedman, thought that the official value of the British pound was too high. In fact, he knew that the pound had been kept at artificially high values only because governments were colluding to avoid facing reality.

In Britain's case, maintaining the value of the pound in 1967 was a sensitive issue of national prestige. However, the British government wasn't willing to do the tough, politically unpopular things it would take to make the pound worth the official value. Great Britain had built up a big, inefficient, heavily regulated, uncompetitive, and wasteful economic structure. The government lived beyond its means, ran deficits, and lost reserves. Under the old nineteenth-century gold standard, when a country lost reserves, its money supply automatically shrank, and the economy adjusted by going through a painful recession or depression. Under Bretton Woods, though, a country could postpone its day of reckoning by borrowing from the IMF and imposing capital controls to keep people from pulling their money out of the country. Those measures did not solve the fundamental problem, but they made it possible to procrastinate at the price of making the ultimate solution more difficult.

Eventually, there would be no escaping the choice of either devaluing the currency or deflating it by choking the economy. Governments don't usually like to devalue their currencies. Currencies are like national flags—they have a symbolic value far beyond their economic worth. On the other hand, governments don't usually like to deflate their economies either—people who lose jobs take out their frustrations in the voting booth. In democratic societies, there was always a temptation for governments to let these hard choices ride until after the next election, when they might become the problems of the opposition party.

Britain had wavered between the devil of inflation and the deep blue sea of depression for years. By 1967, time was running out, and it was inevitable that the pound should sooner or later go down. Friedman was sure the British government would have to throw in the towel and devalue the pound sterling. He wanted to borrow pounds from the bank; sell them on the market for the high, official value; and, when the British pound took its inevitable plunge, buy them back cheaply to repay the bank. If Friedman was right, he would pocket a handsome profit on the so-called short sale. But the banker refused to cooperate, not because of Friedman's credit rating but because of the Bretton Woods agreements. Only big corporations and massive financial institutions were allowed to deal in foreign currencies, the banker said. The bank couldn't allow just anyone to short the pound. The Federal Reserve and the Bank of England would object.

Deal or no deal, Friedman's analysis was correct. The British government did devalue the pound. Friedman would have made a killing had he been allowed to do what he planned. Instead, he wrote a series of articles for *Newsweek* magazine explaining what he had tried to do and why he had been unable to do it. The articles inspired a young man named Leo Melamed to organize the markets that would, in a scant two decades, ensure the supreme independence of money from any effective government control.[2]

The organizers of the Bretton Woods system had promised to throw usurious bankers out of the temple of international finance. Yet now it is the banks, investment banks, hedge funds, and other private financial institutions that judge governments and punish them financially. Their vigilante economics acknowledges no national border, bows to no regulatory authority, accepts no rule but the rule of financial power, and enforces rough justice against those who violate the law of the market.

The revolutionary Friedman eventually won a Nobel Prize despite, not because of, the theories that ushered in the era of the vigilantes. In writings as passionate as an anarchist's bomb, he equated capitalism with democracy, and economic choice with freedom of speech. Friedman is credited with almost single-handedly overturning the Keynesian orthodoxy, although the odds were against him all the way.

Born in New York City in 1912, his father a tailor, Friedman was an outsider from the start. He took his bachelor's degree at Rutgers University, in New Jersey, in 1932, then moved on to Chicago, where he completed his master's a year later. A peripatetic progress then took him through a fellowship program at Columbia, a research assistantship at Chicago, posts with the National Resources Committee and with the National Bureau of Economic Research, a visiting professorship in Wisconsin, a wartime post with the U.S. Treasury Department in Washington, and statistical research at Columbia, where he received his Ph.D. in 1946; then, after a year teaching in Minnesota, he returned to Chicago, where he taught for the next forty years.

It was no accident that Friedman did his most influential work in Chicago. "New York City at that time and still today regards itself as an outpost of Europe," he says. "It is much more rigid and orthodox in its opinions, and much less tolerant of divergent opinions. People in the East regarded me as a complete nut. They wouldn't have paid attention to me. But Chicago was and still is sort of a crude, frontier, anything-goes town. It is much more tolerant to eccentrics, nuts, and crazy people."[3] The University of Chicago was so tolerant that during the 1964 U.S. presidential elections, when the lines were drawn sharply between Lyndon Johnson's Roosevelt-style Democratic party and Barry Goldwater's laissez-faire Republicans, one of Friedman's colleagues at Chicago noted that theirs was the only university in the country that could field from its own faculty a council of economic advisors for either candidate. While Chicago is most closely and memorably associated with the market-oriented monetarism of Friedman and George Stigler, it also had a contingent of Keynesians and even a sprinkling of genuine socialists.

Ask an economist about Friedman's greatest contribution to science and you will hear about two things: the consumption function and the quantity theory of money. Keynesians had designed an analytical theory of consumption that said, essentially, people spend more or less depending on whether their current income is more or less. Friedman proved that this was not true. In fact, he established that only permanent changes in income are likely to cause people to change their spending habits. In other words, the long term was much more important to most people than Keynes had recognized.

Although academic economists generally consider Friedman's work on the consumption function to be the high point of his career, his battle to resurrect the quantity theory of money was arguably the hardest and longest fought. The notion that the quantity of money in an economy had an important effect on economic growth and on prices had fallen into disrepute during the Keynesian ascendancy. Friedman contended that growth of the money supply had to be stable and steady if the economy itself was to grow and prosper. However, fixed exchange rates, as under Bretton Woods, made this kind of stable growth impossible. "His analysis was amply justified when by the 1960's, due to the change in monetary policies, the dollar shortage had turned into a dollar glut," says one commentator.[4]

As early as 1950, Friedman's maverick ideas had led him to propose an alternative to the Bretton Woods system. He predicted that it would be impossible for governments to maintain both fixed currency rates and independent monetary policies. He proposed that instead of fixing their exchange rates, governments ought to let them float, on the principle that a fixed exchange rate would ultimately not be a very powerful incentive for governments to force their populations to undergo painful economic adjustments. Instead of taking the harsh medicine required to maintain stable exchange rates, countries would be more likely to restrain trade to keep domestic employment high. They would either restrict imports, promote exports, or control the flow of capital—and in fact, countries did all three under Bretton Woods. However, from 1950 until almost 1970, this advice was ignored. Friedman was viewed as a brilliant eccentric, a man whose intelligence and analytical power commanded respect but whose conclusions were decidedly odd.

Friedman's eventual vindication came about as a result of his attack on another theoretical fixture of Keynesianism, the Phillips curve. This curve expressed a relationship between inflation and unemployment that was particularly influential during the 1960s. In essence, it said that government planners faced a trade-off between inflation and employment. In other words, governments could solve their unemployment problems by inflating their currencies. To Friedman, this seemed a ridiculous proposition. He predicted that rational people would *not* build new factories and hire workers to make and sell things if the money they received was steadily decreasing in value, and if people didn't invest and produce more, there wouldn't be any new jobs. So Friedman said that a point would be reached at which the alleged trade-off between inflation and unemployment broke down, and an economy directed by the Phillips curve would find itself plagued by both high inflation and high unemployment. This prediction came true in the United States in the 1970s, during the infamous period of "stagflation."

Friedman's economic science, statistical expertise, and cool analytical method impressed his academic colleagues, but it was his impassioned promarket rhetoric that made the public take notice of him.

Economic democracy, the notion that people can best determine the value of things by their free decisions to buy or sell, was not itself a new idea. In fact, Adam Smith taught that an "invisible hand" combines free decisions to produce the wealthiest possible society. Putting the ideas of Adam Smith to work in nineteenth-century England meant uprooting much of the aristocracy, destroying the royal monopolies that kept efficient competitors out of lucrative businesses, and opening up the political life of the nation to many new participants. It was a natural step to conclude that free markets could bring similar benefits to international finance in the twentieth century. Freeing money from government control would allow individuals to make their own decisions on where to invest or borrow, so the invisible hand could guide international financial affairs to the best possible economic result.

Yet despite the evident benefits of free markets and free trade, money and finance had never been free. A currency and an army had historically been the twin pillars of national sovereignty. So, when the international financial system broke down between World War I and World War II, governments acted to fix it, rather than scrap it. The objectives of the Bretton Woods system were noble and, to those who had just lived through the Great Depression, unquestionable: to ensure international economic and financial stability and to finance reconstruction after the war.

After two decades of bureaucratic failures, the world needed a dose of democratic discipline.

But in order to supplant the dictatorship of central banks with pure economic democracy, Friedman's thought needed muscle.

The muscle came from Chicago.

There, in the mid-1800s, grain merchants had invented the futures exchange. Crowded, noisy, rough, and sometimes corrupt, invariably cursed by farmers, the futures exchange stamped its seal on the rich black earth of the corn belt and changed forever the world trade in agricultural commodities. In the twentieth century, futures trading would also change the financial structure of the world.

Throughout history, in times of turmoil or distress, merchants and farmers faced the terrifying risk of losing all they had spent a lifetime building. Throughout history too, speculators had been willing to take on this risk, for a price. In Japan during the seventeenth century, as ragtag armies burned and looted their way across the country, the price of rice rose and fell with dizzying speed. A merchant might decide to buy rice when battling samurai bands cut supply lines and prices rose steeply. He expected scarce supplies to drive prices even higher, making his purchase a good investment, but he could be wiped out if a quick victory resolved the battle, opened the lines, and let abundant supplies of grain into the city. Sketchy records show that when the shogun at last established a modicum of order in the land, Japanese merchants developed a mechanism to protect themselves against sudden price changes. They would buy and sell rice for future delivery. If most merchants expected prices to rise in the future, the price of rice for future delivery would be high, and if they expected prices to fall, the future price would be low. The existence of future prices meant that merchants were not completely in the dark. They could make a decision on whether to buy or sell today with some clear indication of where the market as a whole expected prices to be next month.

In Holland during the seventeenth-century tulip mania, a futures market appeared again. Like the market in Japan, this one came about because of uncertainty about future value of the wild, erratic market for these exotic new bulbs—bulbs for which more than one aristocrat had staked and lost a family fortune.

Little wonder that futures should have appeared in a rough, wooden town on the nineteenth-century American frontier. The steel plow had just begun to slice through eons of prairie sod. Railroads were spanning a still-wild West. Drought, flood, Civil and Indian wars, locusts, grasshoppers, and prairie fires did for the corn and pork and beef supplies what marauding samurai had achieved in distant Japan centuries before. Again, merchants bought and sold the future for comfort in the present.

In 1841, a grain broker named W. I. Whiting and an elevator operator named Thomas Richmond formed the Chicago Board of Trade (CBOT), an informal club with no legal charter or corporate structure. About a dozen of Chicago's leading merchants joined them. During its early history, the board worked on establishing inspection standards and grading criteria for grain, pork, beef, lumber, and other commodities and set up a daily telegraph report of market conditions and prices for its members.

Trading of securities began in 1858. At that time, currency was issued by banks and secured by their investments. When war broke out between the North and the South, the prices of Southern stocks plunged. Banks that had issued currency secured by investments in Southern stocks were in trouble, since the value of their investments had plummeted. People who happened to hold currency issued by these banks tried to get rid of it as quickly as they could, before the banks failed, by using it to pay their bills. Meanwhile, they held on to the safe, sound currency issued by banks that had not invested heavily in the South. "The bills of the sound banks rapidly disappeared from circulation, while those which were distrusted were passed from one anxious holder to another," writes one historian.[5] Gresham's law— the discovery attributed to Queen Elizabeth's advisor in her effort to restore the British currency after her father's Great Debasement—was in full force: bad money drove out good. In order to keep commerce from becoming paralyzed—as it surely would be, if bad money continued to be given in settlement of debts—the CBOT members agreed among themselves to establish values at which the notes of the various state banks could be exchanged. In other words, they arrived at a fair price for each currency based on the degree of risk that the bank would fail. If a bank was sound, its currency traded at full face value. The currency of weak banks traded at a discount from face value because of the additional risk.

By the 1870s, the CBOT had already become a major force in international trade. In 1857, no wheat had been raised in the western United States, and American exports to England were negligible. By 1871, America exported twenty-three million bushels of wheat to London and Liverpool, almost three-quarters of it raised west of Lake Michigan, graded by CBOT standards, and bought and sold by English traders who received Chicago market reports by telegraph.[6]

Already, two great evolutionary streams of traders had diverged in Chicago. The first stream was the genus of the visionaries who predicted the grand sweep of political and economic fundamentals, forecast how the markets would react, and took trading positions that would win spectacularly if their judgment proved true. These were the ancestors of the fundamental traders. The second stream was the genus of what we now call technicians, the traders who focus their attention on the moves of the market itself, rather than supply, demand, and politics in the world at large. Most of their descendants are little known outside of financial circles.

The great nineteenth-century exemplar of the first stream, that of the visionaries, was Philip D. Armour. Born in northern New York in

1830, he was indentured to a farmer after a few years of the most rudimentary education. He bought his freedom at age twenty and joined the California gold rush, where he accumulated enough of a stake to return east as far as Milwaukee and establish himself in the grain business. After a few years, he diversified into pork packing. "Just before the close of the war, in the spring of 1865, pork was selling at $40 a barrel, and the New York operators thinking it would go to $60 were buying it right and left. Mr. Armour thought that the Rebellion was on the eve of collapse, and that if the war should suddenly end, pork, instead of being worth $40 a barrel, would suddenly not be worth $20."[7] Armour caught a train to New York and began selling pork short. Soon after, the Confederacy surrendered, and the price of pork fell from $40 to $18 a barrel. The speculation made Armour a millionaire. He subsequently built his pork-packing operation into one of the biggest meat processing companies in the United States.

Less well known, because he built himself no corporate monument, is B. P. Hutchinson. A farm boy from Danvers, Massachusetts, he left the farm as soon as he could get away and moved to Lynn, where he learned to cut leather for the shoe factories. He eventually opened his own factory but was wiped out by the recession of 1857. He left Lynn, heavily in debt, and made his way to Chicago, where he paid $5 to join the Board of Trade:

> He had the genius of a careful speculator, but was not a daring one. He understood fully, and acted upon, the first half of Ricardo's great maxim, "Cut short your losses." He had no pride of opinion, but could change with the varying tide of the market. He was at one time a bull, and at another time a bear, and often both by turns, within the compass of an hour. No man ever had a keener perception of what the crowd was doing, as well as what the particular operators were doing. No man on 'Change, who dealt largely, could long hide his schemes from "Old Hutch," as the boys soon began to familiarly call him.[8]

Hutchinson eventually accumulated a fortune of $5 million, the equivalent of $94 million in 1994 dollars.

Chicago's half-literate grain traders, led by men like Hutchinson, built something entirely new. Their exchange had features that made it much safer than anything invented in Japan or Europe. Most notable of these was the clearinghouse, a central authority that made sure everyone participating in the market could be trusted by treating each as if none could be trusted. The prices of corn or wheat or beans for future delivery rose and fell many times within a day. When the market expected drought to tighten supplies and drive up future prices, the appearance of a cloud in the sky over Chicago was enough to drive prices sharply down. What would prevent a speculator from gambling on a price trend and simply not paying up if he lost? There was a fortune to gain from being right, and nothing to lose if one could just walk away from contracts when wrong. Unlike Japan or Amsterdam, America was big and full of newcomers. A man could skip out on his debts in Chicago, make his way to St. Louis, and never be tracked down.

So the Chicago merchants ruled that at the end of every trading day, every contract or commitment would be reexamined in light of the day's price moves. Losers would immediately pay a sort of security deposit, called margin, and the deeper in the hole they went, the more margin they would pay, even if the contract had months to run. The invention of the clearinghouse made the Chicago market safe, at least as far as credit risk was concerned, and helped to establish it as the central point for agricultural trade. Farmers as far away as Nebraska, a far distance indeed in the nineteenth century, saw the selling price of their corn crops determined by the Chicago trading pits. The populist politicians of the day, when they railed at the speculators of Chicago, found ready listeners among the impoverished farmers. But futures exchanges provided a central point where the prices of a whole nation's crops could be determined not by fiat but by what hundreds of traders, in the purest Adam Smith fashion, decided. Chicago's futures exchanges set the price for corn from Minnesota to Mississippi, for beef driven from Abilene to the east-bound trains at the Dodge City railhead, and for soybeans in the Ohio, Illinois, and the Missouri River bottomlands. In Chicago, America's widely dispersed farmers were drawn into one economic unit.

Economic Darwinism inspired the architects who built the Chicago exchanges. Their simple, expressive design has endured, so that even today, traders fight for economic survival in trading pits that look like miniarenas. Concentric rings of stairs descend from floor level down to a flat, round open space where one could imagine cockfights being held.

At the world's most active trading pit, the Treasury Bond Pit at the Chicago Board of Trade, five hundred traders squeeze into an arena originally built to accommodate only one hundred. They arrive early, well before the market opens, and mark their stands by dropping a badge or ticket to the floor. The most successful traders occupy the top stair, where they have a clear view of all the activities in the pit below and of the phone clerks who are their link with the outside world.

These top-stair plutocrats dominate their territories, and the crowd defers to their dominance. Perhaps the biggest trader in the bond pit is Tom Baldwin, who left a job in the meatpacking industry to trade bond futures in 1982. He had no prior trading experience. "His market operations have gotten so big," a journalist wrote in 1984, "that many believe he has become one of the dominant forces in pricing U.S. Treasury bonds, which is rare for an independent floor trader. He pits himself daily against Wall Street investment banks, wirehouses, primary dealers, major banks, and the Fed."[9] Baldwin stands on the top stair of the bond pit. One day, a newcomer challenged him for his spot. Baldwin is five feet, ten inches tall. The newcomer towered over him. "He looked at Baldwin and said, 'The hell with you, pal, I'm standing here,' " an exchange official relates, "so Baldwin moved. When Baldwin moved, everyone else moved with him. Well, if you're the guy who used to stand next to Tom Baldwin, who do you want to stand next to—Baldwin or this new young Turk? You want to watch a guy like Baldwin, to see where he's trading."[10]

Neophyte traders squeeze in where they can, often finding themselves stuck in the ebb and flow of bodies on the floor below, where broken bones are an occupational risk. Traders stand chest to back, shoulder to shoulder, "so close you can tell what the guy in front of you had for dinner last night," says one former trader. A team of paramedics stands by. Traders sometimes keel over from heat stroke or heart attacks or shock at a big win or a big loss. In fast markets, the crowd surges against rails built along the top of the pit to keep people from falling out.

The traders are divided into two categories. Although everyone in the pit is there to buy or sell, not everyone is, in the jargon of the exchange, a trader. Those who take orders from customers outside the exchange, buying and selling on behalf of someone else, are called brokers. In the pits, the title of trader is reserved for those who take risk for their own account.

The risk takers have many approaches to making their decisions. Fundamental traders analyze piles of data about crop reports, weather patterns, government policy shifts, and other information in hope of making big money on long-term trends in supply and demand. Technical traders merely watch the line that traces prices from point to point on a graph, and when the line makes a certain shape, they buy or sell. They base their decisions on historical records documenting how prices have moved in the past and believe that the market operates according to patterns and cycles, so that one who understands the cycles can forecast the behavior of the market. Still other traders may glance at the fundamental data and briefly peruse the technical charts but base their real decisions entirely on visceral intuition, sparked by the intensity of noise in the pits, the strain in the face of a trader on the top stair, the sensation of a stampede, the overall feel of the market.

At any moment, the futures price represents the sum of all of the traders' decisions taken together. Traders in the pits are often backed up by big international financial firms that provide hedging services to farmers or manufacturers. In order to know how much to charge for hamburgers, McDonald's has to know what the price of beef will be. Yet no one can predict the fluctuations in prices. So McDonald's might buy a futures contract to guarantee an acceptable future price. The decision of McDonald's to buy a futures contract gives traders important information about the future demand for beef. Traders adjust their own expectations in light of this new information, and the market price moves accordingly. In this way, each decision to buy or sell is like a vote on the future direction of prices. "The marketplace is the most democratic forum ever invented," says Leo Melamed, former chairman of the Chicago Mercantile Exchange (Merc) and founder of the modern currency futures market.

The Birth of Currency Futures

The Chicago exchanges depend on risk. When the agricultural markets became stable and predictable, the exchanges almost ceased to function. By the middle of the twentieth century, the Deere plow and McCormick reaper had long ago tamed the prairie, the Indian wars were a child's game, and the only trace of locust swarms was in a mural at the Mormon tabernacle in Salt Lake City memorializing the westward exodus of those polygamous pioneers. Not only railroad but highways and airlines crossed the corn belt. More efficient communications, advances in agricultural science, the development of interna-

tional trade, and a comprehensive system of government price sup-
ports had stabilized crop prices. Stability meant less need for futures
contracts.

The Merc was the smaller and younger of the Windy City's two great
trading arenas. It traced its roots to the Chicago Produce Exchange,
founded in 1874 by butter and egg dealers. By 1954, when Leo
Melamed bought a seat on the Merc, it was a quiet place. In fact, almost all of its business revolved around one commodity: eggs. The
price of eggs still rose and fell seasonally, but even there the writing
was on the wall. "They were getting chickens to lay eggs all the time,"
recalls Melamed. "Futures were not going to be needed. You need futures markets when there is change in the price, not when it is constant."[11]

Born in Poland, the son of a prominent scholar, Melamed had come
to America as a refugee. When he was six years old, his father fled the
Nazis, taking his wife and children across the border into Russia. But
Stalin's Russia was no friendlier to intellectuals than Hitler's Reich. For
two years, Leo Melamed's father moved the family from hiding place
to hiding place. They escaped to America and settled in Chicago shortly
before bombs fell on Pearl Harbor. Leo studied hard and eventually
went to law school. To help pay his tuition, he worked at the Merc as
a runner, carrying messages back and forth for the Merrill Lynch
traders.

Having seen the effects of economic dictatorships during his childhood in Poland and Russia, Melamed was convinced not only of the
efficiency but of the moral virtue of free trade. As a student, he had
read the writings of Milton Friedman, and the resonance was profound.
"To me, he was an economic god, and he has remained a god, and I
guess the Nobel people thought so too, eventually," Melamed says.[12]
Although Melamed attended John Marshall Law School, he made
arrangements to audit Friedman's lectures at the University of Chicago.
He practiced law for a while after graduating, but in 1954 Melamed
purchased a seat on the Merc and decided to become a trader. Eventually, his trading skills would carry him from the bottom of the pits
to the exchange's board of governors, and finally, in 1969, to the position of chairman, Chicago Mercantile Exchange. He had gotten to
the top the hard way.

In 1967, like millions of other Americans, Melamed read Friedman's
articles in *Newsweek* magazine about his effort to sell the British pound

sterling short. Melamed was shocked and offended by the affront to Friedman's liberty—but at the same time he smelled a great business opportunity. "Here was a great economic mind told he could not do something in the market. I was flabbergasted. I was looking for viable instruments of trade, and you didn't have to be a genius to figure out that if Bretton Woods did come apart, it would create a big era of volatility in currency and interest rates. It seemed you needed a futures market to give an opportunity to everyone to take part in the movement of price," he recalls.[13]

By early 1971, when Leo Melamed began to put together the world's first futures market in currencies, the strains on the Bretton Woods system were unmistakable. Events moved much faster than he had anticipated. In August of that year, President Nixon stated that the U.S. government would not exchange gold for dollars, officially closing the "gold window" and pulling the plug on the Bretton Woods system.

The time was ripe. Currency chaos would provide the perfect environment for a flourishing futures market in currencies. At the time, the futures industry was almost completely unregulated, and no government authority could refuse permission for the Merc to begin trading currency futures. But nothing of the sort had ever existed before, and Melamed had two worries: either that no one would take him seriously enough to use the exchange or that central bankers would take him very seriously and demand that the market be shut down. "I was frankly a nobody," Melamed says, "chairman of a small exchange in Chicago. I needed some credibility. Milton Friedman was absolutely the right man, highly respected, well known internationally. A lot of people looked up to him as an international idol. It was absolutely necessary for me to say, 'If you think this is a good idea, would you write a paper and say so?' "[14]

In 1971, Melamed and the president of the Merc, Everett Harris, made a pilgrimage to the idol's summer residence in Vermont. Friedman listened carefully to their proposal of a futures market in currencies. As Melamed recalls the meeting, Friedman replied, "I like your idea and I'll write the paper for $5,000. I'm a capitalist, remember that."[15]

Melamed wasted no time sending the paper to Nixon's treasury secretary (later Ronald Reagan's secretary of state), George Shultz, who agreed to meet with him. "At the appointed time, I went in. It was the first time I was ever in the Treasury Department. I was thirty-something, scared to death, awed by everything. I was born in Poland, and I was still awed by the United States and in particular by Washington, D.C. After the amenities were over, I asked him about the idea of a futures market in foreign exchange. He said, 'I read the paper from Milton Friedman that you sent, and if it's good enough for Milton, it's good enough for me.' "[16] Arthur Burns, chairman of the Federal Reserve Board and a former teacher of Milton Friedman, also endorsed the idea.

On May 16, 1972, the world's first futures market in international currencies officially opened for business. The Merc built a pit for currency trading, just like the pits where traders standing on concentric stairs shouted bids and offers for egg, butter, and livestock futures. But at first, hardly anyone shared Melamed's zeal for currency futures. Wheedling, cajoling, and twisting arms, he managed to persuade a few experienced traders to stand in the currency pit, but they weren't dedicated to the market. A good commodity trader could make a living trading cattle and hogs, but who ever heard of trading deutsche marks? No one. Exchange traders don't just trade with each other. Much of their business depends on executing orders for customers outside the exchange who have a reason to buy or sell futures contracts. Since the currency exchange was brand-new, outsiders weren't yet using it. Nor were they eager to begin. In fact, the big New York and London banks, which held most of the world's money and bought or sold currencies for their clients, laughed it off. "I'm amazed that a bunch of crapshooters in pork bellies have the temerity to think that they can beat some of the world's most sophisticated traders at their own game," one New York foreign exchange dealer told the *Wall Street Journal*.[17] Because there were no orders flowing in from outside, traders in the currency pits had long stretches of quiet time. Traders don't make money in quiet times, so they wandered away from the currency pits and returned to trading the more established markets.

Melamed knew that the absence of traders could kill off his creation. What if outsiders tried to send orders to the exchange but there were no traders in the pit to take their orders? Word would quickly get around that the Chicago market lacked liquidity; that is, it could simply not handle orders to buy and sell. So he first persuaded the exchange to establish a new category of ultracheap, limited memberships and then swept the streets for cab drivers, steelworkers, discontented lawyers, or just about anyone who had always had a burning desire to make a fortune playing the commodity markets but couldn't afford to buy a full exchange membership. "We sold these memberships for only $10,000, and then there were 150 traders committed to the currency market, because they couldn't get into the cattle pits," he recalls.[18] With a true promoter's instinct for the grandiloquent phrase, Melamed decided to call these new members the International Monetary Market (IMM). Starting with these traders, and capitalizing on the tremendous instability of currencies in the post–Bretton Woods era, the IMM would emerge as one of the most powerful international financial institutions in the world. During the 1980s, when the full force of market power hit the economies of the world like a tidal wave caused by an undersea volcano, evening news shows in places as remote as the Missouri Ozarks would carry reports of currency values on the IMM.

Meanwhile, just across town, a young professor from the University of California was at work on a project that would rescue the fortunes of the other exchange, the Chicago Board of Trade—a project that would change the way every homebuyer in America bought a house, and permanently rearrange the power structure of the banking industry.

Richard Sandor had spent the late 1960s teaching economics on the front lines of America's cultural revolution: Berkeley, a radical mecca on the Bay, where free speech, teargas, acid trips, ROTC burning, Ho-Ho-Ho Chi Minh, the Magic Bus, the Grateful Dead, pot, free love, revolution, and one-two-three-four-we-don't-want-your-fucking-war all swirled together in a Peter Max pastel paisley whirl of the weird and the wired. Yet Berkeley gave the world more than all this.

Even more weirdly, Berkeley also gave the world program trading and junk bonds. Sandor's finance faculty colleagues included a Tibetan Buddhist meditator named Barr Rosenberg, whose research into randomness and volatility led him to start a program trading operation that eventually managed $9 billion for investors, who put up a minimum of $75 million each, and made him the "pope" of program traders everywhere.[19] There was also Hayne Leland, a finance professor best remembered for inventing portfolio insurance, the program trading technique that two decades later would be blamed by U.S. Treasury secretary Nicholas Brady for contributing to the great stock market crash of 1987. Out on the campus, minding his own business, quietly hurrying past the demonstrators on his way to finance class, was a sedulous, clean-cut young student named Michael Milken.

Sandor was a cautious academic, wearing long sideburns but not long hair, and sporting traditional leather patches on his tweedy jacket. Nonetheless, in his way, he had caught the revolutionary spirit. "You just had to look around at the deficits, the Vietnam War, et cetera, to recognize that we were setting the scene for a whole new economic environment as we moved into the seventies and eighties," he recalls.[20] Government spending was cosmically extravagant: "I served on the scholarship committee. My wife tells me I came home one night screaming 'This can't last; it's out of control.' Two of the scholarship committee meetings that day had been for somebody who wanted financial aid because their sports car had broken down and another person who had wanted financial aid because their stereo wasn't working."[21]

Sandor taught what he says was the first futures course ever offered in a business school. At most universities, if futures classes were offered at all, they were part of the agriculture curriculum. Sandor was also one of the first academics to look into the question of whether futures could be used for something completely different. He applied for a grant to study the possibility of a futures contract in mortgages. After all, they were something like crops. It took three months for a loan officer to handle all the paperwork—that was something like the time it took to grow a crop of beans. Prices changed too, as interest rates moved. A mortgage loan made at high interest rates would be worth more if interest rates went down three months later. The changes in interest rates were as unpredictable as the changes in corn prices. Also, the more money the government printed to finance the unpopular war in Vietnam, the more likely it was that inflation would break out. When that happened, the Federal Reserve would have to raise interest rates again, and when interest rates eventually went up, anyone who had invested money in mortgage loans would be in trouble because the loans would be worth less. Just like the banks that had invested in Southern securities before the Civil War a century earlier, the mortgage lenders would see the value of their portfolios collapse. So it seemed to Sandor that a futures market made sense for banks and S&Ls to hedge against interest rate risk.

Yet after sorting through the loan portfolio of a large California-based S&L, he decided that a futures contract couldn't work for mortgages. Unlike corn, beans, pork bellies, or any other commodity that can be sorted into grades and bought or sold by the truckload, mortgages were full of idiosyncrasies. People repaid them at different rates depending on what neighborhood a house was in, on whether the owners were married or single or divorced, on income levels, and on many other factors. Mortgages didn't have enough in common to turn them into a commodity. Sandor published those findings in 1971.

They were almost obsolete as soon as they were printed. The government was on its way to turning mortgages into a commodity.

The Great Depression had been over for almost thirty years. Every American could think of owning a house as an ordinary part of life. There were new problems, though. It had become clear that money for mortgages could no longer come primarily from local bank depositors. Institutional investors like insurance companies, pension funds, and investment banks were buying bonds issued by government agencies, and the government agencies used the proceeds to buy mortgage loans. It was a natural step when, in 1970, a government agency issued a security called a Ginnie Mae. This security was really an ownership interest in a pool of mortgages: an investor who bought a Ginnie Mae received the right to principal and interest payments from mortgages in the pool. Ginnie Maes helped connect Wall Street more closely with Main Street. Since Americans now held so much of their savings in the form of insurance policies or pension funds, it made sense to tap that source of capital for mortgages.

Ginnie Maes were reasonably successful, and they solved the problem that had vexed Sandor. Assembling mortgages in a pool and issuing government-guaranteed securities based on them meant that mortgages could now be as standardized as any other commodity. Shortly afterward, the management of the Chicago Board of Trade approached him with an offer to set up an economics department at the exchange. He told them about his idea for a futures market in mortgages. They liked it. Sandor took a sabbatical from Berkeley and joined the Board of Trade for what he expected to be a one-year stint.

It lasted a lot longer. Sandor worked out the idea of a futures contract in mortgages and went to call on big New York banks and investment banks to see if they would use it. "I got thrown out of a lot of places," he says, "They looked at me and said, 'Berkeley, free speech, drugs, Vietnam War, student activists, and you're from the Chicago exchange.' "[22] Bankers presumed that he was not only weird but provincial. They dismissed futures as something that might work for corn, beans, or wheat but was as out of place on Wall Street as a herd of Holsteins.

Then there was the government. When Sandor began his work, futures markets had been regulated by a small group in the U.S. Department of Agriculture. In 1974, a regulatory reshuffle rolled the regulatory authority into a new agency, the Commodities Futures Trading Commission. At first, the CFTC still had an agricultural mindset. "They sent out their standard form, and they asked how much storage space there was in Chicago for these Ginnie Maes. We said we didn't need silos or barns or anything like that, it's just pieces of paper," he recalls.[23] It took time for the agency to outgrow its agricultural roots.

By 1975, Sandor had finally assembled from financial institutions enough support for the new contract to make it worthwhile to try trading it. But his problems weren't over. "Twenty-four hours before Ginnie Mae started trading on October 20, 1975, the SEC sought an injunction to stop the Chicago Board of Trade from trading the securities," he says.[24] A turf war had broken out between the SEC and the CFTC. A higher court ultimately overturned the injunction, and trading began—but the jurisdictional dispute continued to simmer.

Sandor's timing, like Melamed's three years earlier, couldn't have been better. By the mid-1970s, everybody could see that the economy was falling apart. Milton Friedman had been right about the Philips curve—inflation was racing, unemployment climbing. The chart of interest rates was beginning to look like an electrocardiogram of a heart attack victim. Sandor started work on other interest rate products. Treasury bills futures began to trade in 1976, and then treasury bond futures.

Although futures were already trading on commodities, currencies, mortgage securities, and T-bills, bond futures were a tough sell. Dominated by the most Wall Street elite, the long-term bond market was a white-shoe club. The prestigious money lords in New York didn't favor the idea of the Chicago outpost meddling in their affairs. So when long-term bond futures began to trade in 1977, they got off to a slow start. Then in 1979, Paul Volcker, the new Federal Reserve Board chairman, made an announcement that Wall Street remembers as the "Saturday Night Massacre." With that announcement, the Fed signed on to Milton Friedman's revolution. Abandoning a decades-old policy of controlling interest rates, Volcker said that the nation's central bank would focus its attention instead on controlling the money supply. If inflation was indeed a monetary phenomenon, as Friedman had said, then getting inflation under control meant choking back on the supply of money. Choke back on supply and the price goes up. The price of money is expressed in interest rates. Therefore, in that year, interest rates started a stratospheric ascent that soon would carry the prime rate to an astonishing 20 percent.

As interest rates went up, the value of the investments held by Wall Street houses plunged. That was the best thing that ever happened to the Chicago Board of Trade. Says Sandor, "IBM had a bond issue come out that Friday, the weekend of the Saturday Night Massacre. Salomon Brothers had taken the deal away from Morgan Stanley in a major confrontation with the old-line investment banker." Instead of selling the IBM bonds, Salomon Brothers had kept them. When Volcker made his announcement, there was quiet gloating in the corridors of Morgan Stanley. It looked as if Salomon Brothers had been hoisted with their own petard—the runup in interest rates had sent the value of the IBM bonds crashing down. But wait . . . why wasn't anyone jumping out of windows at Salomon Brothers? Says Sandor, "People started reading that Salomon Brothers had been fully hedged. That's what altered the whole nature of the market."[25] By using Sandor's long bond futures, Salomon had been able to protect itself against a catastrophic event in the interest rate markets, much as farmers protected themselves against catastrophic drops in the price of corn or wheat. Interest rate futures had at last arrived.

Wall Street used to be a cozy warren of old boys from the right schools, relying more on the nod and the wink than on any substantive economic analysis. It had changed little since the days when periwigged traders lifted glasses of port to toast the health of U.S. Treasury secretary Alexander Hamilton. Then the Chicago futures markets established a second center of financial power, where nothing mattered except the price. Now math and physics Ph.D.'s relied on the prices set by futures traders to craft new equations and economic models that could be run only with another new tool, the computer. Futures and options became the basic building blocks of a whole new genus of financial products, called derivatives—financial abstractions, their value mathematically derived from changes in the value of interest rates, commodities, stock prices, currency exchange rates, and other factors. Suddenly, on Wall Street, "who you know" became less important than "what you know." By 1990, at the top of the big financial houses, chairmen and presidents and directors noticed that most of their revenues were coming from a business they did not understand. Although the old boys had grand titles, they didn't really control their businesses. Power had passed them by.

The new finance whose foundations were laid by Melamed and Sandor is ubiquitous in its effects. It even shapes and reshapes neighborhoods. In the heartwarming Christmas classic *It's a Wonderful Life*, Jimmy Stewart urges local neighbors to leave their money in the bank so that there will be capital available for ordinary folks to get mortgages. The notion that bank deposits fund mortgage loans is now almost as dated as the film.

When the financial system was neatly segmented, homeowners sometimes found it impossible to borrow for mortgages, not because the rates were too high but because there just weren't enough local deposits to fund loans. But now, for the right price, anyone whose mortgage fits into the definition of "creditworthiness" can borrow. That definition is determined by a massive "securitization" industry. Financial engineers strip down mortgages into an array of risks, the way a butcher divides a carcass. An American pension fund may buy the principal payments, a Japanese life insurance company may buy the interest payments out to three years, the borrower's option to pay off the mortgage before it matures may be excised and sold to a German universal bank, and the interest payments from three to thirty years may be sold in turn to any number of other investors. The need for standardization to support this industry has affected who can get mortgage loans and what they can buy with their mortgage loans. In short, the international capital markets decide what houses will be bought and sold, in what neighborhoods, and by whom.

Yet the influence of the new markets didn't stop in the United States. In what may be the only case of Paris borrowing fashion ideas from Chicago, by 1992 a crowd of French traders bellowed, flashed hand signals, and jumped around frantically in colored jackets just like the ones the traders wear at the Board of Trade and the Merc. The French, with government encouragement, of course, had in 1986 established a futures market to trade French government bond futures. Not wishing to meddle much with a successful formula, they faithfully copied everything they had seen in Chicago. The British had launched the London International Financial Futures Exchange shortly before. The

Italians were trying to thread through Parliament a bill to allow a futures market to trade Italian government bond futures.[26] Singapore and Hong Kong, Osaka, Shanghai, Switzerland—almost everywhere, a futures market had become the badge of a modern economic structure, a statement to the world that here was a free market open to investors and plugged in to the international flow of capital.

But not everyone welcomed the new wave.

Trouble in Paradise

An architectural monstrosity in the shape of a dull white concrete box sits among pretty flower gardens on the outskirts of Frankfurt. It is the headquarters of the Bundesbank, and it contains thousands of German central bankers.

From a window near the office of Mr. O., a man with a passion for anonymity, a visitor can easily see the domineering yellow headquarters of the American occupation army in Germany. In a relaxed, conversational moment, Mr. O. lets slip his hope that someday the American soldiers will leave and the yellow building will become the new headquarters of a united Europe's central bank.[27]

Mr. O. is a placid, stocky man with gray hair and correct manners. He grew up in a tidy Bavarian village. To be a banker was his childhood dream. After a brief stint in private banking, he entered the service of the Bundesbank at a level commensurate with his age, education, and experience. He has moved laterally within the bank ever since. It's not that he has failed to move up, but in the Bundesbank, moving up isn't done. Depending on how much education they have when they enter its service, the central bank assigns recruits to higher or lower career tracks. Ever after, their professional lives unfold between a certain floor and an unquestionable ceiling. Mr. O. has traveled in Western Europe, and several years ago he even took his wife to America. They rented a car and drove across the country. It was an adventure he will always remember. Everyone should have an adventure once, he says.

Mr. O.'s job is to monitor the new financial instruments that let foreign speculators in trading pits gamble with the national debt of Germany. The German mark is an international currency, and German bonds and stocks attract investors from all over the world.

Though futures exchanges had been illegal in Germany since the Great Depression, during the 1980s international investors decided that there was money to be made trading futures on Germany's national debt. So the London International Financial Futures Exchange (LIFFE) listed a German Bund contract. "As a national bank, we are not happy about such contracts in our own currency that are traded outside of Germany," says Mr. O. "Our partners in policy are the German banks and not the market participants abroad. If we try to exercise our influence on the market, we cannot reach the market participants abroad." Traditionally, a small number of German bankers worked hand in glove with the government to maintain stability in Germany's financial system. London shattered their tight little club. The traditional whispered suggestions and raised eyebrows that the Bundesbank had used to keep German bankers in line just didn't work with London's traders. All they cared about was the price.

Mr. O. knows that the vandals don't care about protecting German monetary stability. They use futures to protect their own investments against changes in interest rates. Futures speculators, like insurance companies, make money by taking risks. Because this insurance is available, more people are willing to invest in German securities, and Germany is able to borrow more money, more cheaply than it could if there were no futures exchange.

Notwithstanding these practical benefits, Mr. O. doesn't like speculation, especially when foreigners control it. In 1990, Germany changed its laws to permit the establishment of the first futures exchange since the 1930s. Mr. O. shrugs, and shakes his head, for there was really no choice.

"Futures are like gunboats," says Michael Hoffmann, senior vice president of DTB Deutsche Terminborse, Germany's new futures exchange. "Fast—you're in and out in seconds."[28] He stabs the air with a cigarette. Mr. Hoffman speaks colloquial English with a Southern California accent, thanks to a childhood and adolescence spent in the United States. "The fact that the biggest contract in London was the German government bond contract was a sore spot," he continues, slouching in his chair with a devilish grin. Then the telephone rings. Mr. Hoffman snaps erect, grabs the receiver, and answers in strong, pure Deutsch. The transition is eerie, as though two distinct personalities inhabit the same body. Mr. Hoffman bellows a final "Jawohl" into the receiver, hangs up, and slouches back to California. German authorities were under the gun, he says. They saw greedy traders in London, responsive to short-term price moves rather than long-term economic fundamentals, shaping the financial destiny of Germany without any guidance from the German government. Perfectly bicultural, Mr. Hoffman used to trade futures for an American bank. Now German bankers and even Mr. O. trust him to do what can be done to save German finance from the foreigners.

Like the Colt .45 on the western frontier, derivatives command respect. But like the Colt, they are most useful in a lawless land. Friedman's disciples, the champions of economic liberty, have created a free financial world where governments must stand daily for a vote of confidence. *Vox populi suprema lex esto* could be graven in stone beside the entry to every trading room, so thoroughly has the Friedman revolution democratized finance.

Yet in a suburb of Boston, a distinguished scholar raises a troubling philosophical question. "Friedman and all of those fellows believe that people are rational, that over time they do what is in their best interest," Charles Kindleberger, a professor emeritus at MIT, told a reporter who phoned one day.[29] Kindleberger has spent his career analyzing the evolution of Western financial and economic systems. He has written most extensively on crises and panics. "They think, you know, that everything will work out fine. But I think there's plenty of evidence in the history of the world that people act sometimes out of malice, sometimes out of ignorance, sometimes out of panic. I'm not quite so sanguine." Is there an invisible hand? If there is, does it really do what Adam Smith said?

THE ATTACK ON THE EUROPEAN MONETARY SYSTEM, PART II

In September 1993, near Fontainbleu, in a small office at INSEAD, Europe's leading business school, economist Charles Wyplosz is having a nightmare. However, he is awake. Flaming barricades block the highways leading into France. The farmers are rioting. Among the masses of the unemployed, the racist demagogues of the far Right find a receptive audience. Antiforeign sentiment reaches to the highest levels of French government and society, where officials talk publicly and unashamedly of an Anglo-Saxon conspiracy to wreck Europe. The project of a generation, the unification of Europe, has fallen into ruins.

The European Monetary System's Exchange Rate Mechanism (ERM) is effectively defunct. In August, the last of three waves of speculative attacks succeeded in breaking the link between the French franc and the German mark. The ERM had kept currencies in a tight band, allowing them to fluctuate in a margin of only 2.25 percent. Now the margin has been widened to 15 percent. Currency traders laugh at calling that a margin. Clearly, the franc floats in all but name. Privately, everyone agrees that this is true, even the bureaucrats at the Banque de France and the French treasury. Officially, however, they deny that anything very serious has happened to the ERM at all: it is dressed in its usual clothes and seated in its usual chair, and if one does not look closely, it looks almost as though it were alive.

Official France is studiously behaving as though nothing has changed. Although France has effectively floated the franc, the government is still trying to maintain the *franc fort* (strong franc) policy of the previous decade by keeping interest rates high. So the franc has devalued only 3 percent.

Thanks to that policy, France is in recession. Unemployment is at 12 percent. Jobs have been disappearing steadily for almost ten years, ever since the *franc fort* policy was introduced. Now it is worse. A year ago, after a speculative attack pushed Britain out of the ERM, the pound devalued steeply. Shortly afterward, an American manufacturer of vacuum cleaners closed its plant near Paris and relocated to Scotland. The "Hoover affair" eliminated seven hundred jobs near Dijon and made front-page news. Now French industrialists say that only a steep currency devaluation will make them competitive with their rivals abroad.

On the Spanish border, French farmers are overturning trucks and setting fire to produce shipped north by Spanish farmers. The Spanish peseta has been devalued, and Spanish produce is so cheap that French farmers cannot compete.

It is beginning to look more and more like the last time France had floating exchange rates, in the 1930s. Wyplosz wonders, in his darker moments, whether history will repeat itself.

In the 1930s, the nations of Europe yielded to the temptation to boost employment and give their industries a competitive edge. Competitive devaluation turned into trade war, with tariffs and other trade barriers to protect local industrialists against their foreign rivals. Trade war turned into total war.

The Common Market, the European Monetary System, the Europe without borders, even the United States of Europe, as some called it—this project was no frivolous matter. It was not about the franc, lira, pound, and peseta; it was about war and peace, nothing less.

There are those who say, of course, that times have changed. There are those who say that Europe learned some unforgettable lesson fifty years ago. However, on this crisp autumn day, the morning news carried the usual grisly report from Sarajevo, and if one believes that Europe has changed, then how does one account for that?

"I'm deeply concerned that if the ERM explodes now, the next attack will be on the Common Market," Wyplosz says. "We have completely open borders and cannot allow frictions to come into play, because frictions are the beginning of suspicions. When you start suspecting the others and public opinion gets inflamed, blaming foreigners for problems of unemployment, recession, missing markets—it's very, very dangerous."[1]

Wyplosz is a Cassandra. That is what makes his nightmare so troubling. In 1990, when, as part of the program for European unification, all capital controls were removed by the countries of Europe, he began to predict that the ERM could not survive a major speculative onslaught. Like Cassandra he was ignored, and like Cassandra, he was right all along. Will he be right again?

In fact, the ERM lasted only as long as the markets were willing to let it endure. They were willing to let it endure because it was quite profitable for them. Essentially, the European central banks offered them a low-risk, high-return, subsidized investment opportunity. Investors took advantage. They poured capital into Europe, buying bonds from Spain, Italy, Sweden, the United Kingdom, and other high-interest-paying countries.

Anyone with a basic knowledge of economics knew that these countries had inflation problems and that their currencies would probably have to be devalued someday. But the central banks of Europe, through the ERM, had promised that the currencies would not devalue against the deutsche mark. As long as the ERM kept Europe's currencies in a tight relationship to the German mark, investors could enjoy high interest rates on their capital. Usually, high returns meant high risk of devaluation. However, since the governments of Europe had promised to do everything necessary to prevent devaluation, it looked as if investors could get risk-free returns. That is, a free lunch.

"Awfully tempting to stick around and eat," says Dave Williams, chairman of the Alliance funds group in New York.[2] The most astute traders had discovered this so-called convergence trade opportunity as early as 1980, just a year after the ERM was established. It was called the convergence trade because it depended on the commitment of Europe's governments to "converge" their separate currencies into one group, and eventually into a single European currency. In 1989, Williams approved a proposal to make the same opportunity available to countless American investors through a mutual fund. In the first year, the fund attracted $1 billion—mostly from small investors. Alliance's success with the concept led Merrill Lynch, Kemper, and other Wall Street institutions to launch copycat funds.

Collectively, these mutual funds attracted almost $30 billion. That was only a fraction of what pension funds, banks, insurance companies, and other investors were putting into the convergence trade. Altogether, they invested as much as $300 billion in this trade.

But there's no such thing as a free lunch. That's the first rule of economics.

Why did Alliance and other fund companies pretend there was? "We were so imbued with the idea that the governments were determined to make this work that we were swept up in their propaganda. We just got carried away by that and failed to heed what the fundamentals were telling us—namely, that these economies were diverging and it was going to be hard to maintain currency values," Williams now says ruefully.[3] In the end, it became clear that the governments and central banks of Europe could not maintain the commitment to a stable currency indefinitely. Investors realized that those who stayed at the table too long would be stuck with the tab for the "free lunch."

What went wrong? In a word, doubt. People—corporations, investment managers like Williams, insurance companies, bankers, all of those who had blithely accepted the notion that the governments of Europe had temporarily suspended the laws of economics—suddenly reconsidered their faith. They decided that perhaps economic law might prevail after all. They didn't set out to demolish the ERM. They merely wanted to protect their property. In fact, most of them would have preferred that the ERM continue to exist. It was very nice to enjoy a free lunch. However, the ERM could not survive without their faith, and they no longer believed.

The bureaucrats had taken faith for granted. They did not really understand the extent to which they depended on the goodwill and confidence of people who could easily withdraw not only their goodwill and confidence but their capital. They had been remarkably obtuse. In fact, the end of the ERM had begun to happen as early as 1989, when the promise of a united Europe suddenly expanded beyond the wildest hopes of the original planners.

In 1989, the Berlin Wall fell. West and East Germany were to be unified. Faced with the prospect of absorbing an impoverished, inefficient, and largely unemployable population, the government in Bonn voted to spend a fortune on social services. If the Bundesbank created the money necessary to cover this spending, it would lead to certain inflation, and German memories of the Weimar inflation are still strong. In no other country is popular feeling on the subject of inflation so intense. What's more, the only real role of the Bundesbank is to keep the mark sound. So instead of printing money, the Bundesbank hiked interest rates to attract capital from abroad. The unification of Germany would be, in effect, the biggest leveraged buyout in history.

Countries that had linked their currency with the deutsche mark in accord with terms of the ERM had two choices, neither one particularly appealing.

On the one hand, they could keep their currencies in line with the deutsche mark. This would mean matching or exceeding Germany's interest rates. Matching Germany's interest rates didn't make sense for the other European countries. None of them was in the process of absorbing a former socialist state. Running their interest rates up to or even beyond German levels could devastate their economies.

On the other hand, they could devalue their currencies. Devaluation, however, was embarrassing. A currency that devalues buys less, so devaluation means a country is less powerful economically. No politician wants to be blamed for sacrificing the wealth and power of the nation. What's more, devaluation could also derail the process of European monetary union. According to the timetable for monetary union, countries were to maintain their currencies in a tight relationship to each other, and especially to the deutsche mark. The population of countries like France had already begun to accept the need to suffer hard economic times for the sake of monetary union. It seemed politically unwise, just as people were beginning to agree that the sacrifice was worthwhile, to tell them now that devaluation was suddenly acceptable and even necessary.

Germany made an informal proposal that could have eliminated the problem, but for reasons of national pride and politics, its fellow European countries rejected the proposal. The Germans offered to revalue the mark. That is, instead of France and Belgium and Holland and the United Kingdom announcing that their currencies had gotten weaker, the Germans would consent to announce that the deutsche mark had gotten stronger. No stigma would attach to the other European currencies, although there is no economic difference between revaluing the mark and devaluing the franc. The ERM structure could be preserved, and the countries of Europe would not have to kill their own economies with high interest rates. The revaluation could be explained as a consequence of the unique historical circumstances of Germany, especially the need to fund the reconstruction of the East.

The Germans broached this proposal informally. Wyplosz says that the French blocked it. A source in the French treasury says it was not the French but the Belgians and the Dutch who refused to go along. However, the proposal was turned down. When the countries of Europe insisted on tying their currencies tightly and inflexibly to the deutsche mark, they sealed the fate of the ERM.

As Germany raised its interest rates, the mark grew stronger. In order to maintain the tight relationship with the deutsche mark, other countries raised their rates even higher. The higher their interest rates went, the more attractive the convergence trade opportunity looked to international investors. Alliance and others profited by investing in the high-interest-rate countries and selling the mark to hedge their investments in lira, peseta, sterling, and other bonds. Paradoxically, the very high interest rates that made the convergence trade more attractive were a sign that the ERM was becoming more and more fragile. Most European countries needed lower interest rates in order to promote economic growth. They were sacrificing jobs on the altar of the ERM. Sooner or later, voters were bound to notice.

On June 2, in a referendum, Danish voters turned thumbs down on the blueprint for European unification known as the Maastricht Treaty. The next day, the French president announced that France would hold a referendum in September. The markets, unsure of what the future would hold, began to shift. If the plan for European union were rejected by voters, the whole logic of the convergence trade would disappear. The ERM could just fall apart.

European corporations had been confident that the plan for European unification would proceed and the ERM would work, so confident that they had stopped hedging their foreign currency revenues. Before the Danish referendum, French exporters to Italy were not at all anxious about what the lira would be worth next month or six months from now, thanks to the ERM. American corporations also treated the European currencies as, in effect, a single currency. European companies didn't hedge, and Americans did all of their hedging in deutsche marks, which they used as a proxy for all European currencies.

The Danish referendum changed that. No longer confident that the European unification project would proceed, corporations began to protect themselves against the possibility that the ERM might break down. Kodak and Intel, two large American corporations with extensive business in Europe, stopped treating the ERM as a single unit. Instead of hedging with the deutsche mark, they hedged directly by selling lira, franc, escudo, and other currencies on the interbank markets or on the options and futures exchanges. European companies like Ciba-Geigy did the same thing. Suddenly, the world's biggest corporations were selling off the weakest currencies in Europe. In the early stages, selling by corporations for the purpose of hedging dwarfed sales by hedge funds, mutual funds, and other investors. Who was buying these currencies? Ultimately, the central banks that issued them. As the central bankers in Italy, Britain, Spain, and other countries paid out dollars and marks to buy back their own currencies, their reserves began to shrink. It was as if they had sprung a slow leak, only they were leaking cash, and the cash they were leaking was the very stuff that backed their own currencies. People believed in the lira and the pound because they knew that if they needed to, they could exchange it for a known quantity of marks, dollars, yen, or Swiss francs. When the central banks began to run low on hard currency, people began to wonder when they would run out completely.

At Alliance, Robert Sinche ran the bond mutual funds that had invested the most in the convergence trade opportunity. In the summer of 1992, he began to have some misgivings. He wasn't alone.[4]

In May 1992, Gavyn Davies, an economist with the investment bank Goldman Sachs, had infuriated the Italian central bank by suggesting that time was running out for Italy, and that the markets would soon force the Bank of Italy to devalue the lira. Sinche had a close relationship with Goldman Sachs, and a lot of money invested in lira bonds. He invited Davies to a long breakfast.

Davies told Sinche and his colleagues at Alliance that it didn't matter how committed the Italians claimed to be to the ERM. The Bank of Italy just didn't have enough marks and dollars to keep buying lira. The Bank of Italy bought lira for its high official value. Traders were borrowing lira to sell them to the Bank of Italy. A similar situation had occurred in Great Britain some years before, Davies explained. British monetary officials announced their intention to maintain the value of the pound. They bought pounds from all comers, exchanging them for dollars and other currencies at the high official price. Since no one else was willing to pay so much for pounds, everyone sold pounds to the Bank of England. Eventually, the Bank of England ran out of foreign exchange—it had nothing left but pounds.

"That was the clinching line," Sinche says. Secretly, so as not to disturb the markets, he bought a put option from Goldman Sachs. The put option gave Alliance the right to sell $1 billion worth of lira at a favorable rate. If the lira fell, Alliance would not suffer a big loss.

Sinche wasn't the only investor who decided to play it safe. Goldman Sachs and other investment banks were giving the same advice to all of their clients. Better to play it safe. Corporations and investors started to hedge, draining the reserves of the central banks. Most hedged by using the interbank forward markets, agreeing on a firm price at which they would buy or sell currencies at some future date. Others, like Alliance, used options. When a corporation buys a put option, the bank that sells the put option has to hedge its risk. If there is a 50-50 chance that the bank will have to pay out something, the bank hedges by immediately selling half of what it is likely to have to pay. The higher the chance that the bank will have to pay out, the more it sells.

Investors were selling, but who was buying? Ultimately, the central banks who had to buy in order to stand behind the currency. Investors had put $300 billion in weak currencies. Now they were trying to get $300 billion out again. However, that was more hard currency than the central banks had sitting around in their vaults.

The more people wanted to sell the suspect currencies, the more the market price began to fall. The farther the market price fell, the more investors worried. The more they worried, the more they sold. They no longer fully trusted the regulators to keep the ERM together. Almost every investor had the same thought: just in case, just to be safe, it made sense to sell some of those doubtful lira and sterling while there was still time.

Then the speculators stepped in, and what had begun as an orderly withdrawal ended as a rout beyond anyone's control Two decades before, money had proven too strong to be contained in a cage of reason built by the Bretton Woods planners. Then the planners of a united Europe had built a cage of a somewhat different design, and for years money had seemed quite comfortable in it. The planners grew careless. Eventually, they became so confident in the logic of the cage that they decided locks—capital controls—could be left off. The outcome was inevitable.

EASTERN SUNSET

Skirmish in Singapore

The time: spring 1992. The place: Singapore, gleaming city-state, financial center, and monument to the power of a free economy. The occasion: the semicentennial anniversary of the conquest of Singapore by Japanese troops in World War II.

It was an inauspicious time for the arrival of dark-suited Mr. Mitsuo Sato, deputy president of the Tokyo Stock Exchange, and his colleagues. A square-faced, bespectacled, temperamental man of age fifty-nine, Sato had probably expected the Tokyo Stock Exchange post to be something of a respite after his three decades of scaling the rock face of Japanese bureaucracy. His career had carried him through tax administration, his specialty as a graduate student, to the top post in the Customs and Tariff Bureau of the Ministry of Finance. Along the way, Sato had also served as chief negotiator for the "Japan-U.S. Yen/Dollar Working Committee," which led to what his biography called the "complete deregulation of Japan's financial and capital markets."[1] Many would question how complete that deregulation has been.

129

Nonetheless, in 1986, as is said of high-ranking Japanese financial regulators, he "came down from heaven" by moving from government to a prestigious post in the heavily regulated private sector.

Once ensconced in comfortable berths with banks, insurance companies, or stock exchanges, former financial regulators often enjoy something of a sinecure in Japan.[2] Their main role is to facilitate good relations between their new employers and their old. Good relations are a matter of the greatest importance for Japan's financial institutions, because the Ministry of Finance ultimately must approve every important decision they hope to make. But his years in the all-powerful Ministry of Finance had ill prepared Mitsuo Sato for the great challenges soon to be brought by the tsunami of international capital markets.

From the trading pits of the Singapore International Monetary Exchange (SIMEX), foreign investors were attacking the Japanese stock market. They had made a mockery of Japan's once-omnipotent financial regulators. Nikkei stock index futures traded on the SIMEX allowed investors to vote on the true value of the Japanese stock market, and the vote was going seriously against the preferences of the Japanese Ministry of Finance.

So, fifty years after the expulsion of Japanese troops, Sato had come to Singapore to reimpose a measure of Japanese discipline on this errant, erstwhile conquest.

There was more than pride at stake. The entire Japanese banking and financial system depended on the artificially high value of Tokyo's stock and real estate markets. In order to keep those values high, the Ministry of Finance (MOF) had historically allowed, even required, that banks publish inaccurate and misleading financial statements that hid more than they revealed about the financial stability of Japan's banking system. For example, banks were virtually forbidden to write off bad loans and report losses. Even if debtors were defaulting by the hundreds, no one could tell by looking at banks' annual reports that there was any problem. Banks were also among the biggest investors in the Japanese stock and real estate markets, and they were allowed to count unrealized stock market gains as capital. In other words, Japanese bank capital consisted not of money they really had but rather of money they might make if they decided to sell their stocks. As long as the stock market kept going up, so did the capital base of the Japanese banking system. The banks looked healthy, so they kept lending, and the steady expansion of the money supply kept land and stock prices spiraling upward in a speculative mania. By 1989, it was said that the market value of the land under the Imperial Palace in downtown Tokyo exceeded the total market value of all the real estate in California, and the stock market value of one Japanese telephone company topped that of the entire German stock market.

Regulators manipulated the market in other ways too. Japan's biggest investors could easily be cowed by a single telephone call from the Ministry of Finance. It was not even necessary for the bureaucrats to give specific orders. A carefully phrased question, even an intonation; was enough to make the managers of multitrillion-yen portfolios do what the MOF desired. The MOF had total power to approve or disapprove all important business decisions of financial institutions, and no one dared risk giving even the slightest offense to ministry bureaucrats by questioning their express or even their tacit intentions.

In the early 1990s, what the MOF mainly desired was an end to a financial nightmare. From out of nowhere, something new and strange had entered the Japanese financial system.

Japan's stock market was crashing. To the Japanese, this was unthinkable. For two decades, almost three, the proposition that the stock market rises was as sure a thing in Tokyo as the rising of the sun. Then, in the early 1980s, foreigners had been allowed to enter the protected Japanese financial market. They had brought with them new financial technologies, new ways of moving money around the world, new ways of investing, new ways of raising funds for corporations. For Japan's regulators, there was a historical analogue to these new financial technologies: the nineteenth-century Black Ships of Commodore Perry. Those threatening marvels of advanced technology had floated ominously in the mists of Tokyo Harbor during the waning days of the Tokugawa period. Splendid, invincible feats of engineering, they spoke forebodingly of the power of the society that produced them. The Black Ships opened Japan to international trade in 1853; a century and three decades later, the new financial technologies once again hinted ominously of outside power and opened Japan to international capital. The Black Ships sparked a revolution in nineteenth century Japan that deprived the samurai of their power and privileges. In twentieth-century Japan, the new financial technologies sparked upheavals that could end in . . . no one knew what.

The foundation of Japanese prosperity was in a slow, sickening slide, still spiraling down when the three officials of the Tokyo Stock Exchange arrived at Singapore's brilliant international airport and made their way through the impossibly clean avenues and boulevards of the Southeast Asian city-state. Convinced that derivatives were responsible for the stock market's unprecedented collapse, Japan's regulators had already nearly put a stop to Nikkei stock index futures trading in Osaka, Japan. They had not expected that traders would be able to move so quickly and so easily to Singapore. The Ministry of Finance and the Tokyo Stock Exchange were now face to face with, but refusing to see, the grim reality of the borderless world of contemporary international finance. They naively expected to discipline the Singapore International Monetary Exchange and choke back the trading of Nikkei stock index futures by speculators in the SIMEX pits.

They were confident of success when they arrived at the exchange headquarters at One Raffles Place, so confident that they dispensed with courtesy.[3] Behind closed doors, beginning at 10:00 A.M., Deputy President Mitsuo Sato of the Tokyo Stock Exchange made two demands. First, he wanted Singapore to agree to exchange information with the Tokyo Stock Exchange in order to better police the trading in Nikkei futures and underlying stocks. To this, the Singaporeans had no objection. "As a-self-regulating organization and an exchange, we don't want illegal activities to take place," SIMEX president Ang Swee Tian explained.[4]

The second demand was more problematic. The Japanese demanded unification of rules and regulations, so that Nikkei index futures trading in Singapore would be subject to the same restrictions as trading in Osaka. "We did not know how we could agree to this. We must be the ones who decide on our rules," said Tian. But Sato persisted, haranguing the Singaporeans for over two hours, refusing even to break for lunch. The Japanese seemed to expect that the power of Sato's lungs would exhaust the quiet but firm resistance of the Singaporeans.

Insulted by the arrogance of his Japanese guests, and firm in his conviction that both money and principles were at stake, Tian refused to yield. A slightly built man, Tian was far more steeped in the rough-and-tumble of free markets than his counterparts from Tokyo. English and Chinese were his native tongues. He grew up in Singapore, the quintessential entrepot, free port, one of the world's most cosmopolitan cities. After earning his MBA in Chicago at Northwestern University, he had returned to join a civil service modeled on that of Britain but imbued with a sense of the value of markets. Tian worked his way up through the Monetary Authority of Singapore, eventually reaching the post of deputy director for insurance before leaving to take command of SIMEX. He had the cunning of a Singapore trader and the fighting temper of a bantam cock.

As the meeting dragged on, bringing him no closer to achieving his goal, the former taxman Mitsuo Sato grew more impatient, and his temper turned ugly. Abandoning any pretense of negotiation, he pounded the table and shouted commands at the SIMEX president. At one point, he picked up an ashtray and threatened to throw it at Tian's head.[5] Still, Tian refused to yield. When threats failed, Sato tried cajolery. He told Tian that even the American Stock Exchange had backed away from trading certain derivatives when the Tokyo Stock Exchange had objected. Why not Singapore?

Tian was unpersuaded. He saw himself as the guardian of the integrity of the international financial system, fighting on the front lines against a new kind of Japanese imperialism. "They wanted us to be subject to Japanese rules," he says. "How could we agree to that? Singapore is an international financial center. If we were going to subject ourselves to Japanese regulators, the impact would go far beyond SIMEX. It would affect the entire international financial community. Frankly, if the Japanese objective is to depress and kill futures trading while ours is to develop that very market, it would be difficult to find a common basis for cooperation."[6]

After the meeting broke, Tian spoke to reporters, leaving no doubt in anyone's mind that Japan's emissaries had failed: "We have not agreed on anything. There are still wide differences in our views and further discussions will be necessary before any agreement can be reached. We are an independent exchange incorporated in the Republic of Singapore and I don't think we can subject ourselves to the jurisdiction of any foreign exchange."[7]

In Japan, as regulators continued to strangle trading of Nikkei index futures in Osaka, business continued to migrate to Singapore.

Nothing in their previous experience had prepared Japan's financial regulators for the new, global marketplace. They were accustomed to control, and the notion that control was no longer theirs to exercise was altogether new and strange. The heretofore impregnable Japanese financial system depended on a careful balance of interests, and some of its elements were centuries old. Now, quite suddenly, it had become an anachronism.

The Black Ships

In 1600, the warrior Tokugawa Ieyasu won a major battle, assumed the ancient title of shogun, and founded a dynasty that would rule Japan for over two hundred years. Tokugawa put an end to the unremitting war of the previous centuries, centuries whose atmosphere is most easily absorbed by spending a few hours with the films of director Akira Kurosawa. In place of roving, battling samurai, Tokugawa brought a hermetic peace. Under his rule and that of his heirs, the samurai became bureaucrats, their twin swords more ornamental badges than functional weapons. But Tokugawa's peace came at a steep price.

Already, in 1543, Portuguese merchants had arrived at the southern tip of Kyushu island seeking trade. They were accompanied by Jesuit priests seeking the salvation of souls. The missionaries succeeded in converting nearly a half-million Japanese by the turn of the century. Tokugawa feared this faith, and so he intensified a bloody persecution that his predecessor had begun. One effect of the persecution was to turn Japan into a hermit kingdom, similar in some respects to contemporary North Korea.

"Overseas Japanese were prohibited in 1636 from returning to Japan for fear that they might reintroduce the virus of Christianity, and Japanese ships were limited to coastal vessels unsuitable for ocean voyages," wrote Edwin O. Reischauer.[8] By 1638, Tokugawa had stamped out Christianity and established a nearly impermeable barrier around Japan.

Tokugawa's era was an era of absolute peace in Japan. But Japan's isolation kept the island pacifically ignorant of advances in commerce, science, and philosophy that were turning feudal Europe into modern Europe while Tokugawa's heirs reigned in Edo (later renamed Tokyo). Japanese finance was feudal well into the nineteenth century. Adequate to provide for the borrowing needs of improvident aristocrats, it was incapable of collecting savings and funneling them into the investments required for industrial development.[9]

When Commodore Perry's Black Ships arrived in Tokyo harbor in 1853, they forced open a door that had been firmly barred for ten-score years and more. The sudden confrontation with Western technological superiority shocked Japan's rulers. Foreigners took possession of Japanese ports and gained the power to limit Japanese tariffs. They totally discredited the heirs of Tokugawa, whose power was justified only by their role as defenders of the nation. Now the defenders had failed to defend, and the failure emboldened those who had begun to chafe against the anachronisms of the old Japanese system. Says Takuma Takahashi, an economist who has written extensively on the history of finance in Japan, "When they had seen the warships, many people in Japan realized that behind the warships there should be a good system capable of producing those ships. They tried to import or learn the system of the Western world."[10]

By 1868, the Tokugawa dynasty fell to a coalition of revolutionaries who fought in the name of the emperor. The Meiji Restoration was not a backward-looking phenomenon; nor was it a chaotic rebellion. It was a peculiar combination of central planning, discipline, order, control, and revolution. Once in power, those who ruled in the name of the emperor set about transforming Japan into something it had never been. Dispatching students to Western countries and hiring Western experts at great expense, they sought to copy the best elements of Western law, arms, industry, and finance. In order to establish a modern monetary system, the reformers established a national bank, the Bank of Japan. They established ministries on the Western model, the most powerful of which was the Ministry of Finance, because it controlled the nation's wealth.[11]

Within nine years, these revolutionaries stripped the samurai class of all its special privileges, even the right to wear twin swords as badges of rank. The samurai had traditionally received a tribute of rice from those living under their jurisdiction. The government eliminated this tribute, replacing it with a system of taxation. In order to compensate the samurai for their loss of income, the government offered them pensions instead of tribute. However, the government soon realized it could not afford the expense of these pensions, and issued pension bonds instead. The interest on the bonds was worth far less than the pensions they replaced, and many samurai sold them, illegally, on the black market. The samurai code had taught them to despise commercial affairs, and they often sold for far less than the bonds were worth. Recognizing that the illegal market for pension bonds contained the germ of the capital market the government would need for its own purposes, the Meiji brought in foreign advisors to design an organized exchange. The ideas of the foreigners were adapted to the Japanese setting, and in 1878 the Tokyo Stock Exchange and the Osaka Stock Exchange were founded.[12]

Not all samurai clung to the old contempt for commerce, however. The samurai pension bonds helped launch not only the stock exchange but the Japanese banking industry. "When the government decreed that the bonds could be used as the capital infusion required to set up a bank, many warrior-class families set up small banks around the country, using their pension bonds as seed capital. Thus, many samurai traded their swords and armor for pinstripes," wrote Samuel Hayes and Philip Hubbard in their survey of global investment banking.[13]

Some of the old moneylenders also survived and made the transition into the modern era. Foremost among them was Mitsui. Mitsui had not only financed the Tokugawa but also helped finance the Meiji Restoration. During the early years of the new regime, Mitsui functioned as a de facto Ministry of Finance and central bank After the government established its own treasury, the Mitsui clan established a bank, Mitsui Bank, which survives to this day under the aegis of Dai Ichi Kangyo Bank.[14]

The bank became the core of the Mitsui *zaibatsu*. The *zaibatsu* were powerful industrial and financial groups focused on major industries of military importance, such as transportation, mining, and engineering. Mitsui, for example, controlled the coal mining industry in Japan. It had not been a traditional role for the Mitsui clan. Although coal had been known in Japan for centuries, its power became clear only after the arrival of Commodore Perry's coal-fired Black Ships. On the island of Kyushu, in the Miike coalfields, nine seams of coal from twenty to twenty-five feet thick stretched through 102,000 acres.[15] Thanks to deft backroom political maneuvering, Mitsui won a bidding war against the Mitsubishis and several other moneyed groups vying to buy these fields from the newly installed Meiji government.

As important as the coalfields was a young engineer, Takuma Dan. Dan had been born into poverty, the son of a samurai. An uncle in the clan adopted him and sent him to study in Boston when he was twelve years old. His course of study eventually led to the Massachusetts Institute of Technology, where Dan learned mining and metallurgy. When he returned in 1884, he went to work as a government employee in the Miike mines, earning the equivalent of $400 per year.

Four years later, when Mitsui bought the mines, Takuma Dan went to work for the clan. He had already risen from engineer to superintendent of the fields. Among his achievements was installation of the largest pumping plant in the world to keep water out of the mines and allow deep coal seams to be worked.

Dan's success with the mine started his rise through the Mitsui group. "In the fifteen years that followed his assumption of directorship of Mitsui mining activities, more and more responsibilities were placed on his shoulders, and he became a director in one after another of Mitsui's companies. . . . In 1915, with the World War getting under way, Dan was made senior managing director of the Mitsui Gomei Kaisha, the highest post in the Mitsui organization," writes one chronicler.[16] Now Mitsui's power was Dan's own.

Japan's integration into the global financial markets had been consummated after the 1894–95 Sino-Japanese War, when (thanks in part to reparations paid in gold by China) it joined the international gold standard. Japan for the first time ever was thus linked with Great Britain, Continental Europe, and the United States in a common network of international monetary discipline.

Japan's links to the outside world spurred an economic boom during World War I. The warring countries had been cut off from their traditional export markets, but Japan was neutral, so for the first time in history the Japanese enjoyed a trade surplus with the rest of the world. Prosperity spurred a boom in financial services. Hundreds of new stock and bond issues came to market. But after the war, Japan again faced competition from Western manufacturers. Between 1920 and 1923, the stock market collapsed, a bank panic swept the country, and then one of the worst earthquakes in world history leveled Tokyo, killing 130,000 people.

The central bankers decided that reconstruction should take precedence over any considerations of monetary discipline. They sent forth a flood of easy money. Banks lent without much worrying about risk. The result was predictable. In 1927, a major bank failed, sparking another bank panic.

Takuma Dan and the Mitsui *zaibatsu* prospered throughout these turbulent times, in part by assisting in the corruption of the government. Working as agents for foreign shipbuilders, the Mitsui clan bribed navy officers to obtain lucrative battleship contracts. The ensuing scandal blackened the name of the Mitsui group.

Japan went back on the gold standard in 1930. Dan opposed re-
sumption of the gold standard because Mitsui's extensive industrial
interests would have benefited from a cheap yen on the export markets. Dan laid two plans—one to topple the government and remove
Japan from the gold standard, the other to make a financial killing when
the yen consequently weakened. In 1931, he began to buy dollars.
Soon after, a powerful cabinet official, reportedly in return for a million-
dollar bribe, brought about the fall of the government and Japan left
the gold standard: "The Mitsuis were reported to have profited by
about 50,000,000 yen overnight through their dollar holdings when
Japan went off gold. Other bankers of course benefited. Altogether, it
was estimated that about $200,000,000 was held speculatively by the
big financial interests. The principal holders, according to one estimate, were Mitsui, with $50,000,000; Sumitomo with $20,000,000;
and Mitsubishi with $10,000,000."[17]

But others were not so happy. The fall of the yen meant a rise in yen
prices that hit farmers particularly hard. In northeastern Japan, fertil-
izer and tax bills left farmers with no money to live on. Many ate roots
and sold their daughters into prostitution: The northern provinces
were noted for their pretty girls. In 1931, the number of girls sold into
brothels from these provinces doubled from seven hundred to fourteen hundred. "Villages of these two provinces today have practically
no girls of a marriageable age left,"[18] a contemporary chronicler wrote.
They would be avenged.

On March 5, 1932, as he was stepping out of his car to enter the
Mitsui Bank, Takuma Dan looked into the barrel of a revolver. A peasant boy pulled the trigger. Dan died shortly after noon, on the fifth
floor of the Mitsui Bank, where he had been carried.

The peasant boy was a member of a quasi-mystical secret society
called the Blood Brotherhood. Headed by a Shinto priest and former
secret agent, the Blood Brotherhood intended to purify Japan by as-
sassination, eliminate politics and corruption, and restore the power
of the emperor. They did not succeed. But the military rulers who soon
took power, self-proclaimed heirs of the ancient samurai tradition, were
also disdainful of the money classes. They reduced the number of
banks and tightened financial regulation.

The military rulers wanted a disciplined, streamlined financial
system that would efficiently turn household savings into guns and
bullets. In 1931, there were seven hundred banks in Japan. In 1936,

there were four hundred, and by 1944, only seventy-two. Over the same period, sixty-one life insurance companies were concentrated into twenty-one. Non-life insurance companies numbered sixty-eight at the beginning of the decade, but the policy of concentration had merged them into only seventeen by the end of the war.[19]

The military rulers sought to focus the entire financial and productive capacity of the nation on conquest. The *zaibatsu* became in effect an industrial and financial arm of the military, their executives often seconded to or from government agencies. Some habits of thought and financial structures that developed during this period strongly determined the future shape of Japanese finance and financial regulation.

For example, during the 1930s the government decided that high stock prices were critically important. Because a sharp fall in prices would cause people to pull their money out of the markets and make it more difficult to prosecute the war, the government intervened actively to prop up prices. In 1937, news of a battle between Japanese and Chinese troops outside Beijing sparked a market collapse. The government urged life insurance companies to step in and buy. Subsequently, the Japan Co-operative Securities Company and the Wartime Finance Bank were established specifically to stabilize stock prices.[20]

Nearly sixty years later, a similar operation would be launched. Wags would quickly dub it the PKO—Price Keeping Operation, a pun on Japan's role in a United Nations Peace Keeping Operation (also PKO). "Since August," the *Wall Street Journal* would write in March 1993, "the Finance ministry has twisted arms and orchestrated a buying binge, using government-controlled savings-account money and pension funds to support stock prices."[21] The story could as easily have run in the 1930s, and stressed the opposition of regulators to free markets when freedom might threaten stability. Obviously, the official interest in maintaining high stock prices, by coercion if necessary, had survived through World War II, the U.S. occupation, and three decades of Japan's emergence as a global economic power.

From Zaibatsu *to* Keiretsu

After the war, the U.S. occupation army modified the financial system somewhat. They broke up the *zaibatsu* and tried to redistribute the stocks that had been held by a few big families and holding companies. This concentration of wealth presented a formidable challenge.

The top four *zaibatsu* accounted for 25 percent of the capital invested in Japan's private sector.[22] The objective of General MacArthur's planners was to democratize Japan's financial system by putting these stocks into the hands of individual investors, ideally employees of the firms and residents of the communities where the companies had operations. "They tried to establish a New Deal in Japan," says Takahashi wryly.[23] Among the New Deal reforms introduced to Japan was a version of America's Glass-Steagall Act, which had sharply divided the commercial banking and securities businesses in the United States.

However, the reformers were not as thorough as they might have been. They neglected to require that the banks formerly at the core of the *zaibatsu* divest their holdings of securities. The banks were able to hold up to 10 percent of each of the former *zaibatsu* companies. Later, the permissible holding was reduced to 5 percent, but the practical effect of the reduction was negligible. The banks simply lent each company money to buy shares in its fellow *zaibatsu* companies. So the banks owned some stock directly and controlled other stock indirectly through these stock purchase loans. The old *zaibatsu* returned in all but name. They were now called *keiretsu*.

The banks became the primary engines of finance in Japan. *Keiretsu* corporations had to go to their banks not only for short-term working capital but also for the long-term capital typically obtained in other countries from equity or bond markets. Those markets would not develop in Japan for almost forty years.

Some American scholars consider the reincarnation of *zaibatsu* in the form of *keiretsu* to be the result of an oversight on the part of the U.S. occupation, or of a failure to understand that Japanese society is based on cooperation rather than competition.[24] However, some Japanese authorities believe that the United States consciously chose to allow the *keiretsu* to form. Takahashi explains, "In the early 1950s, there was a general strike in Japan, probably led by the [Communist] International. So the U.S. side had to seek stability first in Japan, rather than the very, very democratic ideal."[25]

Whatever the reason, by the 1950s the mold for the Japanese financial system was set. The Ministry of Finance and the Bank of Japan were at the heart of the system. They guided the activities of banks and other financial institutions. It is said that there has not been a bank failure in Japan since World War II, and some say not since the failure of the Bank of Taiwan in 1927. The Ministry of Finance simply has not allowed banks to fail, although occasionally management might be re-placed or one institution involuntarily merged into another. Moreover, losses, bad loans, or other results that might lead to doubt about the safety, soundness, and stability of the banking system are kept secret. Keeping up appearances requires sweeping problems under the rug.

In other countries, banks have an important fiduciary and mone-tary role. But in Japan, their role has been bigger than that. Banks have not only owned large stakes in *keiretsu* companies but also been the only practical source of credit for these companies. The combination has given Japanese banks great power and influence over Japanese companies. They have had a stake in the long-term success of their borrowers. They have not looked for dividend payments or for short-term stock price gains; they were in for the long haul. "Banks that own equity want their customers to achieve maximum success" is one an-alyst's pithy summation of the relationship's practical effect.[26] Follow-ing this line of thought, other commentators have noted that the ability of Japanese companies to think long-term has had a lot to do with the fact that their investors were patient bankers and fellow *keiretsu* mem-bers.

During the 1960s and 1970s, Japanese manufacturers stormed the West. They were no doubt aided by an improbably cheap yen and by a protected home market that provided a sort of "shock absorber" for price campaigns in export markets.[27] Of course, the cheap yen and the protected home market did not account for the fact that Japanese cars delivered higher quality than their Western competitors, better fuel economy in a period of rising oil costs, and so forth. Much of the Japa-nese success came from the fact that Japanese manufacturers paid more attention to the customer. But it is also certainly true that their banks strongly supported them.

Over the same period, Western and especially American companies went through a wrenching experience of falling sales, plunging stock prices, takeovers, spin-offs, and so forth. The American companies did not have patient, long-term investors willing to see them through the tough times. It began to look as if American companies were failing because they faced the arbitrary, harsh, and sudden discipline of the markets. Pundits declaimed that the myopic markets, run by investors who cared only about quarterly results, were ruining America. Chief executives of some of the biggest and most harshly disciplined corpo-rations—those whose stock prices fell farthest and fastest—raised their voices against a system that they said made it impossible for them to compete with Japan. "Investors' expectations for simultaneously high dividends on stocks, high interest rates on bonds, and rapid growth in the price of securities force managers to forego many of their most promising ventures. Ultimately, these pressures rob consumers of future products, workers of future jobs, and investors of future profits," said Donald N. Frey, former CEO of Bell & Howell, in one of the most succinct presentations of the myopic market argument.[28]

However, the Japanese system also had serious weaknesses that became apparent only later.

Despite the outcry from corporate leaders dismayed by their tumbling stock prices, most observers eventually came to believe that the case for market myopia did not stand up to tough scrutiny. "On the occasions when a company's stock price responds unfavorably to a new capital project, it probably is not because the market is unable to visualize the eventual payoff. The real reason is that the market predicts that the long-run return will be inadequate, and its judgment will prove to be right more often than not. The record shows conclusively that betting against the market is simply not rewarding," says consultant G. Bennett Stewart III of Stern, Stewart & Company.[29]

Far from being a source of strength, Japan's protected system of finance weakened the country in several ways. It blinded banks and corporations to one of the most valuable sources of information available to Japan's competitors: the considered opinion of thousands of astute investors who analyze every available scrap of information about companies and markets in order to arrive at a price. Because of their efforts, the market price of a company's stock contains as much truth as is knowable at any given point in time about a company's prospects.

This weakness became critical when Japan's financial system began to crack under the shock of international events beyond the control of Tokyo's ministries.

Bubbles, Pretty Bubbles

By the late 1970s, domestic pressures began to whittle away at the labyrinth of controls and restrictions, eroding the power of Japan's financial regulators. Real financial markets at last began to evolve in Tokyo and Osaka, decades after they had developed in New York and

London. Regulatory barriers fell, opening Japan to the rest of the financial world. Soon Japanese capital was financing the deficits of the United States, Japanese stocks were hot, and international financial institutions brought their most innovative financial techniques to Tokyo. However, Japan's corporations and financial institutions were ill prepared for their introduction to the global market in financial risks. During the 1980s, they behaved like drunken gamblers on a lucky streak, piling up a mountain of chips on one impossible bet: that the Japanese stock market would never fall. Outside Japan, sophisticated traders who had seen bubbles come and go knew better.

Despite Japan's tight regulatory system, these traders found ways to express their view that the Japanese market was bound by the same rules as any other. Trading in exchanges beyond the jurisdiction of the Japanese regulators, they proved the impuissance of government to contain the ebb and flow of international capital.

The inevitable, sickening collapse of the Tokyo stock market began in 1990. Two years later, Japanese stock prices had been halved. The crash did more than enrich foreign investors at the expense of the Japanese. It also humbled Japan's vaunted industrialists, both by the fall in their stock values and by the revelation of their too-clever-by-half financial schemes.

The politicians and regulators who had guided Japan's postwar economic course were also discredited. Many had been swept into a culture of corruption fueled by the stock market boom. The Liberal Democratic party was swept from power, but there was no clear successor.

In the Land of the Rising Sun, the sun had set. It was an astonishing triumph for the vandals. A financial system under construction for over a hundred years came unraveled in less than ten. Japan's regulators thought themselves stronger than the market, and Japan's borrowers and investors thought themselves smarter. This was sheer hubris—known in the West for over two millennia to be the tragic flaw.

What went wrong in Tokyo? Japan's stock market had traditionally not been an important source of capital for Japanese companies. However, during the 1980s, it became the cornerstone of Japan's financial system. Banks held substantial shares of the stock of *keiretsu* companies, so stock market values were critical to the safety and soundness of Japanese banks. In fact, stock prices were so important that in negotiations over international capital standards at the Bank for International Settlements in Basle during the late 1980s, the Japanese bank regulators put forth a shocking demand.

Central bankers of the world's strongest economies, troubled by the fragility of the international financial system, hoped that stringent capital standards could protect the system from a recurrence of shocks. The decade had already seen the Third World debt crisis, and many feared that a financial panic could lead to chained bankruptcies of financial institutions.[30]

So the central bankers formed the Basle Committee on Banking Regulations and Supervisory Practices, to draw up rules to keep weak financial institutions from playing the international banking game. The rules required that banks maintain minimum capital reserves to support each line of business they pursued. The riskier the business, the more capital it demanded. The central bankers hoped that by keeping weak players out, they could avoid the financial crisis that occurs when a collapse of a bank escalates into a worldwide panic. The consequences of such a panic could be devastating—some economic historians believe that the collapse of the Austrian bank Creditanstalt in 1931 sparked an international bank panic that spread the Great Depression throughout the world.[31]

The purpose of the Basle Committee was to make the international financial system safer. So Japanese bank regulators sparked controversy when they demanded that Japanese banks be allowed to count as capital the difference between the price at which they had bought stocks and the current market values of those stocks. The Japanese regulators argued that the banks had owned their stocks for decades, that the market had soared far above the level at which they had purchased the stocks, and that therefore the gain in value should be recognized as "hidden reserves" and counted as capital. In essence, they were arguing that the stocks were as good as cash.

The non-Japanese central bankers raised their eyebrows at this demand. Because the stock holdings, or "hidden reserves," were not disclosed on the bank financial statements, only the Japanese bank regulators and the banks themselves were in a position to know how many "hidden reserves" each bank had. So Japanese regulators proposed not only to count their chickens before they hatched but to rely on hidden eggs that no one else could see. What's more, international bankers familiar with how markets worked knew that if stock prices fell, the "hidden reserves" would simply vanish.[32] Nonetheless, the international central bankers bowed to the Japanese demand and worked out a formula that allowed these phantom assets to be counted as Japanese bank capital.

Outside Japan, most bank capital reserves took the form of government securities or cash. Only Japanese banks counted as capital the profits they had not yet made on stocks they had not yet sold. This volatile capital would simply disappear if the stock market bubble popped.

So stock prices became the unstable foundation of the Japanese financial system. During the 1980s, stock prices rose, and on the strength of their "hidden reserves," the Japanese banks expanded both domestically and internationally.

High stock prices not only kept Japan's banks looking strong; they also helped keep Japan's industrial companies looking profitable. Foreign bankers showed Japanese corporations how to borrow money internationally at impossibly low rates—even at negative rates—provided that they gave lenders an option to take their payments in stock rather than cash when the loans came due. Between 1986 and 1989, Japanese issuers raised over ¥60 trillion, most of it by bonds tied to their stock price performance, with coupon rates far lower than American or European companies could achieve. Many international investors, willing to believe that Japan's market could only go up, eagerly bought the bonds.

American industrialists noted with alarm that their Japanese competitors were pouring these cheap borrowings into new production facilities, R&D, and marketing campaigns.[33] Not all of the lending went for expanding capacity, however. Some Japanese companies were losing their competitive advantage as the yen strengthened against the dollar, and they tried to make up lost profits from their ordinary business by extraordinary financial speculation. This practice became so widespread that a new word—*zaitekku*, or *zaitech*—was coined to describe it. *Zaitech* literally means "financial engineering," but in fact it referred to the practice of trying to make money by speculating with borrowed funds.

More than half of the companies listed in the first section of the Tokyo Stock Exchange engaged in *zaitech*. In the fiscal year ended March 1988, almost 38 percent of Toyota's profits came from financial speculation. Matsushita Electric earned 59 percent of its bottom line by such speculation, Nissan 65 percent, and Sony 63 percent.[34] Not all *zaitech* was profitable. In September 1988, the chemical company Tateho Chemical was completely wiped out when interest rates moved suddenly. It had taken a position approximately twenty-four times its net worth in highly volatile Japanese government bond futures.

Japan's regulators were not entirely comfortable with the wave of *zaitech*. In 1987, the Bank of Japan instructed banks to stop lending to companies for the purpose of speculating in bonds, stocks, and real estate.[35] But the instruction was widely ignored. By April 1988, corporations accounted for 7.2 percent of the dealing in Japanese government bond futures. Banks were unwilling to tighten the screws on customers who could easily raise money from other sources.

Showdown

At the offices of Merrill Lynch in Tokyo, economist William Sterling was watching these developments with skepticism. Sterling assembled compelling evidence that the financial situation in Japan was quite similar to other historical episodes, such as the apparent prosperity in France when John Law used the Banque Royal to issue a flood of paper money and engineer the Mississippi Bubble. In an article published in 1989, at the height of Japan's stock market surge, Sterling said that the Japanese boom looked like a classic example of speculative mania. In 1985, the dollar collapsed, oil prices plunged, and the yen's value soared. "Large shocks usually alter the outlook by changing profit opportunities in important sectors of the economy," Sterling wrote.[36] In Japan, this was certainly true. The high yen threatened to devastate Japan's export economy, so the Bank of Japan opened the money supply spigots and flooded the country with liquidity. Discount rates— the rate at which banks could borrow from the central bank—went down as far as 2.5 percent, a historic low.

"If credit is too readily available, its use can become excessive and result in highly leveraged financial speculation, boom-like economic conditions, and general euphoria," Sterling further wrote.[37] Money was easy. How easy? Sterling outlined how Japanese homebuyers could buy houses without using any money: "Step 1: Find house worth $1 million. Step 2: Go to bank, get loan for $1.2 million. Step 3: No need to use any of your own money. Step 4: With this 'infinite leverage,' pay all closing costs and interest payments for two years. Step 5: Repeat Step 1."[38] So many people borrowed to buy real estate that prices soared. Sterling calculated that Japanese real estate was priced, on average, at a hundred times the value of U.S. real estate.

During the 1980s, Japan became an important source of credit to finance the U.S. deficit. Japanese financial interests bought not only bonds but also American real estate—landmarks like New York's Rockefeller Center, and the Pebble Beach golf course in California. Sterling also marshaled impressive statistical evidence to support his opinion that these massive purchases of U.S. Treasury bonds and other foreign assets were simply fueled by easy money in Tokyo. Once money tightened, the Japanese house of IOUs would come tumbling down. In Japan, at the end of 1987, general government debt was 74 percent of GNP, household debt was 69 percent of GNP, and nonfinancial corporate debt had surged to 185 percent of GNP. By contrast, in the United States, the debt-to-GNP ratios for the federal government, the household sector, and the nonfinancial corporate sector were at 42 percent, 60 percent, and 40 percent, respectively.[39]

There were some signs that Japan's financial regulators understood just how fragile the boom really was but did their best to hide the truth from investors. Take for example one of the most popular *zaitech* investments, the *tokkin* funds. Tokkin funds were stock market investments similar to mutual funds. They often came with a guarantee of performance from the securities house that put them together. That is, the securities houses promised minimum returns of 7 to 8 percent no matter what happened on the stock market. In 1987, the international stock market crash caused the value of *tokkin* fund investments to plunge. In an attempt to prop up the Tokyo market, regulators changed the accounting standards for *tokkin* funds. In January 1988 the Ministry of Finance announced that nonfinancial corporations with *tokkin* funds investments could value their investment at the higher of cost or market value—exactly the reverse of standard, conservative accounting, which demands that investments be valued at the lower of cost or market. The accounting change allowed companies to ignore the effect of the stock market crash on their balance sheets.

As long as Japan's financial system had been closed, of course, regulators could manipulate investors' confidence by such changes to the accounting system. However, Japan was no longer closed. Although regulators did not yet know it, they were about to confront the new economic vandals head-on and their old system was doomed. "Internationalization . . . made possible arbitrage transactions that took advantage of differences between Japan's regulatory regime and those existing overseas, and began to give further impetus to the spread of market principles in the Japanese financial system," wrote Shinichi Muroi and Yukihiko Endo of Nomura Research Institute.[40] Nowhere was the victory of markets over regulators clearer than in the battle for control of the stock market.

In 1986, the Singapore International Monetary Exchange began to trade its futures contract based on the Nikkei stock index. At first, Japanese fund managers were not allowed to use overseas exchanges, so only institutional investors from the United States and Europe could use the SIMEX contract to hedge their investments in Japan. These foreign investors were buying and selling the Japanese stock market with a foreign contract traded on a foreign exchange, completely beyond the jurisdiction of Japan's Ministry of Finance. Within Japan, financial institutions were at a disadvantage. Their foreign competitors had access to a powerful new financial instrument, but they did not: "The initiation of Japanese index trading outside of Japan was a form of 'gaiatsu,' or foreign pressure, that was used by those Japanese parties interested in stimulating political and bureaucratic movement at home."[41]

So, in May 1987 Japanese regulators allowed Japanese investors to use the SIMEX contract. Although they started slowly, trading volume soared after the international stock market crash of October 1987. On the morning of October 20, after the shock of Wall Street's Black Monday crash, Japan's stock market could not open. Price limits restricted how far stock prices could fall, and sell orders so far outnumbered buy orders that the limits were broken before trading even started. However, traders on the SIMEX continued to buy and sell the Nikkei futures contract. Already, the borderless global financial markets offered a way around the regulations that governed stock trading in Tokyo.

In response, in 1988, in a move they would later regret, regulators approved an application from the Osaka stock exchange to launch a futures contract in the Nikkei stock index. "When the Ministry of Finance approved the Nikkei contract, I don't think they knew it in depth," says Keikichi Honda, economic advisor to the president of the Bank of Tokyo, Ltd. "It happened to be a Frankenstein, beyond their control."[42]

The desire to bring futures trading under their regulatory jurisdiction was doubtless a motive for Japanese regulators to approve index futures trading in Osaka. It worked. Trading began in Osaka in September 1988, and from September to December, monthly trading volume was about 473,099 contracts. In Singapore, by contrast, average monthly volume for the year was 48,910 contracts. Not all of the increase was for good, clean business. Says Honda, "Unfortunately, in this equity market we still had Mafia who could mobilize lots of money and artificially raise and lower prices."[43]

The Nikkei index was a simple average of 225 Japanese stocks. Launched in 1949, it contained a number of stocks that had long since faded in importance. It was therefore a simple matter for an astute futures trader to manipulate the Japanese stock market. "For example," Honda explains, "one shipping company is known as a scarce stock in the market. It is illiquid, so when they put a big chunk of money on the stock, the price just shoots up. This easily pushes the entire Nikkei 225 index upward. It is so easy to manipulate, many politicians obviously took advantage of such moneymakers."[44]

This kind of market manipulation became commonplace. Traders bought a thinly traded stock (on the cash, or "spot," market), drove up the Nikkei index, and consequently drove up the price of Nikkei futures. Then they sold the futures. "Anything could ignite the crumbling of such a fictitious price structure," says Honda. "Then they made a huge profit buying back the future and selling spot. Regulators came to them asking why they were selling when the market was bad. The response was 'We sell it because we make money,' but regulators did not understand how they made money."[45] When regulators finally did catch on to the game, they were so embarrassed to publicly admit that the Tokyo stock market could be so easily manipulated that they did not take action for years.[46]

Although manipulation was a source of easy money, it was small change compared to the really big money made by those who dared to bet that the Japanese market was about to take a major fall.

Bursting the Bubble

In the offices of Salomon Brothers Tokyo, a young Japanese trader explained one of the techniques used by foreign investors to accumulate vast, short positions in the Japanese stock market (that is, bets on a market fall) without arousing the suspicions of Japanese regulators. Dressed in a starched white shirt and a dark tie, he is almost indistinguishable from any salaryman, except that his bearing is both arrogant and furtive. He insists that his name not be mentioned, and he forbids the single reporter present to use a tape recorder. He is speaking, he says, only because the Japanese press came to treat traders with so little understanding when they seemed to be making obscene profits from the collapse of Japan. But he insists they did no more than help Japanese life insurance companies find a way around an inconvenient, outmoded accounting regulation by using an innovative financial technology.[47]

Japanese insurance companies were the biggest investors in Tokyo. As the Japanese stock market rose during the late 1980s, representatives of various American investment banks approached these insurance companies with a novel proposal. The insurance companies, like most Japanese investors, believed that the Japanese stock market would continue to rise forever. The foreign investment banks, which did not share that faith, wanted the insurance companies to sell them put options. The put options would require the Japanese insurance companies to pay the American investment banks if the Nikkei index fell.

It certainly looked like a no-brainer. It was as if the Americans were offering to pay handsomely if the Japanese would commit to buy stocks for less money than the stocks were selling for on the Tokyo Stock Exchange.

It seemed that the investment banks were offering something for nothing. The promise would be worthless unless the Nikkei fell. But like everyone in Japan, the insurance company employees knew that the Nikkei would never fall, because the government wouldn't let it fall. So, knowing a good thing when they saw it, they took the Americans' money and sold them put options.

However, they sold their options in a carefully designed package. Most of the investment schemes engaged in by Japanese life insurance companies came in carefully designed packages. They faced a stringent set of accounting regulations and legal restrictions on what they could and could not do. But Japan's insurers were used to getting around restrictions, and they did so with ease in this case, by disguising the option income as though it were a bond.

Although Japanese insurance companies accounted for their option income as though it were a bond, financial engineers at American investment banks quickly stripped the options out of the bonds. They kept some for themselves; others they sold in the vast, liquid, and largely secret over-the-counter (OTC) market. No one knows with certainty how many such put options the Japanese insurers sold. In 1991 a commissioner of the U.S. Securities and Exchange Commission estimated that there were from $10 billion to $75 billion worth of them in the market. "But, at this point, no one, including the regulators, knows for sure," she said.[48]

In New York, a former navy jet pilot named Ivers Riley was watching these developments with considerable interest. Riley knew little about Japan. The closest he had been to the country was when he had flown patrol missions over the South China Sea from a base in the Philippines during the late 1950s. Although he was no Japan expert, he knew a lot about financial risks. Riley had been a key man in building the new global markets that turned financial risk into something by which a clever trader could make a fortune. He had overseen the growth of equity options trading as senior vice president of the Chicago Board Options Exchange during the late 1970s. After a stint as a senior vice president of the brokerage firm Paine Webber, he founded an options consulting group, then joined the American Stock Exchange (Amex) as executive vice president in 1983.

Short, sandy-haired, and intense, Riley had seen enough market cycles to be suspicious of the notion that the Nikkei had nowhere to go but up, forever. "It was a big bubble and should have burst long ago," he says.[49] The rapid growth of the OTC market in Nikkei "puts" meant that there ought to be a good opportunity to develop a successful new product at the Amex. The Amex badly needed new products. Dwarfed by the New York Stock Exchange for most of its history, it could survive only by being quicker, more innovative, and more focused than its giant competitor. Like the Philadelphia Exchange, the Amex had made a strategic commitment to the derivative markets, but it faced an uphill battle to establish a niche. Although it had been one of the pioneers of equity options, there wasn't much growth potential left in equity options by the 1980s. Philadelphia had scored a major success with currency options, but the currency options business was already migrating to the OTC market. What was left?

The Nikkei index, of course. The big investment banks that had bought scores of billions of dollars of Nikkei index options from Japanese insurance companies would certainly welcome a chance to sell them to the public at much higher prices than they themselves had paid. Contrarian American investors who delight in going against the trend would welcome an opportunity to place a small wager on the failure of Tokyo. In cooperation with Goldman Sachs, Salomon Brothers, and Paine Webber, Riley devised a tradable product that could use as its raw material either the put options sold by the Japanese insurers or the futures contracts traded in Osaka and Singapore. After nearly a year of review, the U.S. Securities and Exchange Commission approved it, and on January 12, 1990, the first Nikkei put warrants began to trade at the Amex.

The structure of these warrants showed just how difficult it would be for regulators to control them. Three American investment banks— Goldman Sachs, Paine Webber, and Dean Witter—underwrote the issue, but the issuer was the Kingdom of Denmark. The buyer of a warrant had the right to receive from the Kingdom of Denmark a cash payment if the Nikkei 225 index fell below 37,516.77. According to the prospectus, the Kingdom of Denmark raised about $23 million by the warrant issue but did not take any Nikkei market risk. Unlike the Japanese sellers of put options, it was fully hedged. Even if the Japanese market completely crashed, the kingdom would lose nothing, and in the meantime it was making money from lending its name to the new security. There was also plenty of profit in the transaction for the underwriters. The prospectus stated plainly that the price the public paid for these warrants was much higher than the price the bankers paid for the Nikkei options on which they were based.[50]

The Kingdom of Denmark put warrants began to trade on January 12. Five days later, Salomon Brothers issued similar warrants. Bankers Trust and Paine Webber rapidly followed. Between January and April, nearly fifty-six million warrants were distributed to the public. All of them had a three-year life—the payoff to the warrant holder would be calculated according to the difference between the current value of the Nikkei and the strike level indicated in the prospectus. The odd thing was that the Nikkei index began to fall just weeks after the first put warrants were issued on the Amex. The coincidence was not lost on officials of the Tokyo Stock Exchange. They blamed foreigners and their derivatives for toppling their invincible market. The lowest strike level on any warrant was the Paine Webber issue set to expire in April 1993. The strike was 29,249.06. The current market value of the Nikkei in April 1993 was roughly half the strike, making the warrant a very profitable investment indeed.

In fact, the Japanese market collapse was largely made-in-Japan. In the last quarter of 1989, the Japanese central bank decided to tighten up on the runaway credit expansion that had fueled the boom. Says Yoshio Suzuki of Nomura Research Institute, "The leaders of the Ministry of Finance and the leaders of the Bank of Japan didn't think the bubble at that time was very big. They didn't recognize that the burst of the bubble would have enormous destabilizing effects upon the financial system. Rather, in order to encourage the soundness of the Japanese financial system and sound banking, they thought it was good for the bubble to burst."[51] By raising interest rates and cutting the money supply, Japan's financial regulators hoped to remove the fuel that had driven their stock and real estate markets to astonishing, ultimately unsustainable heights. They expected to see a modest market correction—not a rout.

Their motives were, however, broader than merely protecting the banking and financial system. The boom had disturbed the well-ordered social structures of Japan. A society in which the highest-paid executives made only about five times as much money as the lowest-paid factory workers suddenly had to cope with the emergence of real estate and stock market millionaires. A savvy salaryman who bought a house and traded up, riding the boom, could become rich. However property values were rising so fast that it was impossible for newlyweds to have any hope of ever owning their own home. The system benefited those who got in first and rode to the top. There was no connection between hard work and reward. Easy money spurred a culture of greed, and revelations of political corruption soon made headlines. It seemed that politicians and bureaucrats had not stood idly by while traders made fortunes. Scandalous practices by the most august names in Japanese banking, politics, and industry began to give the 1980s something of the flavor of Takuma Dan's heyday. Braking the decay of good order was a powerful motivation for the Bank of Japan to pop the bubble.

In a 1991 address at the Mitsui Life Financial Research Center, University of Michigan, the aforementioned Mr. Mitsuo Sato, deputy president of the Tokyo Stock Exchange, admitted that the initial stage of the Tokyo market collapse was indeed the result of monetary tightening: "Japanese monetary authorities also were anxious to curb the so-called 'asset inflation,' a legacy of the easy monetary policy, because of its adverse effects on the distribution of income and wealth. As a result, long-term interest rates jumped from 5% to 7% around the turn of the year. And this in turn led to a 28% decline in the stock market in the spring of 1990."[52]

However, he blamed derivative markets for luring investors away from the stock, or cash market, and therefore weakening the Japanese stock market: "Futures trading is more attractive to investors because of lower trading costs, higher leverage, and easier diversification. Also, the futures market permits investors to sell short quickly and efficiently," he said.[53] In his view, futures trading was a threat not so much because it caused the market to collapse but because it provided a competitive alternative to actually investing in stocks: "Derivatives are beneficial to the economy only insofar as they contribute to a stronger cash market by providing hedging opportunities that would not otherwise exist. No one, of course, can raise funds in the derivative markets as such, however large such markets have become. In this sense, we should avoid having the tail wag the dog."[54]

The traditional Japanese way to do that was to cut the tail off. Thus, Japanese regulators like Mr. Sato directed their enforcement efforts at Singapore and New York. Although the best available evidence shows that derivative trading did not cause the Japanese stock market to collapse, the battle for control of the market was not driven by the dispassionate search for truth. Japanese regulators like Mr. Sato reacted viscerally and vehemently to the revelation that they no longer had the power to control their market. Says Riley, "We had proved the concept you could trade on the Japanese market even though the market was not open, and you could trade in U.S. dollar terms."[55] In fact, Nikkei put warrants traded on the Amex while regulators slept in Tokyo.

When Riley had negotiated with the U.S. Securities and Exchange Commission for permission to trade Nikkei warrants in New York, the SEC had required him to produce an information-sharing agreement with the Tokyo Stock Exchange. Such agreements make it easier for regulators to cooperate with each other in order to police trading and guard against illegal abuses. At the Tokyo Stock Exchange, however, Sato had insisted on a unique clause in the information-sharing agreement—the right to approve each warrant prior to issue. "In their case, they were using an information exchange agreement to control the issue of warrants," he says.[56]

When the first warrant issues were followed by a market collapse in Tokyo, Sato invoked his rights under the information-sharing agreement and refused to approve any new warrant issues. Threatened with the loss of what had now clearly become the most dynamic product of his career, Riley took two steps. First, he directed the research and development team at the Amex to develop a clone of the Nikkei. They devised a copycat index called the Japan Index, which could mimic the performance of the Nikkei. Thus, the Amex insulated its Japanese derivative business from any damage that might occur should its license to use the name Nikkei suddenly be terminated for some reason. Second, he flew to Tokyo to negotiate a new information-sharing agreement that would allow the Amex to continue trading Nikkei warrants.

"We were saying, 'If you're concerned about the market, we'll just do call warrants, not puts,' " Riley recalls. "We proposed all sorts of different instruments." Call warrants would gain value if the Nikkei rose, not if it fell. Sato shouted, "Mr. Riley, you don't understand—NO NEW PRODUCTS!" He underscored his point with threats. "I felt a couple of times that I was going to get the rubber hose treatment," says Riley. The meeting concluded on a bitter note, with Sato threatening never to speak with the American Stock Exchange again.[57]

Riley returned to New York convinced that the Japanese authorities would use every means at their disposal to prevent him from introducing new instruments. He was also able to convince the SEC of his opinion. When it became clear that the Tokyo Stock Exchange was using the information-sharing agreement as a defensive measure, the SEC decided to exempt the Amex from the usual requirements. "We then set a trading date and informed the Tokyo Stock Exchange that we would begin trading with or without an information-sharing agreement," Riley says. "On the night before trading was to begin, they had a guy from the Ministry of Finance call me. He told me he had just talked to the SEC and they said not to trade the Japan Index tomorrow without an information-sharing agreement. So we called the SEC, and they said, 'We told them you *could* trade without the agreement.' " Riley telephoned Mr. Sato to advise him that the Amex would begin to trade the Japan Index options as scheduled: "He pleaded with us, and said he would lose face if we traded without an information-sharing agreement. So we delayed our trading for two days." The information-sharing agreement came, and in September 1990 the Amex began to trade options on its proprietary index.[58]

After failing to control derivative trading at the Amex, Japanese regulators tried to eliminate it in Osaka. In 1992, as the Japanese stock market reached historic lows, the Ministry of Finance imposed punitive margin requirements, raised commissions on futures trading, and imposed price limits that sometimes meant the Osaka market could be open for only five minutes a day. Although these restrictions did throttle the Japanese futures industry, they were a boon to traders in Singapore. In January, before the restrictions went into effect, Osaka traded over eighty thousand Nikkei futures contracts, while the SIMEX traded about six thousand. In April, after Japanese regulators had imposed their draconian rules on Osaka futures pits, reducing trading to only thirty-four thousand contracts, SIMEX volume more than tripled.[59]

The Japanese regulatory restrictions also brought the U.S. Congress to the aid of its oppressed Wall Street constituents. In 1991, three of the five most profitable brokers in Japan had been American—Salomon Brothers, Goldman Sachs, and Morgan Stanley. Of the top ten most profitable brokerages, six were foreign. "These firms have demonstrated significant technical superiority over their Japanese competitors in futures and derivatives trading. In fact, the better these firms do in these trading areas, the more hostile the atmosphere in which they operate seems to become. Unfortunately, this is yet another example of a troubling pattern which Japanese officials have repeated time and time again with regard to U.S. competition in the Japanese market. It is time that this trend is stopped. We urge you to do everything in your power to see that it is," wrote Congressmen Schumer, Gonzalez, and Dingell in a letter to the Honorable Tautomo Hata, Japan's minister of finance, on March 16, 1992.

Riley sees in the episode an object lesson on the balance of power in the international capital markets: "As securities houses and banks went international, they didn't care which border something traded in; all they cared about was where the demand was. We Americans chased the Eurodollar market offshore by regulation. Japan did the same thing with equity warrants. All of our regulators lost control, because if there was something desirable on an international basis, there was somebody bigger than you to make it happen." He pauses, then grins and says, "We've sort of looked at that as an opportunity."[60]

THE SECRET LIFE OF THE FORTUNE 500

One of the best-kept secrets of corporate America is the degree to which companies are trading sophisticated financial instruments either to protect themselves against currency, interest rate, and other financial risks or simply to make trading profits. Management of such risks is a new discipline for most businesses. During the Bretton Woods era, currencies and interest rates had been stable, so financial risk was not a problem. In the 1970s, after the collapse of Bretton Woods, the initial weakening of the dollar favored American manufacturers, and they understandably did not have great incentive to manage a risk that was working in their favor. But in the early 1980s, American industry was decimated by a strong dollar and relentlessly rising interest rates. The financial markets developed largely because corporations needed protection against these unpredictable, devastating forces.

Unlike the Japanese practitioners of *zaitech*, American corporations by and large approach the financial markets not as a source of speculative profits but as a source of insurance. A study by the Connecticut research firm Greenwich Associates[1] in the spring and summer of 1993 found that only one in twenty large industrial corporations trades cur-

157

rencies simply in order to win money at the game. But for these companies that do manage their treasury departments as profit centers, profits can indeed be substantial. (Intel, the semiconductor chip maker, in some years has garnered as much as 15 percent of its bottom line from speculation in interest rate and currency instruments.) On average, whether for hedging or speculative purposes, large industrial corporations trade $2 billion a year in foreign exchange, the survey found. Although most American companies may not manage their treasury operations as profit centers, even conservative companies don't hesitate to speculate when they think they have a good chance of winning. Occasional speculation is much more common than the Greenwich data, taken alone, indicates. In a November 1993 study, Professor Walter Dolde of the University of Connecticut found much more widespread evidence of speculation: 85.2 percent of Fortune 500 firms use derivative securities,[2] and of those, 87.7 percent speculate at least some of the time.[3]

For the most part, corporations prefer to keep both their hedging and their speculation activities secret, in part because the line between hedging and speculation is seldom clear. While one treasurer hedges by using a sophisticated, highly leveraged derivative contract to remove risk, another may speculate by doing nothing at all and thereby expose the company's assets to enormous risk. Stock analysts look askance at trading gains, because trading gains can easily turn into trading losses when the markets turn, so a company that becomes known as a heavy trader will pay a penalty in the form of lower or more volatile stock prices. Hedging, though, is equally sensitive. A corporation's currency hedging strategy has a direct impact on its pricing and marketing strategies. In order to keep competitors in the dark, most companies reveal as little as possible. Loose and inconsistent accounting standards have made that easy to do.

In 1993, an international committee of bank regulators made the surprising discovery that corporate hedging had been a bigger factor in the demise of the European Exchange Rate Mechanism than speculation by traders like George Soros. After the Danes rejected the Maastricht Treaty on European unification in June 1992, corporations that had previously taken regulators at their word decided that there was a risk the regulators might not be able to hold the system together after all. They used the financial markets to protect themselves against a devaluation of weak European currencies by selling them forward. This selling put immense pressure on the central banks of weak-currency countries and was largely responsible for the collapse of the ERM. "Hedge funds were very aggressive and visible in their operations, but their sales were small as a proportion of total sales," the regulators said.[4]

However, in the spring of 1994, a series of astonishing losses brought this secret, swinging life of the Fortune 500 squarely into the headlines. It seemed that almost every day brought news of a new derivatives trading disaster: Procter & Gamble, $157 million; Air Products & Chemicals, $113 million; Gibson Greetings, $19.7 million; Mettalgesellschaft, $1.34 billion; Kashima Oil, $1.45 billion.[5]

Congress lost no time in taking up the issue. Lawmakers convened hearings to examine the ominous and risk-fraught world of the new finance. Congressman Henry B. Gonzalez, chairman of the Committee on Banking, Finance, and Urban Affairs, together with Congressman Jim Leach, drafted legislation to control the risks of derivatives. Congressman Edward J. Markey, chairman of the Subcommittee on Telecommunications and Finance, also planned to introduce a bill. Although the bills did not move out of their committees before the 1994 elections brought in a new Congress, derivatives legislation remained a priority for the committees to pursue in the 104th Congress.

The hustle and bustle in Washington seemed a little incongruous to some. "Corporations make good and bad decisions everyday. Procter & Gamble made a bad decision. But if they came in with a Pampers line that flopped, you wouldn't have hearings in Congress, would you?" said one puzzled banker.[6] In fact, derivatives trading had quietly become so much a part of the mainstream business world that companies could actually be taken to court by their shareholders if they failed to use the new financial technology to protect themselves against financial risk. In 1991, a class action lawsuit filed when Compaq's stock price fell alleged that the company "lacked sufficient and adequate foreign currency hedging mechanisms."[7]

Derivatives trading and risk management are now as much a part of doing business as marketing, production, or R&D. An entire industry of bankers, consultants, and software designers has grown up to support this activity. Among the most successful corporate practitioners of this new management science is Dow Chemical.

Risky Business

The town of Midland, Michigan, sits athwart a broad highway, so most people who come are just passing through. Midland has all the attributes of any hick town in America, foremost among them the fact that it's a long way from anywhere one might actually want to go. To approach it by car from Detroit means hours of driving, past pine trees, trailer parks, truck stops, and, finally, just outside town, the world's biggest discount outlets for Christmas decorations.

A traveler who comes through in October might stop by for the Octoberfest, held on a field where a round yellow tent snaps in the crisp north wind. Inside, lederhosened grinners squeeze the accordion up on stage while the gray grandchildren of Midland's original Aryan settlers drink pitchers of beer and try to remember the polka. Outside, volunteers run the usual mix of carnival games—throw-a-Ping-Pong-ball-in-a-goldfish-bowl-and-win-the-fish, and so forth. But the crowds are streaming toward the big attraction, a booth where a long-distance telephone company is offering folks a chance to make free long-distance telephone calls anywhere in the world. Farm families jostle in the queue, talking excitedly about whom they might call.

In Midland, the summit of achievement is a good job at Dow Chemical, the biggest operation for miles around. It's been there almost a hundred years since the founder built a plant to make bleach from chemical wastes.[8] Eventually, Dow's business got a lot bigger than bleach, but the company stayed put anyhow. Cheap land, easygoing government, and tractor-trailer access down the highway to the car lords of Detroit all doubtless made Midland a good choice for a headquarters site, but despite the exodus of Fortune 500 companies from city life, no other has been charmed by Midland. Dow sprawls all alone among the pastures. An arriving visitor can't help feeling a strange surprise upon finding this solitary multinational in the fields. Usually, multinational headquarters are found in clusters, huddling together in that security that comes from knowing that if a decision turns out wrong, it will be possible for executives, by way of exoneration, to point to others just as smart who made the same mistake.

In the treasurer's office, the feeling of surprise grows. Instead of the paunchy old boys with pocket protectors and green eyeshades bending over ledger sheets that one might expect to see in a place as out of the way as Midland, Dow has a currency trading floor that rivals in computer power the setup of any major bank. Here is a tribute to the borderless world of modern money, a monument to the power of telecommunications. Here among the rolling, cow-flecked hills of Midland, Dow's finance department trainees match wits with the canniest traders of Wall Street, Marounouchi, Queens Road Central, and the City of London, not to mention the Merc and the Chicago Board of Trade.

Like traders anywhere, Dow's youngsters shout into telephones, stare into blinking trading screens, pore over news feeds, and try to outguess the markets. They use the whole gamut of new financial instruments—futures, swaps, options, and hundreds of elaborate mathematical combinations thereof—all in an effort to move the company's assets quickly and protect them from such threats as inflation, currency fluctuation, interest rate spikes, oil price moves, capital controls—in short, all the thousand shocks that capital is heir to.

It's a tribute to Dow's management that they haven't yet sunk the company. After all, these aren't the finance stars from the nation's best business schools. Those luminaries go to work on Wall Street for bigger paychecks than Dow can afford. Dow's traders are nose-to-the grindstone, house-in-the-suburbs, two-cars-and-two-kids, ordinary corporate citizens on their plodding way up the company hierarchy, hoping to survive long enough to collect a gold watch. Yet despite their unglamorous credentials, the company has a reputation for being one of the most sophisticated and successful traders in the markets. Bankers fight for Dow's business and curse the company for its tightfisted ways. Dow's traders have been known to call several bankers for a price on a currency trade, getting prices both to buy and to sell. If two banks are far apart on their quotes, Dow buys from one and sells to the other, pocketing a trading profit within minutes. That's arbitrage, and bankers hate to be arbed. It makes them look dumb.

Some of Dow's shareholders would no doubt be surprised to learn how much their dividends depend on this trading desk. In some years, trading in the markets has contributed significantly to Dow's bottom line. However, shareholders who wanted to know exactly how much would be hard put to find out. Accounting regulations don't really require that Dow say much about these activities in its annual reports.

In fact, most corporations that trade for profit are quiet about their activities. Dow is one of a handful of companies that are willing to talk publicly about their trading. But there are a lot of reasons why trading currencies makes good sense for Dow, and Pedro Reinhard, a tall, bronze Brazilian who presides over Dow's treasury, found the main one. He has the steady, deliberate air of a man who is sure that, just around the corner, there is a big risk he does not see. He moves slowly, speaks cautiously, insists that anything on which he is quoted be read back to him so that he can be sure he is quoted correctly. He is a very careful man. Reinhard began his career with Dow in Brazil and spent several years moving between Midland and various financial posts in Latin America. Just before he came back to Midland as treasurer in 1988, Reinhard had been managing director for Dow's Italian operations. Reckless men do not survive such environments. Reinhard prospered, winning promotions.

He also found what might be Dow's most extraordinary discovery in decades. In 1987, Reinhard began a study to examine the effect of currency moves on Dow's business. At the time, Dow earned over half its bottom-line income from operations outside the United States.

Unlike most companies, Dow had already established a reputation as a savvy and successful trader. Currency trading was an indispensable part of the management development process for fast-track financial staff, and Reinhard wasn't satisfied just to have his treasury staff meet budgets. The company's reporting system held them responsible not only for the results they turned in but for the results they might have turned in had they made sharper moves in the currency markets. So, at a time when even chief executives like Chrysler's Lee Iacocca couldn't resist the temptation to blame the dollar-yen rates for poor car sales, Dow's management refused to accept such excuses.

When he began his study, Reinhard was troubled. The financial upheavals of the 1980s had unleashed unprecedented volatility on the world's financial markets, and he was sure that Dow's business was suffering from it. He just wasn't sure how. Dow manufactured all over the world, and the chemical business is incestuous. Chemical companies not only compete with each other, but they also sell to each other. Thus, while a strong German mark may hurt Dow's German competitors, it can also erode Dow's sales to these same companies. So to some extent, a threat to Dow's competitors may also be a threat to Dow.[9]

Reinhard assembled a global task force, a gigantic committee that analyzed every aspect of Dow's international business. Treasury staff from Dow's regional operations in the United States, Europe, Canada,

Latin America, and the Pacific joined marketing and purchasing types from thirty groups representing over 80 percent of Dow's products. They took more than a year just to measure the effect of currency rates on each product in each market.[10]

They found that there was a lot more to currency than the short-term market moves that earned so much money for the trading desk. Reinhard discovered that the key to solving the riddle of how currency affected Dow's real economic bottom line was to identify what he calls the "currency of determination" for each product group. The currency of determination is the currency that determines how prices react when currency rates change. When the currency of determination strengthens, prices go up; when it weakens, they go down.

An industry's price leaders—those companies that actually have the market power to determine what prices will be—decide the currency of determination. In the early days of the computer industry, for example, the currency of determination for computers was the U.S. dollar. All important computer suppliers were American, and when the dollar strengthened, they had two alternatives. They could have kept prices constant in francs, marks, or whatever other currency they accepted in payment for a shipment. However, that would have meant decreasing the price in dollars, since foreign currencies buy fewer dollars when the dollar strengthens. The second alternative was preferable: to keep dollar prices constant, which meant raising prices in foreign currencies. Since there were no competitors based in other currency areas who would have a competitive advantage when the Americans raised their prices, they routinely did so, and the dollar's strength and weakness therefore determined prices for the industry. But by the end of the 1980s, the dollar's position as the currency of determination was threatened. Asian manufacturers had moved into the business. Since the Asians measured their own bottom-line performance in terms of yen, Taiwanese NT dollars, Korean won, or other currencies, they had no reason to raise prices when the dollar strengthened. As a result, the Americans found out that they could no longer raise foreign currency prices without losing sales to these competitors. The dollar was no longer the currency of determination for the industry.

The currency of determination is a business concept that did not exist when currency rates were fixed and relatively stable. One of the main objectives of the Bretton Woods system had been to remove currency shifts as a competitive force in international trade. However, after the fall of Bretton Woods, companies on the wrong side of currency moves suffered catastrophic losses and forceful competitive threats.

The international financial system had broken down just as businesses were discovering the global marketplace. The Bretton Woods world had been a basket of separate national markets. When corporations began to expand internationally, they had done so by opening independent operations in several countries, a model that Harvard professor Michael Porter had tagged "multidomestic."[11] Each operation conducted its business as if it were in fact a domestic company in the host country. It concentrated sales activity on the immediate domestic markets and was protected like any domestic company by a wall of trade barriers that kept international competitors at bay.

The erosion of trade barriers changed the way companies approached international manufacturing. The Japanese were the first to devise new business structures and strategies for the new global marketplace. In global competition, it wasn't enough to have the highest quality and lowest prices in the land. In order to compete successfully, it was necessary to have the highest quality and lowest prices in the world. Japanese manufacturers rowed their export boats with two oars: quality control and an undervalued yen.

Americans learned this the hard way.

In the late 1970s, when the dollar was weak, many American companies had confused luck with brains. Despite increasing foreign competition, their margins were holding up. They didn't recognize that the weak dollar had handed them an unearned competitive advantage. Instead of holding their own, the American companies ought to have been beating back competition on every front. Yet they drifted complacently. "As a result, they were poorly prepared for the shift in competitive position vis à vis their foreign competitors caused by the 'dollar shock' of late 1980," noted Professor Donald Lessard of MIT.[12]

Lessard concluded that in order to prosper in the new international financial climate, companies had to consider currency exchange rates as a major strategic factor. Managers had to look at currency effects when they decided where to build plants, where to buy parts and supplies, how to finance their operations, how to set prices, and how to evaluate their own performance. This represented a major change in how companies managed currency risk. "In fact," he wrote, "as now practiced, corporate exchange risk management differs little from stak-

ing the assistant treasurer with a sum of money to be used to speculate on stock options, pork bellies, or gold."[13] Lessard noted that while
American companies had been quite adept at lowering their cost of
capital through sophisticated financial transactions in the Euromarkets
and elsewhere, they had a very limited understanding of how the new
facts of financial life affected their long-term strategies.

Like those at most American companies, Dow's managers had always assumed that the dollar was the currency of determination for
their business. However, as Reinhard's task force dug in to the matter,
they found that it was not. In fact, different currencies affected each
different product in complex, subtle, and various ways.

Oil, for example, is priced in dollars. When the dollar strengthens,
German petrochemical makers have to pay more marks to buy a dollar's worth of oil. So even if the German manufacturers are the price
leaders on a certain product and the product's currency of determination is the mark, the effect of dollar strength on the cost of oil in
German marks might influence their product pricing decisions. It
would be a big strategic mistake for Dow to anticipate a rise in prices
whenever the dollar strengthens, but it would also be inaccurate to
suppose that the dollar's strength invariably has no effect at all on German prices.

The strategic and competitive maze was more complex than three-
dimensional chess. Only after Dow had identified the currency of determination and made allowance for such factors as oil prices could
the company have a clear idea of how the price of each product would
react when currencies moved. If the dollar weakens against the mark,
a product whose price is determined by the Germans might well increase in price for American customers. The price will increase because
German companies report to their own shareholders in deutsche
marks, and they would naturally not want to show a decrease in revenues just because the dollars paid by their American customers are
worth fewer marks. Yet whether the price changes in Europe depends
on the relationship of the German mark with the other European currencies. Whether the price changes in Japan depends on the relationship of the mark with the yen.

Once Dow had identified the currency of determination for each
product, the next stage of analysis was to identify what actions the company could take to cope with currency risk. For example, if Dow can increase prices when the dollar strengthens, or reduce costs by shifting

more production to factories in Europe or Asia, then the company can maintain the same profit margins despite the dollar's strength. Under these circumstances, it might not be necessary to use financial contracts to hedge revenues. However, if only part of the currency effect can be addressed by operational changes, Dow's treasury department swings into action and hedges the balance in the rapidly developing financial markets. As the study was concluded, Dow was about to begin hedging strategic exposures by using swap and option contracts that ran as long as three years. Dow uses these derivatives to insure itself against the risk it is unwilling to bear, much as someone might buy insurance against the risk of burglary or fire, and much as farmers insured themselves against the price risk on their harvest by selling corn futures to the early speculators in Chicago.

However, getting rid of economic risk often means taking another risk—accounting risk. Accounting regulations in the United States require that hedges of most long-term economic exposures be treated as speculative investments. This means that any gain or loss from the hedge has to be reported on each quarterly income statement. Dow might do the right thing by hedging to protect long-term cash flow, but accounting rules can make the company's income statements show erratic profits and losses instead of the real, stable economic truth. This happens because accounting rules require that financial contracts used to hedge long-term risks have to be "marked to market." That is, every quarter, the current market price of the swap, option, forward, or other hedging contract must be calculated. If the current market price is higher than it was the previous quarter, the gain has to be added to the quarterly income statement, and if the price is lower than it was the previous quarter, the loss must be subtracted from quarterly income. In a sense, such profits and losses are not "real," because in fact the company has not sold the contract, so there has been no change at all in its cash position. However, to the extent that investors react to reported accounting results rather than "real" economic results, these strange, unpredictable accounting gains and losses could damage the company's stock price performance. In spite of this, Dow's management in effect bit the bullet. They decided that the cash flow damage Dow incurred by not hedging competitive and economic risks outweighed the income statement volatility created by how the company accounted for the hedges.

It is important to understand that while Dow's hedging program allowed it to get rid of some risks, it couldn't get rid of all risks. Hedging one risk just means taking another risk. There is really no escape from risk. There is just some freedom to choose which risk to take. This, in fact, is the position in which most companies now find themselves.

Of course, corporations had been invented precisely to take risks, especially those risks no individual could afford to take alone. It had long been recognized that without risk, there could be no reward. Even Jesus Christ took the notion for granted, and used it in his teachings. The Gospel of Matthew includes a parable about a man about to depart on a journey who calls his servants and entrusts to each a portion of his property. To one servant, he gives 5 talents; to a second, he gives 2; and to a third, he gives 1. At the time of Christ, a talent was worth about a hundred pounds of silver, or 6,000 denarii. One denarius was a day's wage for a laborer, so 1 talent was a considerable stake.

The man who receives 5 talents and the man who receives 2 go out to the markets and trade their stakes for a 100 percent profit. The servant who receives 1 talent digs a hole in the ground instead and hides the money. After a long absence, the master returns, and praises and rewards the first two servants for their successful speculations. Then the parable continues:

> Last came forward the man who had the one talent. "Sir," said he, "I had heard you were a hard man, reaping where you have not sown and gathering where you have not scattered, so I was afraid, and I went off and hid your talent in the ground. Here it is; it was yours, you have it back." But his master answered him, "You wicked and lazy servant! So you knew that I reap where I have not sown and gather where I have not scattered? Well then, you should have deposited my money with the bankers, and on my return I would have recovered my capital with interest."[14]

The master took the 1 talent away from the risk-averse servant, threw him out of the house, and gave the talent to the one who had turned 5 into 10. Trading involves risk, and investing with bankers also involves risk, albeit less than trading. Either would have been preferable to taking no risk at all, because with no risk there could be no return.

Over the next two millennia, the Western world developed a multitude of institutions to manage risks. These institutions spread risks among a number of investors so that each investor might share both in the risk and in the reward. Germany's Hanseatic traders formed numerous short-term partnerships that allowed them to diversify their investments among several ships, instead of trusting all they owned to one captain and one voyage.[15] Similarly, the first joint-stock companies in England were formed in the sixteenth century to raise capital for long trading expeditions. The Muscovy Company traded with Russia, the Levant Company with the Mediterranean, the East India Company with the Orient, and so on. These companies not only allowed entrepreneurs to raise money for ambitious, risky projects, but they also allowed investors to diversify their risks by investing in more than one trading voyage. Shakespeare's Antonio, the Merchant of Venice, says, "My ventures are not in one bottom trusted, nor to one place, nor is my whole estate upon the fortune of this present year. Therefore my merchandise makes me not sad."[16]

The development of the financial markets was yet another innovation to make risk more bearable by spreading it around. Before the development of these markets, companies had no choice but to take risks as they came. After the collapse of Bretton Woods, such choices came in spades. Dow's own choices kept its name out of the headlines in the spring of 1994, when many of its less cautious peers were reporting their speculative fiascos. Although the company had been one of the most aggressive corporate traders in interest rate swaps and options, it managed to sidestep the interest rate turmoil that cost Procter & Gamble $157 million in pretax losses. Reinhard attributes the company's success to extremely tight controls. These controls prevent any trader from hiding trading positions from management and risking more than the company can afford to lose. Pedro Reinhard, a cautious man, only allows the acceptable risks.

The Corporate Revolution

Charles Smithson, a lanky, drawling storyteller from East Texas, shrugs to make a point. It's a southern shrug that says, "Well there it is; who could deny it? But don't just take my word. It's plain to see."[17]

Whether he stands before a crowd of CFOs or perhaps settles comfortably back in a chair across from some legislator, his "Aw, shucks" manner makes the whole frantic panic of the markets look so plain commonsensical that it's hard to imagine a world without them. Then he gives that self-effacing shrug and spins a yarn, like some Garrison Keillor of finance.

There's the one about Freddie Laker, the British air travel entrepreneur who invented discount flights across the Atlantic. Laker did a great business ferrying Brits to America during the 1970s when the dollar hit bottom. He did so well that he decided to buy a few American DC-10 airplanes. He agreed to pay for them in dollars because after all, dollars were getting cheaper every day. Then the financial markets dealt him a bad hand. The dollar started to strengthen. Suddenly, British travelers didn't want to come to America anymore. It was just getting too expensive. Laker's business fell off, about the time that the bill came due for his DC-10s. They were a lot more expensive now, because the dollar was so much stronger. Laker Air crashed into bankruptcy in 1981.

Shrug.

There's the one about Continental, squeezed by high interest rates on its exorbitant debt load and by high fuel prices. Bankrupt. Shrug. There's the one about Wang, the computer company, whose marketing people were having trouble signing up customers because the company's finances were shaky. Shrug. It's pretty clear, isn't it? Financial risk is a complex, subtle, and potentially deadly thing.[18]

Smithson happens to be a managing director in the risk management education group at Chase Manhattan Bank, but when he speaks, it's easy to forget that his career depends on these markets. Of course, much of what Smithson has been saying for years is now being supported by new, testable academic research into the way stock prices react to currency, interest rate, and other risks.

Leaning back in a chair in his Princeton office one winter day in 1992, he reminisced about how he came to see the light and believe that the derivative markets weren't just a high-stakes crapshoot but rather a critical strategic tool for American business.

He graduated from Tulane University in 1976 with a Ph.D. in economics and remembers a famous economist coming out from Washington to give the commencement speech and saying, "It's a pity you are taking your degrees in economics now, when all of the interesting problems have been solved."[19]

Although the commencement speaker was too close to events to see them clearly, in fact the whole economic system had just come unstuck. The solutions that seemed so sound and reliable to him would soon impress only connoisseurs of anachronism, much as now do the nineteenth-century automatons, those curious specimens of skillful artifice useless for practical work.

Armed with his new Ph.D. in old economics, Smithson ambled forth from Tulane to face a more volatile world than the old economist had ever imagined could be. Inflation was the number one economic problem in the United States.

Oil was priced in dollars, and dollars were worth less and less, so the Organization of Petroleum Exporting Countries (OPEC) had raised prices. The sudden increase in oil prices threw open the U.S. auto market to Japan. American car buyers had never before considered fuel efficiency to be an important feature in a new automobile. After the oil price shock, fuel efficiency mattered greatly to almost every car buyer. So the Japanese share of the American auto market began to grow rapidly.

When regulators tried to fix the inflation problem, they made life even harder for American manufacturers. On Saturday, October 6, 1979, Paul Volcker, the new Federal Reserve Board chairman, announced that the Fed would choke back the money supply in accordance with Milton Friedman's monetarist recipe for inflation busting.

For decades, interest rates had been predictable. No more. The week before Volcker's announcement, IBM had floated a bond issue with a coupon rate of 9.5 percent. Four months later, commercial banks had raised their prime rates to 15.25 percent.[20]

Never had the Fed tightened money so far so fast. However, much to the surprise of Volcker and his colleagues, inflation remained high. So they tightened again, driving the Fed funds rate to nearly 20 percent.[21]

In the spring of 1981, President Carter tried to rally the nation to austerity with a new budget and an economic program that included credit controls and further monetary tightening. He made a televised speech urging people to reduce spending. Americans responded by cutting their credit cards into pieces and mailing them to the White House.

As a result of the drop in consumer spending, the money supply fell sharply. In order to prevent a crash, the Fed suddenly reversed its course and lowered interest rates from 20 percent to 8 percent in three months.[22] The economy responded to this stimulus with another outburst of inflation. The Fed reversed its course again and tightened hard, and commercial bank prime rates climbed above 21 percent.[23]

U.S. interest rates were on the way up, so foreigners sent their capital to America. In 1982, 10-year U.S. treasury bonds were paying nearly 15 percent.[24] However, the supply of dollars was limited. In order to earn those high interest rates, investors had to buy increasingly scarce dollars. So the price of dollars went up too.

Change was everywhere.

Unfortunately, the U.S. economy hadn't really been built for fast changes. Over the years, companies had grown up in a slow, steady environment. Now the world was altogether different. The landscape was getting littered with the ruins of companies that had been blown up by the explosive force of change.

At Chrysler, a competitive analysis team pored over the financial statements of Japanese car makers to find out why the Japanese had a cost advantage of about $2,000 on each car they built. The team discovered that about 60 percent of the cost of a Japanese car was based on the level of the yen. So if the yen weakened by 10 percent, the cost of a Japanese car in U.S. dollars fell 6 percent just because of the currency difference. In one year alone, from 1981 to 1982, the yen had weakened by about 40 percent against the dollar.[25]

The strong dollar gutted America's manufacturing industry and gave a windfall opportunity to European and Japanese companies. In 1981, imported machine tools accounted for 27 percent of U.S. consumption. By 1985, imports took 44 percent of the market. Imported construction machinery had a 9 percent market share in 1981, an 18 percent market share in 1985. Import market share doubled for products as widely different as electrical transformers and household furniture.[26] The only thing these products had in common was that U.S. manufacturers did business in dollars, while foreign manufacturers did business in yen, marks, pound sterling, francs, or some other currency.

In Europe, a source told the *Wall Street Journal* that "everyone is laughing all the way to the bank."[27] The United States went from a trade surplus of $15.8 billion in 1981 to a deficit of $129.5 billion in 1987.[28]

One of the things Charles Smithson had learned to do when he studied economics was to make forecasts. When the rules that governed the economic system were clear, forecasting wasn't too difficult. When the rules broke down in the early 1980s, economic forecasts started going badly awry. "There was a time during this period when I went to parties and when people asked me what I did, I told them I was in the plumbing supply business," he says. "I didn't want to tell them I was an economist and sit there and listen to them nag on, saying, 'What good are you guys? You can't forecast.' "[29]

American business responded to the crisis by demanding government action to control the exchange rate of the dollar. Caterpillar chairman Lee Morgan was the first and most vocal executive to step forward, but the chief executives of U.S. Steel, Honeywell, Ford, Motorola, TRW, Chrysler, and eventually General Motors joined him. Even IBM and Xerox demanded a change in the international monetary system. The chairman of the pharmaceutical company Pfizer told the Reagan administration that exchange rates should take precedence over trade negotiations.[30] For almost five years, Washington turned a deaf ear. Companies began to look for their own solutions, and trading in hedge instruments boomed.

However, the strength of the dollar was playing into the hands of protectionist forces in the U.S. Congress. There was a real threat of a trade war. To avert it, on September 22, 1985, at the Plaza Hotel in New York City, finance ministers and central bankers from the United States, Britain, Germany, France, and Japan met and agreed to take steps to bring the dollar down. The markets endorsed their decision, and within three years, the dollar fell back to the levels at which it had begun the decade.[31]

Unfortunately, it was too late to help most American manufacturers.

In some cases, the dollar's decline did stem imports. The chairman of Porsche, the German maker of luxury automobiles, had focused the company's marketing efforts on the United States during the early 1980s. Now he slashed prices to try to hold market share, but it was no use. Profits dwindled, and he was forced to resign.

Yet others who had established a beachhead in the U.S. market managed to hold much of the ground they had gained. Japanese automakers had built factories in places like Ohio and Tennessee, so when the dollar turned down, they merely cranked up their production runs at these factories. They also used the high profits they earned in their protected home market to absorb the losses they incurred by keeping dollar prices low in the United States.[32] The dollar was weak again, and the yen was strong, but American companies found that their competitors were adept at managing currency risk.

Economists were puzzled by the fact that currency exchange rates did not do more to solve America's trade deficit problem. When American products had gone up in price, people had stopped buying them. The fall in the dollar was like an across-the-board price cut on all American products. The economists expected that this price cut would make American products more competitive and help reverse the trade deficit. But people still weren't buying American.

In fact, the influence of currency had grown more complex with the growth of international investing and offshore manufacturing and with the ability to source products from many countries. Academics at various universities began to investigate the implications of currency for business management. What they found launched a whole new field of management and was largely responsible for the rapid development of the derivative markets.

Beyond the ivory tower, in the real world of making, buying, and selling, companies found that in many cases their own internal systems made it impossible for management to understand the changes that were taking place. Monsanto's experience was typical. The St. Louis–based chemical maker's agricultural division began an international push just as the dollar was starting to strengthen.

Monsanto kept its books in dollars, but it sold its products to farmers who paid in their own national currencies. As the dollar strengthened, management raised the local currency prices it charged farmers, simply in order to keep dollar revenues from falling off. Monsanto's prices went up much faster than the rate of inflation in the countries where it was doing business, so the farmers who faced higher prices for the Monsanto products couldn't pass the cost increase along to their own customers. Monsanto's sales fell off.

When management in St. Louis saw that sales were falling, they prescribed the old-fashioned cure—more advertising, more promotion. Local managers in Europe threw money into sales and marketing. However, they were throwing francs, sterling, marks, and pesos, all of which were rapidly declining relative to the dollar. In fact, the dollar was rising so fast that when the local marketing budget was translated into dollars and sent to St. Louis for review, it looked as if the European managers hadn't followed instructions. It looked as if the European managers were doing nothing about promotion. "We were spending more, but because of the dollar strength it looked like we hadn't grown at all," a Monsanto executive recalled.[33]

When the world had been stable, Monsanto's management could tell at a glance what was happening in the field, simply by looking at the accounting statements. It didn't matter that the statements were in dollars. Now that the world had changed, Monsanto's systems were obsolete. So management eventually tried a new approach.

As an experiment, Monsanto sold its anticipated French franc revenues forward on the interbank market. When the dollar strengthened against the franc, the company pocketed a gain of $2 million on its forward sale. Instead of raising French franc prices to compensate for the strength of the dollar, Monsanto was able to keep French prices stable. Management expanded the hedging program. In 1988, the company spent $700,000 to buy an option on British pound sterling. Monsanto was launching a price war in Britain, cutting prices in order to increase market share. That would reduce both pound sterling and dollar income, but the company had calculated what it believed would be an affordable price cut. The wild card was the currency markets. There was a good chance the pound might weaken, in which case Monsanto's dollar income would be hit twice—once by the carefully planned price cut and again by the unplanned and unaffordable currency shift. The option protected Monsanto's battle plan from the risk of surprise attack.

These early experiments worked so well that soon Monsanto was routinely using options to hedge its budgets and business plans against currency risk.[34]

Other companies found similar surprises. Merck, for example, learned that fluctuations in the dollar-mark exchange rate were interfering with its research and development efforts—even though all of its R&D is done in New Jersey. Merck is one of the biggest American pharmaceutical makers, and about 40 percent of its sales were to customers outside the United States, often national health plans and other buyers who pay for medicines in their own national currency. Merck translates those foreign revenues into dollars when it calculates its annual budget, and that's where the trouble began. When a team at Merck was assembled to study several years' worth of data, they found a curious relationship. When the dollar strengthened against European currencies, the R&D budget in New Jersey would be cut. Conversely, when the dollar weakened, the R&D budget increased. Digging deeper, they found out why.

When the dollar strengthened, Merck's European revenues bought fewer dollars. Merck couldn't raise prices to make up the difference, because in most of its markets, prices were negotiated under long-term contracts or otherwise controlled. The only way to keep profits high and shareholders happy was to cut expenses. But pharmaceutical companies don't have much manufacturing expense—it's just not that costly to pour powder into a gelcap and pinch it together. The biggest expense for a pharmaceutical company is R&D. So that's what Merck cut when the dollar got strong.[35]

Of course, R&D is the most important long-term investment a pharmaceutical company can make. So by raising and cutting its R&D budget in tandem with exchange rate fluctuations, Merck was gambling its future on the currency markets. Hedging let Merck proceed according to plan instead of according to luck.

Multinational companies with significant foreign sales were by no means the only ones affected by the new currency world. Exchange rate fluctuations were also beginning to affect stock prices. Take Eastman Kodak, for example. The Rochester, New York–based company is best known for its photographic film, a business in which it has one major competitor, Japan's Fuji. The dollar's surge during the early 1980s meant that Fuji could easily underprice Kodak and seize market share. According to one estimate, the strong dollar cost Kodak about $3.5 billion in lost earnings.[36]

At the time, Kodak's currency management was primarily an accounting exercise. When a customer in Germany or Britain ordered a shipment of Kodak film, Kodak's accountants booked the order at prevailing exchange rates for marks or sterling. It took some time for the order to be prepared, shipped, and paid for, and if the dollar strengthened during this time, the marks or pounds that Kodak received would not be worth the dollar value at which the order was booked. So Kodak used currency hedges to lock in the value of the dollar, in effect selling its marks and sterling in advance so that it would not have to register a loss on its accounting statements.

Although this type of hedging protected the company against short-term moves in currencies, the big risk to Kodak came from long-term moves. By 1985, Fuji had a major competitive advantage, thanks to the dollar's strength. Investors recognized that Kodak's value as a corporation depended largely on the value of the dollar versus the yen. Research conducted under the supervision of Charles Smithson at Chase in 1992 found that during most of the 1980s, Kodak's stock price had moved inversely to the dollar.[37]

Obviously, Kodak's problem with currency was much bigger than the problem of whether an order booked at $1,000 would be worth a couple of dollars less in a month or two. Kodak's problem was whether the company could survive another five-year period of dollar strength. The company first tried to reverse the effects of currency on its bottom line by emulating the Chicago floor traders who speculated, rather than the farmers who hedged. By 1985, Kodak was known to be one of the most active traders of currencies in the markets. In fact, Kodak even sent some of its treasury employees to train on the trading desk at the Bank of America in New York.[38]

In 1988, however, Kodak changed its approach to currencies. Instead of just managing the short-term impact of exchange rate moves, the company began to look at long-term strategic effects of the floating dollar. Kodak addressed these long-term effects both by operating measures and by means of financial contracts. Operating measures included such tactics as buying materials from Japan so that the company would benefit from a reduction in costs when the yen weakened.

However, operating measures could do only so much—Kodak could hardly switch its sources of supply around completely every time the dollar-yen rate took a major jump or plunge. So Kodak was also one of the earliest and most active users of foreign exchange hedging contracts.

Kodak's director of foreign exchange risk management, David Fiedler, explained Kodak's strategy by reference to a hypothetical corporation, located in the United States, that bought all of its supplies from U.S. manufacturers; paid for them in dollars; did all of its own manufacturing in the United States, paying in dollars; and sold all of its product in the United States, receiving dollars. Did that company have foreign exchange risk? Yes, he said, provided that the company has one foreign competitor shipping to the U.S. market. Kodak developed a strategy to manage this risk using the financial markets.[39]

Managing the risk meant protecting the company against the negative effects it suffered when the dollar got strong, while taking full advantage of the positive effects it experienced when the dollar got weak.

It meant hedging "selectively." If the deutsche mark was likely to strengthen, there was no point in hedging deutsche mark revenues. However, it made a lot of sense to hedge deutsche mark liabilities. Selective hedging meant taking a view of which way currencies were likely to move and positioning the company accordingly. It meant taking some risks, perhaps considerable ones, since anybody who could be sure about which way markets were going to move probably wouldn't be working for a salary at Kodak.

In order to reduce the risk of loss from adverse moves while keeping the benefits of favorable moves, Fiedler and his small hedging team relied heavily on options and other new hedging instruments. They brought in consultants to design special computer programs that could track their hedge positions, measure their risks, and forecast how different currency scenarios would affect the company.

As a result of Kodak's changed approach, Smithson's study found, the company immunized its stock price from the effects of currency moves. Stock investors no longer bid Kodak down when the dollar went up.[40]

Yet Kodak's case was relatively simple—one big competitor, one big currency risk. Most companies faced a much more complex set of risks. Moreover, currency risk was just one of many risks that threatened business managers. Interest rate risk was just as important. All businesses needed money, and most businesses borrowed at least some of what they needed. Companies that borrowed cheaply had a competitive advantage over companies that had to pay more for their money. The less money a company spent paying interest, the more money it had for research and development, advertising, new factory machinery, customer rebates, or some other productive purpose.

Previously, borrowing had not been particularly risky. Now every borrowing decision meant taking a big risk with interest rates. Companies that borrowed long-term, at fixed rates of interest, took a risk that interest rates might fall. Then they would be paying a high price for their money, while competitors who borrowed short-term would be paying less. Companies that borrowed short-term, at floating rates of interest, took a risk that interest rates might surge suddenly, leaving them worse off than their competitors who had borrowed long-term.

Sometimes interest rate risk wiped out whole industries. The savings and loan industry, for example, had grown up in an era of controlled interest rates. Throughout the 1960s and 1970s, S&Ls made thirty-year, fixed-rate mortgage loans at rates as low as 6 percent. The money they loaned out came from depositors whose savings accounts earned less than 6 percent. When short-term interest rates surged in 1979 and into the 1980s, depositors pulled their money out of the S&Ls because they could earn higher returns by putting their money in other accounts—money market funds, for example. S&Ls were caught in an interest rate risk dilemma. The only way they could attract more deposits was to pay higher rates—but they were earning low rates on their long-term mortgage loans. The result: massive failures, taxpayer bailouts, and countless reports on "The S&L Mess."

In the late 1980s, bankers and investment bankers who dealt in derivatives became the insurance companies for interest rate and currency rate risks. Companies paid them to take the risk of rising interest rates, volatile currency rates, or other risks that were too dangerous to bear alone. The security and stability were not free, however. Sometimes the price was steep. Kroger, the grocery story chain, shelled out $9 million in just two days for a "cap option" to protect a billion dollars of debt against rising interest rates in the late 1980s.[41] This option put a ceiling on the company's potential interest rate costs. If market rates rose above a certain level, the bank would pay Kroger the difference between the ceiling rate and the market rate.

But at such high prices, most companies couldn't afford to insure themselves against all of their risks. They had to make economic decisions about how much protection they wanted to buy, when, and at what price.

These decisions led to the development of the field of financial risk management. They also blurred the lines that separate hedgers from speculators. If a speculator is one who takes risk, then every company was a speculator because every company took some kind of risk. The company that did *nothing* to manage its financial risks was the most flagrant speculator, because it retained every risk. Risk management meant an analytical approach to deciding how much and what kind of risk to take. The terms *hedger* and *speculator* lost precision, for every company became, to a greater or lesser degree, both.

The development of markets in risk allowed companies to decide which risks to take, which not to take, which to buy, which to sell. Many firms learned to use these markets to focus their business on the risks they were best able to manage.

One of the most important of the new risk management markets, the swap market, started in 1981 when IBM and the World Bank found a mutual interest in avoiding certain government controls on borrowing. The World Bank borrowed about $8 billion a year and lent it to the world's poorest countries to build dams, highways, hospitals, and other projects. The rate the bank charged its own borrowers depended on its borrowing costs. The Bank borrowed by issuing bonds in twenty countries. These governments strictly controlled how much money the World Bank could borrow in their capital markets, when it could borrow, and what it could do with the money.

At the time, U.S. dollar interest rates were about 17 percent, while Swiss franc interest rates were about 8 percent and deutsche mark rates about 12 percent. The World Bank decided to borrow Swiss francs and deutsche marks to fund its loans to the developing world. "The Bank staff felt that for the intermediate term it was better for its borrowers to be saddled with Swiss francs at 8% rather than dollars at 17%," says former World Bank treasurer Eugene A. Rotberg.[42] There was a problem, though: the bank had already borrowed the maximum that the Swiss and German governments would allow.

It happened that IBM had borrowed Swiss francs and deutsche marks sometime previously. After IBM had borrowed, those currencies had depreciated. The mathematical relationship between currency values and interest rates made IBM'S Swiss and German borrowings worth much more than the company had paid for them. If there were a way for IBM to sell its Swiss franc and deutsche mark obligations at their current market value, the company could recognize a hefty profit on its books.

So IBM and the World Bank agreed to "swap" obligations. The World Bank would borrow in dollars, issuing a bond that paid 17 percent. IBM agreed to pay the interest and principal on this dollar loan. Meanwhile, the World Bank agreed to take on IBM's Swiss franc and German mark borrowings, paying principal and interest to IBM.

Presto—the World Bank's borrowers got Swiss and German currencies despite the government controls in Switzerland and Germany. IBM got to recognize a fat profit on its books.

The swap proved to be simple, fast, and completely beyond the control of government regulators. And once the first swap had been done, there was no stopping this market. Corporations could borrow wherever costs were lowest, and swap their borrowings into whatever currency they needed. It was no longer necessary to line up a borrower on each side of the trade. Bankers became the swap counterparties and hedged their own risk in the rapidly developing interbank swap market. By 1989, the swap was so much a part of corporate finance that when General Electric Capital borrowed in Europe and did *not* swap, it made the news.[43]

The swap market exploded. By 1989, by one measure, there was nearly $2 trillion of swaps outstanding, and in just three more years, the market more than doubled in size, to $4.711 trillion.[44]

The swap proved to be remarkably versatile. Once the early interest rate swaps had been done, financial engineers found many other applications. Oil, for example. Like currency and interest rates, oil prices are volatile, and in some industries this volatility made planning difficult. So bankers began to market oil swaps to freight companies and airlines. These swaps gave the companies a guaranteed, fixed price for oil over a period of one year, three years, five years, or longer. The companies agreed to pay the bank the fixed price for oil, and the bank in return paid them the current market price. The corporations used the money they received from the bankers to buy oil on the market. If corporations were unwilling to bear the risk of oil prices, neither, in most cases, were the bankers. Usually, they hedged their own swap obligations, using oil futures contracts that trade at the New York Mercantile Exchange.

Companies don't have to be big to use these markets. Qualex is a small photographic-film-development company with outlets at K-mart stores throughout the American South. Yet Qualex used an oil swap to hedge the cost of gasoline used by its delivery trucks that picked up film from the Kmart outlets and returned developed photographs. Qualex agreed to pay a bank a fixed price and receive a floating price. Gasoline prices subsequently went down, but although Qualex's fuel costs would have been lower had it not entered the swap, the treasurer was happy. "We're beating our budget," he said.[45] The fixed price he paid on the swap was still lower than the price the company had originally budgeted for fuel, and it was guaranteed, unlike market prices.

The only limit to the potential applications of financial tools was the imagination of the corporate treasurer. Kaiser Aluminum developed a series of computer models to analyze the effect of raw material prices, interest rates, currency rates, and energy costs on its income statement and balance sheet. Kaiser then negotiated agreements to link its labor costs and energy contracts to aluminum prices. Financial instruments, swaps, and especially options hedged the balance of its risks. Because the hedges removed an element of considerable uncertainty from the company's financial outlook, bankers considered the company a better credit risk, and Kaiser could borrow at more favorable terms.[46]

In 1987, financial engineers in New York combined the swap with the option to create a new financial instrument called a "swaption." The swaption made a flexible tool even more flexible. It gave a company the right to enter into a swap if it chose, but didn't force an immediate decision. It was an option on a swap. Swaptions were popular because when treasurers were doubtful about the direction of interest rates, they preferred to defer decisions on whether they wanted fixed or floating terms. In one year, the swaption market grew from zero to $20 billion.[47]

Corporations used swaps, options and similar tools to capture every possible economic advantage. Some traded in and out of swap positions aggressively. At Sequa Corporation, for example, a conglomerate in the aerospace, chemical, and machinery businesses, the treasurer, Kenneth Drucker, was one of the most active users of swaps and swaptions in New York.[48] His goal was to get the best cost of funds possible for his company. He tried to do it by guessing right about the direction of interest rates. Drucker wanted floating rates when he thought interest rates were going to go down. When he thought they had hit bottom, he wanted a low fixed rate. He used swaps to switch back and forth, easily and cheaply.

He also used the new financial markets to protect his company against the economic fallout of political events. Shortly before the Gulf War in 1990, Drucker surveyed the managers of Sequa's many businesses and found that the company had about $100 million exposure to oil prices. He reduced the risk by using an oil collar, buying an oil option at one price while selling another at a different price. The mathematical effect was to establish a floor and a ceiling on what the company would pay for oil no matter how the war went.

Drucker emphasized that he did not speculate, but used financial instruments only when he had a legitimate, business hedging purpose to do so. Yet he used some of the most sophisticated swap and option combinations available, not only to reduce what he paid in interest or to lock in a guaranteed price for oil but to make timely bets on the direction of the markets. He used a complex combination of swaps and options that would pay off handsomely if the yield curve—the difference between long- and short-term interest rates—changed. He justified this transaction as a hedge, noting that the company borrowed at short-term floating rates, and if short-term rates went up while long-term rates came down, Sequa would suffer. However, he allowed that it was hard even for him to see the difference between this hedge and a straight speculative bet.

In fact, it was getting hard for anyone but an expert to tell the difference between hedging and speculation. In some cases, the distinction was so fine that even the experts were confused.

In 1988, a small company called Albany International shocked the stock market when it reported a $4 million loss on a swap. Albany sold fabrics used by papermakers, and its revenues were only about $500 million a year. So, securities analysts were stunned to learn that the company had entered into a complicated swap transaction worth $100 million. The reason for the swap? Albany's treasurer thought the yen was about to strengthen against the dollar, and believed the company's business might suffer. Soon after the swap was put on, the yen weakened instead of strengthening. Accounting regulations required that Albany International treat its swap as a speculative transaction and report a loss that knocked about 10 cents per share off of the company's earnings. "No one expected it, and all of a sudden, boom!" an analyst said.[49] Albany's stock nose-dived. The next year the yen strengthened as the treasurer had predicted, and Albany cashed out of its swap for a profit of $14 million. The treasurer criticized inconsistent accounting regulations for making the company report such volatile results.

If accounting regulations treated Albany too harshly, they seemed to let other companies hide more than they revealed. In 1992, a Wall Street analyst heard rumors that Dell Computer Corporation was speculating heavily in foreign currencies. He hired a team of currency experts and accountants who spent months reviewing Dell's published financial statements. Despite high-powered analytical techniques, they couldn't figure out exactly where some of Dell's revenues had come from. The company refused to cooperate by providing information the analyst requested. He went public with his concerns in a conference call to over a hundred brokers. Dell's stock plunged.

Afterward, a reporter obtained a copy of the résumé circulated by the trader who had been managing Dell's foreign exchange during the period in question. According to the résumé, the trader had traded over $1 billion a week in currency contracts. That was an astonishing sum of foreign exchange trading, especially considering that Dell had earned only $52 *million* the previous year.[50]

In 1993 and 1994, a series of spectacular losses began to focus attention on corporate losses in derivatives. Japan's Showa Shell lost $1.58 billion on currency and interest rate contracts in early 1993.[51] Later in the year, Germany's Metallgesellschaft suffered losses of over $1.34 billion in the oil futures markets.

In the first quarter of 1994, when Procter & Gamble reported its loss of $157 million, it was on a swap contract leveraged, by some reports, as much as 80 to 120 times. Bankers Trust, the bank that had sold Procter & Gamble's contract, had sold similar deals to Gibson Greetings, which lost $19.7 million; Mead Corporation, which lost $12.1 million; and Air Products & Chemicals, which lost $113 million.[52] A spokesman for the bank said that the swaps were highly speculative and that the companies had bought them because their treasurers had a strong view that interest rates were about to fall and wanted to profit from the market move. Instead of falling, however, rates rose.

It seemed that an orgy of speculation was occurring in corporate boardrooms.

How had things gotten so badly out of control? Most companies that reported heavy losses refused to elaborate or explain. In some cases, like Procter & Gamble's, they justified their silence by claims that they expected to take legal action against bankers who had sold them inappropriate investment contracts.

Yet for students of the history of derivatives, the great losses were all variants on a theme. It might be called the Allied-Lyons theme, after the British food and beverage company that counts Baskin Robbins ice cream and Canadian Club whiskey among its brands. In March 1991, Allied-Lyons announced that it had lost £150 million, or about $270 million at then-current exchange rates, through wild speculation in the currency markets. Allied-Lyons's chairman, Sir Derrick Holden-Brown, had the nobility to take full responsibility for this catastrophe, tendered his resignation, and explained in a detailed letter to shareholders exactly what had gone wrong. His letter remains the fullest explanation to date of how an otherwise responsible corporate management was seduced by the apparently easy gains to be had by market speculation.

He explained that his treasurer had been turning in very respectable profits from activities in the market, and that as chairman of the company, he was naturally pleased. He did not understand the risks the treasurer was taking to earn these profits. The treasurer, the better to please the chairman, expanded his market activities. Profits from the treasury department became even more impressive. The chairman was not one to look a gift horse in the mouth.

Then rumors began to circulate about extraordinarily risky bets being made by the Allied-Lyons treasury. The chairman heard about these bets from a banker, who was warning him about the risk to his company. Apparently, the treasurer had encountered a run of bad luck and incurred some small losses. Confident that his underlying analysis of the market was correct, the treasurer was reluctant to accept these losses. Instead, he made another, bigger bet, expecting to win back what he had lost, and on top of that make a profit, the better to please the chairman. When that bet lost, the treasurer increased it again, over and over.

By the time someone finally stopped him, the damage was irreversible. "It is now evident that the Allied-Lyons treasury was dealing in foreign currency instruments which were inappropriate, and in which it lacked the requisite trading skills, and also that the scale of trading was excessive," Sir Derrick Holden-Brown's letter read. "The reporting systems for measuring and monitoring activity in these instruments and the nature and level of management control exercised over the Allied-Lyons treasury—as well as communication of its activities and difficulties—were insufficient."[53]

Risk and Reward

Despite the headline-making speculative fiascos that often send stock prices tumbling, stock market investors demonstrably approve of companies that use derivatives in the context of responsible risk-management strategies. When corporate treasurers remove risk from their business, they add value to their corporations. Investors pay for safety—so reducing a stock's risk makes it a more attractive investment and gives the firm a lower cost of capital than its riskier competitors have.

In the field of corporate finance, however, this was not a self-evident proposition. The basic principles set forth by Nobel Prize laureates Franco Modigliani and Merton Miller in a 1958 paper, informally referred to as "M&M theory," guided most orthodox thinking on corporate values. M&M theory said that hedging did nothing for the value of a corporation, because if investors had wanted to hedge they could do so themselves, simply by diversifying their investment portfolio.

In 1994, though, results of research undertaken by Professor Eli Bartov of the Stern School of Business at New York University, Professor Gordon M. Bodnar of the Wharton School at the University of Pennsylvania, and graduate student Aditya Kaul of the Simon School of Business at the University of Rochester began to shed some light on how the volatile international economy affected stock prices. They discovered that when the Bretton Woods system was breaking down, the stocks of U.S. multinational corporations became much riskier investments.

The most important measure of stock price risk is beta. Beta measures the risk that cannot be overcome by diversification. If a company has a high beta, it is risky, and no amount of diversification can overcome that risk. High beta means that investors can't rely on the company's ability to keep generating cash. Investors demand to be paid for taking risks. Consequently, companies with high beta have to offer higher expected returns to attract investors to their stock and have a higher cost of capital than their low-beta peers.

In a paper entitled "Exchange Rate Variability and the Riskiness of U.S. Multinational Firms: Evidence from the Breakdown of the Bretton Woods System," the researchers noted that as exchange rates became more volatile, the stock prices of U.S. multinationals also became more volatile.[54] The stock prices jumped around, instead of trading in a steady band. Investors demanded to be paid more for investing in multinationals, since their earnings were now subject to an additional (and in some cases unavoidable) risk from the uncertainty of currency values. Beta went up for these companies. It cost them more to raise the money they needed to develop their business.

This research was complemented by research conducted by Charles Smithson's team at Chase Manhattan Bank in New York. They were studying large public companies that had issued complicated bonds called hybrids. Hybrids don't pay ordinary interest. Instead, they pay according to a formula that may be linked to commodity prices, stock prices, or something else. One of the earliest examples of hybrid debt was issued in 1988 by Magma Copper, a mining company. Magma's bond paid bondholders more when copper prices were high, and less when copper prices were low. In other words, when Magma received less for the copper it sold, it had to pay less to its creditors. Magma's margins were thus protected against the effect of fluctuating copper prices.

As a result of issuing this debt, Magma reduced its vulnerability to copper prices. It removed two types of risk from its stock. Before this bond issue, Magma's stock had moved up and down with copper prices. Now, after the bond issue, Magma's stock was only half as sensitive to copper prices. Copper price risk belongs to a category called "idiosyncratic," or "alpha," risk. Investors can diversify this risk themselves, simply by diversifying their portfolio of investments. One of the most forceful arguments against hedging alpha risk is that investors may invest in companies like Magma precisely because they want the company's alpha risk in their portfolio. Perhaps these investors are hoping that a runup in copper prices will make their Magma stock more valuable, the argument goes.

So it was much more significant from a corporate finance perspective to learn that Magma's beta fell by about a third after the bond issue. In fact, Magma reduced its overall cost of capital by reducing its exposure to copper. Investors were willing to pay Magma to hedge a risk that they could have diversified away by simply changing the mix of stocks in their portfolio. This finding was at variance with classic M&M theory.

Smithson continued to expand the study, separating hybrid debt issuers into two groups. The first group contained firms whose business was exposed to copper, oil, or other risks that the hybrid debt had hedged. The second contained companies that were not exposed to these risks but had issued hybrid debt anyway, perhaps as a speculative measure. He found that when hybrid debt reduced a genuine business risk, it consistently reduced the beta of the company's stock, but when it did not hedge a genuine business risk, the reduction in beta did not occur.

The research was still ongoing in 1994. However, preliminary conclusions were that stock market prices react to a company's financial risks, and when firms act to reduce the risk, their cost of capital goes down and their stock prices should, logically, improve. That is, the firm's stock should no longer be tossed like a cork on the waves of currency rates, market trends, interest changes, and fluctuating commodity prices. The implications for the field of risk management and for the further development of financial science were strong. Investors now expected corporations to do something about the risk they faced. Companies that did manage risk were rewarded with better stock prices. Companies that did not manage their financial risk could expect to pay more for capital.

In fact, corporate executives now have the means to control their financial environment. They can negotiate a financial contract that will lock in the prices they pay for raw materials, interest rates, and the value of their international revenues and can even protect themselves against a wide range of taxes by moving money around the world smoothly and secretly. They can also take massive financial risks that can, in a matter of days, destroy their companies. One phone call to a banker can accomplish all of this.

Whether corporations are using the new financial markets to hedge a business risk or to take a speculative chance, they are casting a vote that helps determine the direction of currency exchanges and interest rates throughout the world. By the funds they provide to bankers and investment managers, they determine what countries money will flow into and what countries it will flee.

When corporate managers stick to hedging risks that immediately affect their own business, risks that they know and whose effects they fully understand, the outcome is predictable: they stabilize their business, and investors are likely to reward them. However, when corporate executives become convinced that they understand the direction in which markets are moving well enough to predict the future, and decide to bet their shareholders' capital and their employees' jobs on their view of the markets, they step onto uncertain ground.

The bankers and brokers from whom corporate executives buy the highly leveraged swaps and options used for such bets seldom if ever take such extreme risks themselves. In fact, the real experts in risk take as little of it as they possibly can. If they bet on a market trend, they do so carefully, backed by powerful analytic technology, and constantly monitor their positions. In fact, much of the investment in technology by banks and investment banks has been for the purpose of measuring and monitoring risk in order to prevent inadvertent or deliberate bets that could cause serious damage to the firm. This is a field of finance as demanding as astrophysics. What these adepts do is not mere, old-fashioned investing—it is nuclear finance. Yet the markets remain, even for them, a bewildering blend of passion and reason, as the following chapters will show.

INTERREGNUM

THE ATTACK ON THE EUROPEAN MONETARY SYSTEM, PART III

SEPTEMBER 1993. In the lobby of the Grand Hotel in Paris, under a gilt-domed ceiling, among the mirrors and the nude statuary, the senior vice president of an American bank takes a long slow drink of beer.

Then he waves his arm and shouts, "I'm a free-market animal. Period. Supply and demand. That's it, that's the name of the game!"[1]

The banker's name is Jon Peabody, and although he did not directly speculate on the crisis that finally demolished the European Exchange Rate Mechanism, Peabody had been trading European currencies for as long as there was an ERM. In 1992, he was somewhat distracted by the need to help arrange the sale of the options trading firm where he worked to Nations Bank for over $200 million. But although he didn't have his finger on the trigger this time, he still sees the collapse of the ERM as a victory for his side—a victory for speculators, who enforce the pure law of supply and demand, against regulators whose motives are less worthy.

So his euphoria is understandable. Just a month ago, the ERM was decisively vanquished by speculators. It took almost a year. In the first wave, Britain and Italy had folded. France, though, hung on for almost a year, enduring three full waves of speculation before the central bank finally ran out of reserves and gave up the fight. "The markets *love* to run the spec," he laughs. "Sterling down, lira down, what are you going to go for next? Well, the French franc!"

Peabody is still somewhat amazed at the way Europe's regulators acted when the attack started. They just didn't get it, somehow. When the markets moved against the pound, Great Britain borrowed $14.5 billion worth of deutsche marks and made an announcement of its intention to defend the currency. Peabody laughs scornfully at the thought. The markets ate it up in a matter of days and came back for more. Only there wasn't anymore.

As usual, the whole time that the ERM was under attack, officials kept promising that there would be no devaluation. That was a signal to those who knew how to read it. The more loudly the officials proclaimed that their currencies were sound, the more certain speculators could be that they were on the edge of devaluation. Peabody had been paying close attention to such official statements for years—betting against the officials every time, and winning every time.

For most of the history of the ERM, countries had been pretty reasonable about facing up to the economic facts of life. Something changed about five years before the collapse. Germany kept boosting rates, and other countries kept following, but it was clear that there had to be a limit. Meanwhile, an average of one in ten people in Europe were unemployed. How high could the rates go? How long before the people threw the rascals out?

Sterling was a no-brainer. "You die for opportunities like that," he says. The pound had entered the EMS at a rate that almost everyone who didn't work for the British government said was too high. It was just a matter of time. France was a little more challenging. French inflation was low, all right, thanks to the high interest rates. Yet the French were not the Germans. Germans drink beer and worry about inflation. Germans seem to think it's better to be unemployed than to be paid in inflated marks. French drink wine and think perhaps it's better to have some inflated francs than no francs at all.

So one thing was very clear to a reasonable man like Jon Peabody. "The Germans hold all the fucking cards," he says. "They need interest rates high for their own reasons. They need to fund what's happening in the East. The French don't need high interest rates. So there's no fundamental reason to own French francs."

In the end, it came down to a judgment about what the people really wanted. The regulators in Italy, Britain, Scandinavia, Spain, and France swore that they would stay the course. When the speculative attacks began, one after another, the central bankers took the same futile steps.

When their currencies fell, they borrowed massive sums of German marks. They told the markets all about their war chest. That was very useful information. It was like knowing exactly how much food and water there was in a city under siege. From Paris to London to New York to Chicago to Hong Kong to Tokyo and back, traders passed information about the dwindling central bank reserves.

"It was like throwing down a gauntlet, insulting our manhood," Peabody says. "When you're new, it's an ominous thing. After you've been in the markets awhile and you've seen interventions, then it becomes a challenge. It makes the game spicier. Ultimately, the economic forces prevail. When the central banks had spent half their money and hadn't had much effect on the currency, the game was really over."

At one of the biggest French banks, a division manager found an interesting difference between the world outside France and the world inside. He was puzzled when he talked about the franc to all of his traders scattered around the globe. From September, when Britain and Italy dropped out of the ERM, until August, as the waves of speculation pummeled the Bank of France, he got the same answer. "All of our traders outside of France, whether they were French or foreigners, said, 'We don't see any economic reason why the franc should be devalued, but it will be. When we talked to French traders in our Paris operation, they said, 'We don't see any fundamental reason why the franc should devalue,' and they stopped there. Outside France, they knew the market, and they knew that it starts in a way and it finishes in a way. But inside France . . ."—he shrugs, and draws pensively on a fine Cuban cigar.[2]

How did the market work?

The attacks were very simple. To attack the lira, speculators borrowed lira and sold them for marks—often borrowing from and selling to the same bank. The bank sold the lira to the Bank of Italy, also for marks. The Bank of Italy then lent the lira back to the banks, where speculators borrowed them again, sold them again, over and over.

When the Bank of Italy ran low on marks, it turned to the Bundesbank. The Bundesbank started buying lira for marks. However, it didn't want to buy too many. The Germans really thought that the Italian lira was overvalued anyway. They really thought it should be devalued somewhat. So they didn't pull out all the stops. They just made a good show of it.

In fact, they felt the same way about the pound. Bundesbank president Schlesinger told the world on September 15, 1992, that he thought there should be further realignments in the ERM. "That was like taking out an advertisement telling the world to sell pounds," says a report prepared for the U.S. Department of the Treasury.

Schlesinger had all but told the world that the Bundesbank didn't intend to support the pound. The speculators already knew that the Bank of England was running out of money.

The only thing the Bank of England could do to stop the speculative wave was to raise interest rates so high that speculators couldn't afford to borrow. On September 16, the Bank of England raised rates from 10 to 12 percent and announced that they would go to 15 percent the next day. However, the interest rate hike wasn't slowing down the speculators. They had gambled, correctly, that the British people weren't eager to sacrifice their own economy for the sake of a quasi-mystical relationship with the rest of Europe. By evening, Britain had dropped out of the ERM.

Meanwhile, speculators launched an attack on Sweden. The Swedish central bank raised interest rates to 500 percent per year.

Italy, exhausted, dropped out of the ERM.

The Irish central bank, under attack, raised interest rates to 300 percent.

Historically, when central banks raised interest rates, speculators usually retreated. Higher interest rates meant that the central banks were committed to defending their currencies. This time, though, was different. Speculators saw the high interest rates as a sign of weakness. They meant that the central banks were almost out of foreign currency reserves, and their only defense was to raise interest rates. However, speculators correctly decided that those high interest rates couldn't be sustained without killing the economies.

A rate of 300 percent a year works out to less than 1 percent a day, and speculators expected devaluations on the order of 10 or 20 percent. If the countries devalued quickly, the speculators could easily pay the high interest rates and still make a profit.

In November Sweden floated the krona, and it depreciated by 9 percent. The Spanish peseta was officially devalued by 6 percent. In February, after a long but ultimately futile fight, Ireland devalued its pound by 10 percent.

Then attention turned to France. There had been sporadic attacks on the franc during the fall of 1992, but the French currency was only slightly overvalued. There were bigger profits to be had pursuing other prey. By the spring of 1993, the other prey had all been devoured. Then an election swept France's Socialist party from power.

Throughout the spring and summer, speculative pressure against the French franc built steadily. "At one point," recalls a French banker, "an official was saying things he shouldn't have said. He said that the French franc was already as strong as or stronger than the German mark. This was rather stupid to say, first because it's not the truth as the market sees it and second because the people at the Bundesbank were very angry about this."[3]

The French central bank tried all of the usual defenses—higher interest rates, intervention—but as the banker observed, once the market has started a serious attack, there is only one way for it to end. In August, the franc devalued.

It was the fault of the dirty speculators, the regulators said.

In the lobby of the Grand Hotel, under the gilded dome, among the nude statuary, Jon Peabody finishes his last beer. "There's no such thing as a dirty speculator," he says. "You know why I love Chicago? Because in Chicago, a speculator is a respected professional. The markets are geared to people who want to go in and take a risk, and if you're right, you make money. Speculation is a very good thing, because it determines value. I'm a big believer in that."

But what about the ERM, the fate of Europe, the fate of France, the long-term plans of the economists and the government ministers and the central bankers?

"Obviously, the franc wasn't worth as much as they thought," Peabody confides.[4]

There is only one law: the law of price.

Behind the swaggering self-assurance of traders was an array of electronics that monitored, quantified, and computed the effect of every slight shift in market sentiment. Speculators had focused all the power of their analytical technology on the prospects for the ERM. Not so many years ago, the kinds of minds that design this technology were launching satellites toward the outer planets or devising guidance systems for cold war weaponry. Now they're in the markets.

NUCLEAR FINANCE

Near Radio City Music Hall, in an eleventh-floor, windowless, bare-walled room, behind a plain wooden desk, facing a computer screen, a rangy, bespectacled man makes careful notes, in pencil, in a laboratory notebook of the sort familiar to high school chemistry students. His wispy hair flies out in all directions, like Einstein's, except that it is brown instead of white, like the frames of his spectacles. He pauses, looks vaguely at a visitor, and begins to speak, slowly. Douglas Williams is not a man to talk in sweeping flourishes of imaginative exuberance. As befits the inhabitant of such a barren cell, there is something almost monastic about the contemplative timbre of his hesitant voice. It pulses in long waves punctuated by remote, thoughtful silences.

He says, "I was born on the plains, an area where there were no trees indigenous: flat prairie. I often wonder if I like my room like this because of that, or because I work in an electronic environment and what really matters is on the screen." [1]

Williams is working on a series of mathematical models that will duplicate the functions of a human brain, but with much greater power, and enable the firm he serves to anticipate moves in the world's financial markets. This is the philosophers' stone of the new finance, the key to all wealth and power: the ability to know the future.

He is one of a horde of intense scientists who have poured into the banks and trading firms of New York and pushed the frontiers of finance to the limits of mathematical possibility. For almost a decade, the biggest financial institutions have been arming themselves with aeronautical engineers, satellite software designers, nuclear physicists, pure mathematicians, and genetic scientists. They are all seeking the same stone, the one that turns reams of daily price information into a predictor of tomorrow's prices.

Called quants, geeks, or rocket scientists, these number crunchers provide living evidence that investing and trading have changed, utterly, from the old world of stocks, bonds, and hot tips from a brother-in-law in the markets. Economic policymakers and national regulators still base their strategies on economic principles derived from eighteenth-century science. The traders, meanwhile, move in the twentieth-century world of chaos, fractals, and beyond.

The breakdown of the Bretton Woods system, the invention of new financial markets, the discoveries of financial economists at the University of Chicago and elsewhere—all have turned finance into a science as esoteric and inscrutable as quantum mechanics. Forget about finding that undervalued growth stock, that high-yielding but safe bond, or any other kind of sure thing. For that matter, forget gurus, advisors, ingenious money managers, or almost any kind of recommendation to buy or sell. Hardly anyone on Wall Street thinks there's big money to be made by poring over the financial statements of corporations in order to find one with advantages no one else has noticed. As far as recommendations are concerned, those in the know have known for years that no analyst or investment manager really beats the market over the long term. For that matter, forget about investing in a solid company with good management for the long term—even that is too risky. Nowadays, the most successful investors and traders take diversification to the extreme, often using futures contracts to buy a proxy for every company in the stock markets. There aren't any undiscovered investment opportunities out there—none that can be seen with the naked eye, anyway.

Douglas Williams designs the kind of lens that the biggest and best traders now use to spot investments that can't otherwise be seen.

If knowing the future is the philosophers' stone, then Douglas Williams is indeed an alchemist. New to the world of trading, he has no background in economics or finance. As an undergraduate at the University of Edmonton in Alberta, Canada, he studied pure mathematics. He developed an interest in biology, and after taking his master's degree in mathematics, he went on to graduate studies at the University of Chicago, where he earned a Ph.D. in biophysics. Eventually, he found himself designing working models of human brain parts.

Essentially, that was a matter of solving a complicated set of equations. The brain and nervous system are simply a collection of on-off switches called neurons. The on switches are excitatory, the off switches inhibitory. Babies have more of the excitatory kind, which is why they jerk around uncontrollably at first. As they get older, they develop more of the inhibitory neurons. Interestingly, and contrary to popular misconception, the more intelligent people are, the less active their brains seem to be. Apparently, their inhibitory neurons eliminate distractions by toning down the brain so they can concentrate on the problem at hand. But whether the brain belongs to a genius or a goof, it consists of the same basic neural cells, wired together in a sequence and blinking off or on.

The question that scientists like Williams tried to answer mathematically was how this simple wiring of excitatory and inhibitory neurons could produce everything from the theory of relativity to Michael Jordan's jump shot. They decided to find out by trying to make small neural systems of their own—minibrains that could do small, simple things. Williams designed neural networks that could recognize color, for example. He also worked on problems like how the eye sees a snowfall. Although snowflakes move independently, tossed in all directions by the wind, the eye easily recognizes both the motion of the individual snowflakes and the fact that they are all generally moving down. This experience would later prove particularly useful in analyzing the financial markets.

From Chicago, Williams moved in 1983 to AT&T's Bell Labs in Murray Hill, New Jersey, where he continued his research, this time concentrating on texture recognition—making artificial brains that could distinguish between two black-checked scarves, one wool and the other silk. There he inadvertently experienced his first great market shock. During its decades as a telephone monopoly, AT&T had funded Bell Labs as a pure research institution. But after its monopoly was taken away by a federal judge and AT&T was forced to compete for business, Bell Labs was gutted. Management had decided that while knowledge was nice, money was nicer.

Williams and the other vision researchers left en masse, settling at New Jersey's Rutgers University. Shortly afterward, he moved over to Rockefeller University in New York, where he spent a few years designing an eye for a robot. He got as far as teaching the robot to recognize colors and follow a light around a room. Then he experienced his second big tap on the shoulder from economic realities.

In 1989, his wife gave birth to a daughter, their first child. A psychology professor in New York, she knew from both academic studies and maternal inclination that her daughter would get a much better start in life with a full-time Mommy on the premises. She wanted to stay home with the child. Unfortunately, academics who design robots don't make enough money to support families in New York. Williams started to interview with financial houses, and in 1989 he joined Millburn. He found, much to his surprise, that his work designing neural networks could easily be transferred to the markets. "I actually do very much the same thing I did when I was in academics. They bring me problems and see if I can find a solution," he explains. For a hypothetical example, he mentions soybeans and deutsche marks. "At certain times, those totally unrelated markets may begin to move together. Then the question is, Are there rules to say when they move together and when they don't, when do you trade them, how long? We give the neural net parameters for trend, volume, open interest; line up all cases of where past trades would have been profitable or not profitable; and see if the neural network can figure out, buried in the noise, some property responsible, some trading rule."

The example of soybeans and deutsche marks moving together is fictional. Williams guards carefully the real subject on which his neural network is working. It has something to do with currencies and interest rates—not surprisingly, since Millburn is one of the biggest currency speculators in the world. He says that his neural network devours four thousand points of data every day—minute-to-minute prices for the currencies and interest rate instruments under consideration. The neural network he uses here is similar to his previous models of the human eye. It consists of on-off switches that respond to signals. The eye he designed for the robot at Rockefeller University responded to light and color. The eye he is designing for Millburn responds to prices and price moves, to market conditions, to volumes, and so forth.

Curiously, he doesn't know exactly how his neural networks assimilate and respond to all of that information. Every neural network consists of an input layer that receives the data and an output layer that gives the network's response. In between are a series of so-called hidden layers. In the hidden layers, by a mysterious process the networks evolve their own series of connections. No engineer designs these connections. Williams tells of a team of researchers who trained a neural network to recognize colors. When it had duplicated human output—recognizing red, green, blue, purple, blue-green, and so on, much as a human eye would—the researchers carefully disassembled it. They found, much to their surprise, that the internal organization of the hidden layers was very similar to that of the human brain. The neural network had, on its own, devised a pattern of inhibitory and excitatory neurons that mirrored what was known of the brain's patterns.

Williams doesn't give his network a series of rules, the way he might program a computer. It's up to the network to define its own rules, based on the information Williams provides. He begins by feeding the network a mass of data and telling it what happened historically. The neural network then knows that over a period of time, when certain things were happening in the markets, prices went up. It's up to the neural network to figure out which of the thousands of possible causes was actually responsible for the price move. After he has trained the network to reach the historically "right" conclusion, Williams feeds it an entirely new set of data from a different time period. If the neural net can analyze the new data and give the correct result, it goes through a period of dry-run trading, using current rather than historical data. Only after the network has successfully proven itself during this dry-run period is it allowed input into real trading decisions.

Williams is not the only quantitative researcher designing new trading systems at Millburn; nor are neural nets the only example of high technology used by the firm. Millburn's research director, Grant Smith, has also looked into genetic algorhythms. These are trading models designed to duplicate an evolutionary process. Like neural nets, they are "learning" systems. Here the genes are trading rules—mathematical statements that eventually evolve into a trading system capable of producing profitable trades. The genes are tested with historical data. In the first generation of trading rules, those genes that make progress toward the historical result are allowed to survive and duplicate themselves. Those that do not make progress are destroyed and discarded. This process repeats itself through subsequent generations, until at last a system has evolved that can survive the test of real markets.

Millburn also uses nonlearning quantitative systems, such as artificial intelligence and expert systems. Essentially, these are attempts to duplicate the mind of a successful trader with a series of if-then directions. Such systems are already widely used in other financial applications, such as credit approval. To make a system for that purpose, the designers typically interview lending officers at length to determine how they make their decisions, then program a computer to mimic that pattern. The use of artificial intelligence and expert systems for trading means programming intuition and imagination into a computer through so-called fuzzy engineering.

Millburn's quantitative tools have been developed over two decades of active and highly successful trading. Grant Smith joined the firm in 1975. The Bretton Woods system had just broken down. The dollar was sinking steadily. Commodity prices soared, pushed upward not only by the currency shift but also by historically unprecedented Russian purchases of U.S. grain and the emergence of the Organization of Petroleum Exporting Countries as an effective cartel. These upheavals devastated business, but traders prospered.[2]

Fundamental analysts, those who looked carefully at supply and demand and historical prices to make their forecast of future prices, faced a situation unlike any they had ever known. Commodity prices quickly shot past the level that fundamental supply and demand analysis, based on the experience of previous decades, considered reasonable. Since these prices were driven by historically unprecedented forces, fundamental analysts were naturally at a loss to predict where they would finally stop.

By contrast, technical analysts, who looked only at the language of the market, ignoring historical fundamentals, saw the market moving up, invested in the psychology of a bull market, and successfully rode the trend to riches. Because the trend was so pronounced, even the crudest forms of technical analysis seemed to work.

Back then, Smith explains, quantitative investing usually meant tracking two moving averages and trading when they crossed. At first, this method owed more to intuition than to science. "Folklore determined the rules," he recalls. By the end of the decade, though, computers were already being used to identify the best times to trade, the best moving average to use, or the best price series to map—daily, monthly, or minute to minute. Instead of focusing on just one or a few markets, Millburn's traders tracked many markets over many time periods in order to discover which were the best opportunities.

Meanwhile, financial markets began to overshadow commodity markets. Of all financial markets, the biggest was currency. Currency traders could trade billions of dollars in minutes, using a wide variety of instruments: swaps, options, futures, forwards, even cash. They could choose between the interbank markets and the various futures or options or stock exchanges. The relationships among markets and instruments could all be defined mathematically.

Millburn had been one of the first investment companies to trade currencies. Before the Chicago futures market in currencies developed, Millburn had already arranged direct access to the interbank currency markets through a cooperative New York bank.[3] Millburn's approach to currency trading was to forecast price trends, buy before the trend had gathered force, and sell at the top—or, in the case of a declining market, to sell short before prices went down, and buy back the shorts near the bottom of the market. The 1980s were especially favorable to this investment style, since there were two long, strong trends—a strengthening dollar before 1985 and a falling dollar afterward.

At the end of the decade, though, the trends lost their force, and it became much harder to discover what prices were going to do. Instead of one long increase in the dollar for several years, followed by a long fall, the dollar jumped up and down in short sharp spurts. Nonlinear mathematics, especially chaos and fractals, seemed to offer some hope of discovering patterns in these apparently random price moves. Hence Millburn's interest in neural networks, artificial intelligence, genetic algorhythms, and other technology that allows it to analyze masses of complicated data in the quest for patterns.

It is a commonplace of chaos theory that an iron determinism may lie buried at the heart of apparently random events. Given any wildly irregular, serrated price chart of a particular market, chaos theorists immediately explore whether some beautifully simple parabola might explain it. Millburn's purpose has been to identify the function that defines the parabola—the order hidden in the chaos. Like a radar detector, the ideal system will identify the historical patterns, compare contemporary market movements to the stored patterns, and beep when it recognizes a match.

Without the aid of such sophisticated technology, the sheer volume of data would make it impossible to find these patterns. Notwithstanding the math, though, Smith says, "There are so many parameters that can totally change a problem, it's very much an art in applying these techniques. There's no right way to do anything; there's just tremendous flexibility. The skill is in the art of the technique, knowing what inputs are going to create what outputs."

Millburn needs all of this technology for one simple reason: it wants to know whether prices are moving up or down.

The Science of Risk: A Brief History

The techniques Millburn uses may appear radically new, but in fact the roots of technical analysis are over a century old. Millburn, though it does not trade stocks, belongs to a tradition of analysis that began in 1882 when Charles Dow cofounded Dow Jones & Company to promulgate his ideas about how to get rich in the stock market. He saw that the stock market often moves in waves. We call these waves bull and bear markets—long periods in which prices rise, followed by long periods in which prices fall. Dow believed it was possible to predict when prices were about to begin their long climbs and falls. The only information necessary was a chart of the price movements of the market. In order to make it easier to track the movements of the market as a whole, Dow averaged the daily closing prices of a few big companies. The Dow Jones average is still widely popular as a shorthand indicator of the daily market activity, though most professional investors no longer consider it reliable or useful and instead rely on the much broader Standard & Poor's 500 index.

Using his rough and primitive data, Dow invented technical analysis of the stock markets. He believed that an investor could examine a chart of historical price movement, make an informed judgment about the future direction of the market, and win in the market at the expense of less informed traders who couldn't read the future price from the tracks left by past prices.

Technical analysts still share that faith. The extremists among them don't even care about so-called fundamental factors, like whether there's a drought in Brazil or runaway inflation in the United States.

They say that any important information is already reflected in the price, and no information is necessary except price history. They are fond of expressions like "The market speaks in a language all its own." So a technical investor doesn't think he needs to know much about a company whose stock he buys in order to win in the stock market, anymore than he needs to know how to grow corn in order to make money in corn futures.

Technicians need to know only a few things to predict the market. They disagree, though, about precisely what those things are.

Consider the case of Ralph Nelson Elliott, an accountant who in 1924 accepted an appointment from the U.S. State Department as chief accountant for the government of Nicaragua. Two years later, having developed a severe case of anemia, he returned to Los Angeles, where he lapsed into a coma. He spent the years 1929–33 drifting in and out of consciousness. He had blacked out at the height of the Jazz Age, and came to in the depths of the Great Depression. He began to piece together the past—not his own, but the market's. He saw that portentous price waves had augured the bull run of the 1920s and foreshadowed the crash and the depression. Elliott classified these waves into two main groups. In his taxonomy, a five-wave pattern of up-down-up-down-up signifies the beginning of a bull market. A three-wave down-up-down prognosticates a bear. He devised ancillary rules to clarify the basic wave patterns. It takes an adept to understand even the first simple steps of his explanation. For example, in a five-wave pattern, wave three cannot be the shortest and wave four cannot intrude into the territory of wave one, except under rare and narrowly defined circumstances. In 1946, he published the definitive version of his discoveries in a book he called *Nature's Law—The Secret of the Universe*. Elliott's system, delphic though it sounds, survived the test of time. For the period 1979–93, the Elliott Wave Theorist enjoyed some of the highest scores among the investment services tracked by *Hulbert Financial Digest*.[4]

Another very different technician, Joseph Granville, predicted with uncanny accuracy most market moves between 1974 and 1982. From his base in Kansas, he tracked chiefly the number of stocks hitting new highs or lows and calculated the proportion of advancers to decliners. Trends in these statistics revealed to him the esoteric secret of the market's course. Granville soon became a household word. He was blamed for causing one market crash simply by advising his clients to sell, since he had so many clients that when they sold, the market fell. Granville was a guest on national talk shows, a subject for biography, guru of a movement. Then, in 1982, his formula suddenly stopped working. He diversified his forecasts and began to predict earthquakes as well. The quakes did not come; nor did the market move any longer in accord with his predictions. He predicted a market collapse, but the market rose to historical highs. His followers apostatized, leaving him to follow others. Granville toiled over his system. In 1994, he was still publishing his letter for the faithful remnant. Now he understood what had gone wrong, he said, and he had full confidence in his method again.[5]

A century before, Charles Dow had proved that people who used technical analysis could indeed make money in the markets. However, others noted that there is a paradox in trying to predict markets by using price information. After all, every stock or contract was bought by someone who expected prices to go up, and sold by someone who expected prices to go down. If all investors have access to the same information, and they're rational, then the market price on any given day represents a broad, informed consensus that this price is the right price. If sellers expected their product to be more valuable tomorrow, they would demand a higher price today. If buyers expected the product to be less valuable tomorrow, they would be irrational to buy at higher prices today. So at any given point in time, the probability of the price moving up or down has to be 50-50. The first to record this insight was an obscure French mathematician named Bachelier, ignored in his own time but now recognized as the founder of financial science. Bachelier also discovered that prices move randomly, and could be described by the mathematics of Brownian motion, the random movement of particles in physics. Bachelier published his most important work, *Theory of Speculation*, in 1900. It lay unread and unrecognized for a half-century. Then researchers at the Cowles Commission, at the University of Chicago, rediscovered and used Bachelier's insights to build a theory of finance and investing that would eventually overturn the established powers of Wall Street.[6]

The commission was named for Alfred Cowles III, scion of the family that owned a large share of the Chicago Tribune Company. Cowles happened to contract tuberculosis, and while recovering at a sanitarium in Colorado he began to help his father manage the family's investments. The year was 1926. Cowles studied the two dozen most widely circulated investment advisory publications and eventually decided that it was wasteful to spend so much money on so many services. He decided to pick just one—the best one—and follow that. In order to find the best one, he started tracking the performance of the whole group. Beginning in 1928, he analyzed their recommendations and compared them to the market's performance. In 1929, the market crashed. The crash came as a complete surprise to all of the services, and for the most part, the advisors continued to stumble all the way through 1932. Cowles wanted to know why.

He bought the most advanced computer on the market in the 1930s, a Hollerith punch-card calculator made by International Business Machines. Cowles analyzed 7,500 recommendations by sixteen leading financial services: every purchase and sale of stock by some twenty fire insurance companies over a four-year-period, 3,300 recommendations of the twenty-four leading investment advisory publications, and 255 *Wall Street Journal* editorials written between 1903 and 1929 that contained definite market forecasts. He measured the percentage gain or loss for each and compared them to the percentage gain or loss for the market as a whole. In 1933, he published his conclusions in the journal *Econometrica* under the title "Can Stock Market Forecasters Forecast?" His answer: "It is doubtful."[7]

Taken as a whole, the group of advisors showed negative performance. Only one advisor seemed to have any real skill. An investor who had followed the recommendations of Charles Dow's theory as published in *The Wall Street Journal* would have seen the investment multiply nineteenfold between 1903 and 1929. However, if the investor had simply bought into the market and held on through the same period, instead of buying and selling as the Dow theory recommended, he would have done even better, increasing his wealth twenty-six-fold.[8] Cowles found that even the best advisor did no better than one could achieve by simply buying and selling at random.

In 1944, Cowles published another study, this time analyzing 6,904 recommendations made over the period 1929–44. He found that bullish, buy recommendations outnumbered bearish, sell recommendations by four to one, even though the market was falling more than half the time over this period.[9]

Cowles's own research was valuable and insightful, but his most important contribution to financial science was the Cowles Commission.

In 1932, while he was in the midst of his first study, he had contacted the Econometric Society. A newly established association of economists and mathematicians, the society needed money. Cowles offered to finance the publication of an econometric journal and also to establish a research center for financial science. The Cowles Commission was located in Colorado Springs until 1939, when it moved to Chicago. There, in 1952, a young economist named Harry Markowitz demonstrated exactly how the investment process hinges on risk. Markowitz eventually would receive the Nobel Prize for his work. Other researchers would eventually demonstrate mathematically why, given Markowitz's discoveries about risk, the conclusions reached by Cowles in the 1930s had been inevitable.

Essentially, Markowitz's work was a high-tech application of the old adage "Don't put all your eggs in one basket." Buying just one stock, for example, in the hope that it will go up means taking a big risk. A strike, a lawsuit, bad management, or bad luck could sink the company. Investors have less risk if they spread their money among several companies. This way, if any one company has problems, it doesn't threaten the investor's whole wealth, just the part invested in that company. Markowitz also saw that sometimes investors are willing to take more risk than they absolutely have to. When they do take more risk, however, they expect to make more money. Nobody invests in a risky startup biotechnology company to make the same rate of return one could earn on a safe, insured bank deposit. No pain, no gain; no guts, no glory—put it any way you please—there is no return without risk, and in general, the greater the return, the greater the risk.

Markowitz found that it was possible for an investor to own some very risky investments and at the same time have a very low overall risk if the investments were properly diversified. Through statistical analysis, he discovered what he called the "efficient frontier," the combination of investments that gave the best return for any particular level of risk. The key is to pick investments that, while risky in themselves, do not move together. An investor who buys two biotechnology stocks has more risk than an investor who buys a corn futures contract and a biotechnology stock. The reason? The entire biotechnology market might move up or down, but corn futures and biotechnology stocks don't move together. There's a good chance that when the price of one goes down, the price of the other will go up or at least hold steady.

Using computers, it is possible to calculate an efficient frontier for a young investor who prefers to take a lot of risk in the hope of a high return, and another efficient frontier for an elderly widow who wants to take as little risk as possible. The two portfolios will not be utterly different. When investments are combined in the most efficient portfolio, the risk-averse widow could well end up owning a few biotechnology stocks, while the aggressive young investor might even own some stodgy utilities.

In 1964, William Sharpe, who would also receive a Nobel Prize for his work, demonstrated that the most efficient portfolio, the one that gives the highest level of return with the lowest level of risk, is the market itself. The market is, in fact, a superefficient portfolio. The only way to beat the market is by taking a great deal of risk. Over the long haul, someone who buys a representative cross-section of the entire market and holds on to it has, statistically, a much better chance of coming out ahead than the person who trades in and out of the market, now looking for hot small-cap stocks, now looking for growth stocks, now looking for undiscovered values, and so forth.

In any given year, it's possible for an investor to beat the market, but only by taking more risk. Despite the fame of money managers like George Soros or Warren Buffet, scores of academic studies have shown that statistically, over the long haul, the odds against consistently beating the market are astronomical.

Of course, the money management industry is a big one, and Wall Street didn't welcome the theories of Markowitz, Sharpe, and the other researchers who came after them. "These knaves must be driven from the temple!" thundered a senior economist at one consulting firm.[10] No wonder. The logical implication of these theories is a form of passive investing known as indexing, in which investors simply purchase a cross section of stocks and hold them for decades. If investors realized that they would be richer if they ignored brokers, analysts, and touts, there would be a lot fewer yachts cruising the waters off Manhattan.

Fortunately for the brokerage industry, America's biggest investors didn't pay much attention to the science of risk. Pension funds own over a quarter of all of American stocks (28.6 percent in 1992),[11] and by and large they chose to ignore the discoveries of Markowitz and Sharpe, at least until very recently. Like the hopeless, dazed crowds that keep Las Vegas slot machines profitable, pension plan sponsors have wasted scores of billions of dollars trying to pick money managers who can beat the market.

America's taxpayers may end up paying for this negligence. In 1963, the financially troubled automaker Studebaker closed a plant and told five thousand workers they would not receive the pensions they had been promised. In 1974, in order to prevent future pension disasters, President Gerald Ford signed the Employment Retirement Income Security Act. This act, known as ERISA, laid down rules for running pension funds and set up a government insurance agency, the Pension Benefit Guarantee Corporation (PBGC), to protect workers' rights to their pensions. The PBGC protects pensions in much the same way as the Federal Deposit Insurance Corporation protects bank deposits. According to ERISA, companies that promise pensions to their workers are supposed to put enough money aside to cover future benefits. Not all of them do. When a company goes bankrupt, if the pension fund doesn't have enough to cover workers' pension rights, the PBGC assumes them and then squares off with the company in bankruptcy court to recover whatever it can.

Many companies set up ERISA plans, tax-exempt pension funds that were supposed to manage money in accordance with the "prudent man" rule. This gave companies a lot of latitude. Basically, they were expected to make investments that a prudent man would consider to be safe and sound, consistent with long-term growth objectives, and for the sole benefit of the beneficiaries. If the rule seems murky, it is. No one can offer a simple rule of thumb for what is prudent and what is imprudent in all cases, although courts have, from time to time, tried.

However, many pension plans have in fact proven to be less than prudent, even by an ordinarily commonsense interpretation of the term. On January, 6, 1994, the PBGC published a notice that, as of 1992, private pension plans were underfunded by approximately $53 billion. These plans don't have enough money to pay for the retirement needs of their workers. Some of the underfunding came about because companies never put enough money into their plans in the first place, but some of it arose because investments just didn't perform the way the plan managers had expected. Some of these plans belong to financially troubled companies, and if the companies go under, their pension obligations fall on the PBGC. If the PBGC doesn't have enough money to handle these obligations, the American tax-payer picks up the tab. In 1994, the PBGC claimed to have a deficit of $2.7 billion.

If pension fund managers had paid due attention to the discoveries of Markowitz, Sharpe, and others, it's safe to say that there might not be an underfunding problem.

In 1992, the Brookings Institution published a study that calculated the cost of ignoring the efficient market arguments of Markowitz. From 1983 to 1989, money managers hired by the biggest pension funds actually underperformed the stock market by an average of 1.3 percent per year, the study found. Hiring them in the first place wasn't cheap—pension funds pay about 0.5 percent of their investment assets per year in fees to the people who invest the money.[12] The authors of the study concluded that each year, year after year, this underperformance costs pension plans "$15 billion that go to the brokerage industry, the money management industry, and smart investors who trade against the funds."[13] This is money the pension funds could earn if they simply bought the market and held it instead of hiring money managers to beat the market.

Now pension funds are underfunded by approximately $53 billion, and American taxpayers might be on the hook for $2.7 billion of that. Clearly, the pension system in America and the pocketbooks of taxpayers would both be a lot safer had pension funds paid due attention to the Nobel laureates who invented financial science.

No wonder that, in 1991, the giant glassmaker PP&G decided to fire all of the stock market gurus who used to handle the company's pension assets, and index the whole shebang.[14] Few other companies have gone that far. Most pension plan managers still resist the new science because it could cost them their jobs. Slowly, though, economic facts are prevailing. "When all is said and done, we doubt that an industry that has added little if any value can continue to exist in its present form," wrote the authors of the Brookings study. The first company to index part of its pension investments was Samsonite, which invested $6 million in the strategy in 1971.[15] Now index funds account for 36 percent of corporate pension assets and 51.7 percent of government pension investments.[16]

The basic principles of the new financial science, risk and diversification, have also led pension funds into new investments that have nothing to do with old-fashioned stock market investing. Pension managers now trade currencies, commodities, and a whole new universe of complex bond and mortgage derivatives.

Futures, for example, used to be considered a high-risk, zero-sum game—and for most individual investors, that is still the truth. Surprisingly enough, though, some evidence is emerging from academic studies that the new futures markets, which exist largely in order to transfer risk from people who don't want it to people who do, actually function like a giant insurance company. Like the old stock market, the new markets for risk perform a valuable economic function. Since they are not directly related to the stock market, the new markets provide additional diversification, lowering the overall risk of an investor's portfolio.

Pension funds, insurance companies, banks, and other big investors can use the new markets to lower their overall risk while increasing their long-term returns, according to Professor Scott H. Irwin of Ohio State University. His study helped the Virginia Retirement System decide to allocate $640 million to futures speculation.[17] Virginia's state pension plan isn't alone. Futures have also attracted investments from Kodak, the Detroit Policemen & Firemen Retirement System, the San Diego County Retirement Association, and others.

These funds aren't trying to make a killing. They are trying to capture the benefits of diversification by adding a small, high-risk investment to their portfolio, an investment that will not share in the gains and losses of their other investments but will add an increment of return over time.

A number of highly quantitative investment approaches have been developed to supply what these investors demand.

New Risks, New Rewards

While quant shops like Millburn have concentrated on developing new tools to do the old job of recognizing trends in the markets, others focused their attention on ways to make money no matter which way the market went—up, down, or in a trendless sideways drift. They did this by exploiting superior information about inefficiencies in the market—cases where the markets did not work as theory and science dictated they should.

These new techniques are directionless. They allow speculators to profit from flaws in market structure, no matter where they arise. They are not for Everyman. In fact, by the time these new investment styles are handed down to the public, via mutual funds or other generally accessible investment vehicles, the juice has invariably been squeezed out.

Although it is an axiom of the efficient markets theory that all information about the markets is contained in the price, and a corollary that there is no return without risk, the explosion of new financial markets during the 1980s showed that efficient markets theory was not exactly true in all cases. In fact, some opportunities did exist to secure above-average returns with little risk. Those who found them were like the first discoverers of gold in California. They struck it rich—then the hordes came and the gold went.

The most astute practitioners manage to keep ahead of the crowds by delving deeper and deeper into the analysis of markets, seeking new inefficiencies to exploit and keeping them secret as long as possible.

Sometimes these secrets are spectacularly lucrative. Consider quantitative arbitrage.

In its simplest form, arbitrage means merely buying something cheaply in one market and quickly selling it elsewhere for a profit. During the takeover boom of the mid-1980s, arbitrageurs with inside information about the plans of corporate raiders bought stock cheaply and promptly sold it for obscene profits when the raiders attacked. This is illegal, of course, but worse, it is intellectually crude—the investing equivalent of smashing a shop window to grab a necklace. Practitioners of that unimaginative type of arbitrage looked and acted like hoodlums. They imprinted on our minds the indelible image of the successful 1980s market operator—amoral, ruthless, boastful, sleazy, and above all, greedy. Yet while Ivan Boesky and his vulgar coterie were exchanging suitcases full of cash, corrupting the markets, and basking in their mutual adulation, something of far greater historical significance was going on in even deeper shadows.

This other arbitrage was kept carefully and deliberately secret by the handful of investment banks involved, not because it was illegal but because it was so profitable that it makes Boesky's illegal profits look small-time by comparison.

A visitor to the bond floor of Salomon Brothers during the 1980s saw pandemonium. A legion of shouting, swearing, sucker-swindling traders composed the elite of Wall Street. Most visitors failed to notice a tiny island of calm concentration in the midst of this chaos, where not more than a dozen quiet and studious nerds gathered in an anodyne cluster. In 1991, one of these nerds, a young trader named Lawrence E. Hilibrand, pocketed a $23 million bonus for the year and became the reluctant subject of headlines.

Hilibrand was co-chief of the quantitative arbitrage group. He and his small group of fellow traders had designed intricate mathematical techniques to spot and profit from tiny differences in the value of bonds, futures contracts, options, and other inventions of the new science. Because the value of derivatives is "derived" from something else, mathematical formulas could be used to determine what the value of the derivative ought to be. Sometimes, especially in the early days of the markets, the derivatives sold for more or less than their theoretical values. The differences could be tiny—as little as two-hundredths of a percentage point. But for those who knew how to exploit the inefficiency, those tiny variations meant great wealth.

It took more than suitcases of cash to get the information needed to succeed in this game. One afternoon in 1994, Hilibrand agreed to explain what until then had been the secret story of their success.

In a nondescript building in Greenwich, Connecticut, at the office of Long Term Capital Management (LTCM), he and a fellow quant, Eric R. Rosenfeld, sat by a window overlooking a little harbor where sailboats lay placidly at anchor, their canvas furled. It was still early in the season, the air too crisp for all but the most ardent boaters.

LTCM had brought together the glitterati of quantitative investing in a glamorous new hedge fund. Two coinventors of the first widely used option pricing formula, Professor Myron Scholes of Stanford and Professor Robert Merton of Harvard, were on board. So were John Meriwether, former vice chairman of Salomon Brothers; a few key members of Salomon's quantitative arbitrage group; and David Mullins, former vice chairman of the Board of Governors of the Federal Reserve System. The fund was secretive and exclusive. Prospective investors were required to put up a minimum of $10 million. If that didn't keep out the hoi polloi, there were fees. "LTCM's fees—two percent of assets and 25 percent of trading profits—are also ambitious, considering top hedge funds traders like George Soros and competitors charge only one percent of capital and 20 percent of profits," noted the newsletter *Derivatives Strategy*.[18] Notwithstanding, LTCM is said to have received nearly $2 billion from investors and began trading in February 1994.

Across a large room curved a counterlike stand supporting an array of computer terminals, market information screens from Reuters and Bloomberg, speed dialers, telephones, and all the other standard impedimenta of the well-equipped speculator in today's markets. A huge television hung from the ceiling in the center of the room, tuned to a round-the-clock cable television news program.

A loose group of casually dressed men lounged in their swivel chairs more or less in the vicinity of the screens, hands behind their heads, feet crossed, talking in relaxed cadences about the market or their weekend plans. It was Friday afternoon, and the Fed had just announced its quarterly refunding requirements, which usually means a furious market reaction, so their ease seemed somehow incongruous. Farther south, in Manhattan, telephones at Salomon Brothers were no doubt ringing off the hook, as shouting traders deafened each other with curses. But these quants knew how to use their brains to rise above the hurly-burly of the market.

Most of the men had worked together for years at Salomon Brothers. In fact, they constituted the core of Salomon's quantitative arbitrage unit. But in 1991, Salomon had been devastated when a rogue trader named Paul Mozer, who was himself an alumnus of the quantitative group, had been discovered falsifying bids for U.S. government securities in order to take bigger positions than regulations allowed, as if aiming to corner the market. Salomon's chairman and top management knew what he was doing but did not stop him or inform regulators. When the crimes came to light, they were forced to resign. Congress held hearings, and for a time the very survival of Salomon Brothers was doubtful.

The members of the quant group helped hold the firm together during those difficult times. "Nothing would have made us leave Salomon in that period," says Hilibrand. "The organization was under extreme external pressure, and we were committed to seeing it through." Rosenfeld even replaced Paul Mozer as head government bond dealer. "We all pitched in for the good of the firm," he says.[19]

After the crisis had passed, they left Salomon and regrouped in Greenwich at LTCM.

They sit in a small, glass-walled office next to the trading floor. Rosenfeld wears chinos and a white knit T-shirt with a club logo. In 1984, he had been a professor at Harvard, getting a little tired of teaching the same courses year after year and yearning for something new.

A call came in from Salomon, asking if he could recommend any of his bright students for an analytical finance position at what was then the preeminent bond trading house in the United States. Instead, he took the job himself.

Rosenfeld was the first person with a Ph.D. in finance to join the group. One of his most important roles was to build bridges into academia. He was largely responsible for Salomon's effort to recruit, from major universities, engineers, mathematicians, statisticians, and financial theorists for the quant group.

The conversation in these Greenwich offices has much of the feel of an informal chat in the commons of a good university. Hilibrand looks like an earnest young graduate student: horn-rim glasses, white shirt, tie, dark slacks. He seems to lack the swaggering braggadocio of the stereotypical 1980s Wall Street achiever. A shadow crosses his face when the subject of his $23 million bonus comes up. He doesn't like to talk about it, doesn't seem to think it's fair to single him out. "It was a group activity, and I don't stand out from the group and from the best people in the group in terms of contribution in that year or in other years for that matter," he indignantly argues. "It's just totally alien to our concept of ourselves to achieve public identification."

The quantitative arbitrage group was a distinct subculture at Salomon. "We were taking offensive positions in the market," he says. This business had nothing to do with Salomon's traditional role of serving as an intermediary between buyers and sellers of securities. Most traders made their money on the "spread" between the price at which they bought securities from one customer and the price at which they sold them to another; buy low, sell high was the traditional path to riches on Wall Street. But Hilibrand's group put their analytical skills to work to find ways to make money independently of the market's moves. Buying and selling on terms set by other traders, terms the other traders thought were quite profitable, the quants still picked up hundreds of millions of dollars for themselves.

"It was very unusual," Hilibrand reflects. "We were a group of people who had not worked at any other firms. We came in and learned, each person taught by the others before them, each person taking the tools and approach and moving it a little further." He pauses, thinking how to explain it, and continues, "There's a type of loyalty that arises when you achieve all your human capital, success, skill, and enjoyment through one work experience. It was an unbelievably strong bond, and it went toward John Meriwether, who had hired us, trained us, built the group, pulled the people together."

They laugh at the stereotypical machismo of the 1980s trader. Rosenfeld says, "When the hedge vehicles made it easier to go long and short, the macho traders just got beaten up. If you just tried to tough something out and didn't have the analytics on your side, you eventually lost. So the street started to get smarts."

Salomon had several hundred employees selling and trading bonds. No more than a dozen worked in the quant group. Yet those twelve traders were, by all accounts, the firm's most prized human assets. They had the best brains on the street.

A mathematics major from MIT, Hilibrand had taken a summer job in the treasury department of Chase Manhattan Bank in 1978. "It captivated my interest unbelievably," he recalls. He returned to MIT, finished his undergraduate degree in math, then took a master's degree in economics. By 1981, he was back in Manhattan, working for Salomon Brothers in a new group, under the direction of John Meriwether.

In the late 1970s, interest rate futures had provided a new, low-cost way to speculate on interest rates—or, as Hilibrand puts it, to "express a judgment" about the future direction of rates. Prior to the invention of futures, such speculation was cumbersome and expensive. Investors who expected interest rates to be lower in eighteen months could borrow money to buy a long-term security and hold it in the expectation that when rates fell, they could sell the security at a profit. Investors who expected rates to rise could borrow a long-term security, sell it short, and expect to buy it back for less in eighteen months. The value of the security would depend on the level of interest rates, but the investor's profit would depend on a number of other things, such as whether financing was available for the transaction, and at what price, or even whether the security was available.

Futures made life easier for speculators. Now they could bet on interest rates without actually buying or selling any real securities.

Soon the interest rate futures markets were full of speculators betting on rising or falling rates, and hedgers looking to protect themselves against the same. Futures contracts are commitments either to deliver or to take delivery of the so-called underlying—the bond, bill, or other security from which the contract is derived. Usually, a futures contract is written in such a way that it allows a number of similar securities to be delivered upon expiration of the contract. But investors usually liquidate their futures contracts before expiration and do not actually deliver or take delivery of the underlying. Still, by definition, there is a close mathematical relationship between the futures contract and the underlying securities.

Not everyone understood these relationships very well. Salomon's quantitative arbitrage group specialized in analyzing the futures markets and the securities on which the futures were based. Sometimes they noticed small deviations from the theoretically correct value. Perhaps the futures were selling for a fraction of a percentage point more than the strict, mathematically correct, theoretically defined equation between futures and underlying. These tiny differences were so small that most people in the market paid no attention to them. At Salomon, the quants saw them as low-risk opportunities to make fast centimillions of dollars.

In the early 1980s, the U.S. treasury bonds traded on the Chicago Board of Trade were selling for slightly less than the correct value. Salomon's quant group took three steps almost simultaneously. They bought bond futures contracts, which gave them the right to receive bonds in the future. Then they borrowed bonds and, having borrowed them, sold them. When they bought the futures contracts, they locked in the price they would pay when they eventually received the bonds. They were able to sell their borrowed bonds for a higher price than that, so they made a profit. When the futures matured, they took delivery of the bonds and used them to repay the bonds they had borrowed.

Usually, people who sell something short expect to buy it back later for less. They take a risk that the market might move up and they will have to buy it back for more. Salomon's quant group didn't have to take this risk. They had a contractual commitment—the futures contract—that already guaranteed them a lower price than the bonds were selling for. It didn't matter what else happened in the market.

Hilibrand finds it hard to believe now that it was so easy to make money then. Soon he and his colleagues had carried the concept to a higher level of refinement.

The buyer of a bond futures contract might receive any of a set of closely related bonds. Usually, all of the deliverable bonds sold for about the same price. Sometimes, though, for various supply and demand reasons, one of these bonds would be more expensive than the others. So when the quants bought undervalued futures contracts, they decided to sell the expensive bonds short. They were betting that the price of the expensive bond would fall back into line with the others before they had to pay back the party who had loaned it to them.

Effectively, they had chained together two trades, two risks, two opportunities to profit. One was a straight arbitrage trade between the bond market and the futures market. The other was a relative value trade between the bond they had shorted and the bond that would be delivered when the futures contract expired. Taken individually, perhaps neither piece of the trade would be worthwhile. Combined, they would be highly profitable.

"We're talking about very small opportunities that could be levered," Hilibrand says. "We levered in a very large way. In the case of a futures contract trading one-quarter of a percent below the theoretically correct valuation, which was the case during the period when this was an attractive opportunity, it meant that the futures contract trading at 99 should be trading at 99 1/4. If it were a bond, that's actually only worth 0.02 to 0.03 percent per year in terms of excess yield over the remaining life." Yet a difference that wouldn't mean much to the owner of a bond could mean a lot when leverage entered the picture.

Sometimes they lost. Asked to name their worst trade, they cite not the trade that lost them the most money but the trade that taught them the hardest lesson. Sometimes the market has reasons math cannot express.

"It was spring of 1985," Rosenfeld says. "The Chicago Board of Trade came out for the first time with options on ten-year treasury note futures. Since we had been trading in options on bond futures and OTC options on actual bonds, we thought we kind of understood options and how they should be traded." When the Chicago Board of Trade started to trade the new options on ten-year note futures, the quants noticed that some of the options were trading at values somewhat higher than their own mathematical models said were the correct values. The single most important factor in determining the price of an option is volatility. Volatility is the measure of how variable price changes can be. Salomon's quant group reverse-engineered the options traded on the Chicago Board of Trade, much as a computer manufacturer might disassemble and analyze a rival's machine. They found that the volatility component was high—too high, according to their models. "So we sold them," Rosenfeld says. "But we didn't just sell them and hope the market went down. We sold them and bought some of the underlying note futures." By selling options and buying note futures, the group created a hedged position that would allow them to profit from what appeared to be a mispricing in the options, without exposing them to market risk. That was the theory, anyway.

They held the position for two and a half months. Nothing happened to change their minds about the pricing. On the Friday afternoon when the options were to expire, they were set to pocket a handsome profit. Options stop trading at 1:00 P.M., and positions are settled at 5:00 P.M. The market was very stable. Volatility had been, if anything, even lower than Salomon's models had predicted. The profits on the transaction exceeded their expectations. However, something odd was going on.

According to the models, these options ought to have been worthless on Friday afternoon when trading stopped. Yet other traders still seemed to think they were worth something. The prudent thing for the quants to do would have been to buy back the options they had sold, pocket their profits, and close the books on a successful transaction. However, they couldn't bring themselves to pay for options that their own models said should be worthless. "So we sat there, twiddling our thumbs, talking about what we were going to do for the weekend," Rosenfeld says. "Then, totally out of the blue, the Federal Reserve cut the discount rate. The market wasn't expecting it, and it just gapped up. At 1:00, the option was a quarter point out of the money; at 4:00, it was a quarter point out of the money; and at 4:01, it was a point in the money." That is, instead of moving smoothly and regularly, the market took a sudden jump—a jump that the model could not have anticipated or explained—leaving a gap in the price chart.

The group lost not only the profit but three times what they had expected to make, just because the option pricing model they were using assumed that markets move smoothly. Says Hilibrand, "We learned that our models missed something. Though we totally understood the assumptions that went into the black box we used, we learned that some of the assumptions just don't fit reality."

Knowing the limits of theory, which assumptions are reasonable and in what kinds of markets, means knowing the difference between gold and fools' gold.

At LTCM, Salomon's quantitative arbitrage group continues to do much the same kind of work they pioneered at the investment bank. There is one difference, however. While at Salomon, the group had to limit its activities to the U.S. markets. Now they plan to go after opportunities all around the world. They are taking a very long range view—one to three years is about the minimum time an investor will wait for a payoff. Hilibrand says, "We enter into each trade without knowing exactly what will make the opportunity go our way, without knowing exactly when, without knowing exactly how or why. We see the opportunity, and structure the trade as efficiently as possible." Then, when the market finally does become efficient, the group makes a huge profit—but then another opportunity is gone.

Since the U.S. markets have been around for a long time, most of the early, easy, profitable inefficiencies are already gone. Some of the same techniques that succeeded in the early days of the U.S. market may still work in newer markets, however. That's why LTCM is prospecting where the crowds aren't—looking, as always, for what no one else has found.

The half-life of a good trading idea is short, because competition among traders is intense. As soon as opportunity becomes apparent, they rush in like ants, and soon the opportunity has been devoured. As a result, traders must keep pushing back the frontier of knowledge in order to make any profit at all. Since the discovery of a truly new scientific principle is as rare an event in the science of financial risk as in any other science, pushing the frontier usually means applying old principles in slightly different ways.

In 1990, for example, a former college professor and bank currency trader began to solicit funds to invest in an innovative trading strategy. His name was Ezra Zask. A little over a year after he started his company, he had been invited to join the lineup of Mitsubishi All-Stars, a fund that tries to pick the best currency and commodity traders in the world and give them money to manage for Japanese investors. Oppenheimer, Merrill Lynch, Dean Witter, and other big American brokerage firms gave him money to manage for their clients too. By 1994 in his fourth year of business, Zask was managing $190 million.

His was a simple concept. As a former academic and professor of finance, he knew that markets are efficient and that there is no return without risk. Yet when he made his transition from banking to entrepreneurship in 1990, he had a well-conceived plan to exploit an inefficiency he had been eyeing, and profiting from, for years. This inefficiency promised an extraordinarily low-risk source of returns.

Because of a variety of factors, currencies trade at different levels of interest. At a time when investors in U.S. dollars expected no more than 3 percent interest rates, investors in the Mexican peso could expect to earn 15 percent. There was a good reason for this difference in expectations. Mexican inflation was high, and the markets expected that sooner or later, Mexico would devalue the peso. An investor who sold U.S. dollars to buy Mexican pesos found that if he tried to hedge his purchase against the risk of devaluation, it would cost him all but about 3 percent of the high Mexican peso yield.[20]

However, Zask had researched the subject of currency yields carefully and had come to an unorthodox conclusion. He believed that the markets exaggerated the risk of devaluation. He decided that some of the additional yield was simply a "risk premium." Much as companies without well-established names expect to pay more than blue chips for the money they borrow—regardless of their credit ratings—so too do obscure countries have to pay more interest just to get the attention of investors. "When I invest in a high-yield currency, the returns to me are greater than the risk of decline," he explained.

For a time, Zask's risk controls let him profit in some of the world's riskiest markets. He quickly began to attract attention because his trading style was unique. He specialized in trading currencies that most other traders ignored: the Thai baht, the Indonesian rupiah, the Malaysian ringgit, the Greek drachma, and so forth. He also had a unique image. He didn't present himself as a home-run hitter like George Soros, who boasted of winning $1 billion when Great Britain left the European Exchange Rate Mechanism in 1992. In fact, in 1992, Zask earned less than 8 percent for his investors. However, if he didn't have eye-popping gains in his good years, he didn't have hand-wringing losses in his bad years either. Zask boasted of his Sharpe ratio, a risk measure designed by Nobel Prize–winning financial economist William Sharpe to determine how much risk an investor took for each increment of return. Zask's careful approach to risk is what most impressed the management of the Mitsubishi All Stars fund. They were very appreciative of Zask's ability to have only modest declines at times when most other currency traders were devastated.

Zask was looking forward to a long career exploiting his theory about risk premiums to continue delivering modest but low-risk returns. "Once a country is hooked on a risk premium to attract capital from abroad, it's almost like a junky," he told an interviewer in 1993. "Year after year the interest rate pickup is substantially greater than the currency devaluation."[21]

A year later, the situation had changed considerably. In the wake of the European Monetary System collapse, and historically low interest rates in the United States, capital poured into the developing world. Investors couldn't get an adequate return on their capital in the traditional markets, so they were willing to take more risk to get higher returns in less familiar places. Many of the countries whose currencies Zask had considered a mainstay were caught up in an emerging markets investment frenzy, and as a result, they didn't have to pay a risk premium to attract capital anymore. Instead, they were now awash with money.

Zask had lost his raison d'être. With the risk premium gone, his strategy of buying exotic currencies for yield no longer worked. So instead of holding them, he started selling some of them short because he figured that in some cases, instead of overestimating the risk of devaluation, the international markets now underestimated it. Zask still didn't want to make a big one-sided bet that would pay off handsomely if he won but expose his investors to big losses if he was wrong. So he tried to maintain his market-neutral position, but it wasn't as easy to hedge as it had been before. Because of the changes in investors' perceptions, currencies had stopped moving together in their historical pattern. It got riskier to play one country's currency off against that of another, closely related country. Zask scrambled to find new strategies. "Basically I scour the world looking for lower-risk propositions, trying to take advantage of them," he said.[22]

Of course, as a general rule, if opportunities are easy to spot, they've been spotted already. So Zask also decided to acquire a piece of oracular technology called the Market Information Machine. This computer system is actually a database loaded with decades of historical price information, all linked by software that sorts and selects it in any conceivable pattern.

First brought to market in 1991 by a company called Logical Information Machines, the MIM is now being adopted by the biggest traders in the industry. Its units can be found in the offices of George Soros, Paul Tudor Jones, Bruce Kovner, Prudential Securities, the Canadian Imperial Bank of Commerce, and many more.

What does the MIM do? It answers complicated questions quickly. Suppose a trader had a sudden flash of inspiration that the midterm congressional elections in the United States might somehow cause a change in the markets. The MIM could tell the trader in seconds how the stock, bond, or commodity markets were likely to react for a month after the elections. The trader could qualify the inquiry with "what if" questions: what if dollar interest rates are rising, what if the Japanese stock market is down 10 percent, what if the German mark is up 5 percent? Within seconds, the MIM would have analyzed all previous historical occurrences of the precise scenario, noted the outcomes, and calculated the relevant probabilities.

William R. Aronin, executive vice president of Logical Information Machines, makes no bones about the capabilities of the technology: "It does predict the future. It can tell you what's going to happen a year from now, an hour from now, whatever."[23] The MIM also provides statistical probabilities for various investment outcomes. Given a scenario and a proposed trade, it can calculate whether there's a 70 percent chance of the trade turning a profit or a 94.4 percent chance of it turning a loss. Of course, to believe that the MIM actually predicts the future is to believe that there is no escape from the past.

Whether or not they use the MIM, traders, like Macbeth before his witches, are learning from bitter experience that it is important to allow for the unexpected, unstated, unthinkable secret upon which every forecast really depends. Sometimes, under rare circumstances, a wood may indeed march upon a castle, and a man not born of woman may exist.

In 1994, for example, a number of astute financial institutions lost heavy sums of money when historical relationships suddenly stopped predicting the future. Even institutions that did not suffer losses nonetheless made much less money trading than they had made a year earlier. Said one British investment banker, "Most of the things people regarded as being sure-fire went wrong, and violently wrong." The markets reacted quickly. J. P. Morgan's triple-A credit rating was called into question by the credit rating agency Standard & Poor's. The reason?

The bank had come to rely heavily on trading income, and it was becoming clear that trading income was not reliable after all.

Some began to raise an alarm about the extent to which major financial institutions had adopted the technology of nuclear finance to manage their day-to-day business. Most institutions relied on the basic principles set forth by the early pioneers of risk management, and thus it was to be expected that a certain amount of herd behavior was programmed into the financial system. Regulators worried because herd behavior is what causes panics and crashes. If everyone in a boat rushes to the same side of the boat at the same time, the boat capsizes.

In order to understand how this might happen, it helps to consider the stock market crash of 1987 and a financial product known as *portfolio insurance* (also called *program trading*). Portfolio insurance promised investors a low-cost alternative to traditional hedging. No two investors owned precisely the same mix of stocks, bonds, currencies, and other assets. By applying the mathematics of options pricing models to the management of their own investment portfolios, investors could design their own, tailor-made hedges to fit each unique portfolio. They cut out the middleman too. Investors who used portfolio insurance hedged their risks just as a bank hedged its risk.

A bank that sells an option first calculates the risk of the option being exercised. If the bank has received $100 for an option on Swiss francs, and there is a 50-50 chance that prices will change and the bank will have to deliver them to the customer, the bank buys $50 worth of Swiss francs. If the price of Swiss francs rises, making it likelier that the customer will exercise the option, then the bank buys more of them. If the price falls, making it less likely that the customer will want to exercise the option, the bank sells some of them.

People who bought portfolio insurance actually bought a computer model that showed them how to buy and sell just as a bank options trader would. As the market price went up, they bought more of whatever asset they were hedging, and as it went down, they sold more.

Portfolio insurance worked with mathematical exactitude. Users paid no more to hedge their risk than a bank would pay to hedge its risk. As long as markets functioned fairly smoothly, they were well protected.

However, in 1987, for reasons that are still debated by students of finance, a panic occurred. As prices fell, users of portfolio insurance rushed to sell, just as their models said they should. All of the people rushing to sell sent prices down farther, and the farther prices fell, the more the users of portfolio insurance had to sell. Did portfolio insurance cause the crash? No, but it certainly contributed to the selling pressure, and helped make a bad situation somewhat worse.

The same hedging techniques used by portfolio insurance are still used by banks, investment banks, insurance companies, and other big financial institutions to hedge their currency, interest rate, commodity, and other trades. In times of market stress, when they all try to implement similar trades, the effect is like a crowd trying to rush through the same exit at the same time. Some get out, some get trampled. Too great a reliance on the promise of protection can be fatal.

Nonetheless, the development of new markets and new trading technologies has given owners and managers of capital unprecedented power and freedom. For centuries, governments have relied on the power of deception and surprise in the conduct of their monetary and economic policies. Now traders have such sharp electronic eyes that it is impossible for governments to surprise them. Neural nets, quantitative arbitrage strategies, and high-powered statistical analytics mean that the markets can analyze and anticipate every aspect of every possible policy action before regulators have had time to conclude their preliminary meetings.

HIDDEN RISKS

On September 22, 1985, the finance ministers and central bank chiefs of the G-5, the five strongest economic powers—the United States, Japan, Germany, France, and Britain—assembled in New York's Plaza Hotel for what was to have been a secret meeting. Japan's finance minister, Noboru Takeshita, had gone to elaborate lengths to disguise his departure from Tokyo for this session. He made plans to play golf at a course near Narita airport, left his home wearing golf togs, played nine holes, but was whisked off the course midway through his game and rushed to the airport to catch the plane for New York. There he joined the other members of the G-5.[1]

Such secrecy was the norm for members of this group. "Nobody outside a very tight official circle knew exactly where and when the five ministers met, what they discussed and what they agreed," recalls one participant.[2] However, it was no secret that the world was at this point perched on the brink of financial crisis. For five years, high interest rates in the United States had been pushing the dollar upward. Commodity prices had crashed, plunging Third World nations into insolvency, and now powerful forces urged the U.S. Congress to unleash the hounds of trade war against Japan. Clearly, the dollar had gone too far. Even the markets sensed that it had to be stopped. Six months before the G-5 meeting at the Plaza, the dollar had peaked, and now its strength was beginning to dissipate.

When word of the pending G-5 meeting leaked, rumors swirled through the markets. A spokesman for the group confirmed to the press on Saturday that a meeting was scheduled—but said nothing about the agenda. On Sunday, September 22, the G-5 announced their intention to encourage "appreciation of the non-dollar currencies,"[3] and started a stampede in the markets. Suddenly, everyone was selling dollars, and the greenback went into free fall.

Instead of orderly appreciation, there was a rout.

On the other side of the world, in Kuala Lumpur, Malaysia, a central bank went rogue as a result of this G-5 action. Malaysia, like many other developing nations, held much of its foreign exchange reserves in dollars. In 1984, those reserves had totaled $4.8 billion. When the dollar fell, the purchasing power of Malaysia's dollar reserves evaporated.

In order to recover what it had lost, Malaysia's central bank began to wage a sort of financial guerrilla war against the world's leading economic powers. Using all the resources a central bank commands—privileged information, unlimited credit, regulatory power, and more—Malaysia's Bank Negara became the most feared trader in the currency markets. By trading for profit, Bank Negara committed apostasy against the creed of central banking. Instead of working to ensure global financial stability, Bank Negara repeatedly shoved huge sums of money into the most vulnerable market situations in order to destabilize exchange rates for its own profit.

In June 1985, a new governor had been appointed to Bank Negara. Tan Sri Dato' Jaffar bin Hussein, a former Price Waterhouse accountant, mapped the strategy for the central bank's campaign of profiteering in the markets. In a speech given in New Delhi in December 1988, he admitted that "honest-to-God trading" had contributed 40 percent of the bank's total overseas income that year, up from only 20 percent the year before. Jaffar noted proudly that Negara had a reputation for running one of the most sophisticated currency trading operations in the world. He justified this unorthodox activity by noting that "exchange rate volatility since the Plaza agreement of September 1985 has changed the stakes of the game."[4]

Jaffar's profiteering campaign distressed the international financial community, but it had the endorsement of his country's strongman,

Prime Minister Mahathir bin Mohamad. Mahathir taunted Negara's critics publicly, saying, "What is wrong with our protecting our own interest? Why is it when they [rich nations] can protect their interests we cannot? I can't understand it."[5] A self-styled leader of the developing world, Mahathir seldom missed a chance to strike out at Western imperialism. At various times, he had seized the spotlight by criticizing the U.S. military presence in the Philippines, campaigning to ensure that developing countries shared in the mineral wealth of Antarctica, excoriating Western environmentalists for their efforts to prevent the logging of rain forests, promoting nationalist economic strategies like manufacturing automobiles in Malaysia, and threatening to boycott British products in retaliation for perceived slights by the British press. Negara's currency trading made the West fear Malaysia, and that didn't clash at all with Mahathir's agenda. He did not need to read Machiavelli to know that it is better for a prince to be feared than loved.

Negara operated behind a thick veil of secrecy. The bank seldom spoke publicly about its controversial trading activities. Yet it was increasingly clear to foreign exchange traders that Bank Negara's operations in the foreign exchange markets went far beyond simple self-defense. It became the most awesome currency trader in the world. At one point, an official of the Federal Reserve Board in the United States criticized Negara's speculation at a conference attended by the Malaysian central bankers. They coolly denied any speculative activity and said they were merely protecting their reserves. Ezra Zask, who at the time was managing currency dealing rooms for Manufacturers Hanover Trust in Europe, recalls reading this denial in the financial press just as a big speculative order was coming into his trading room from Bank Negara.

Jaffar found it easy to exploit the greed of Western bankers. A bank that did business with Bank Negara could add $20 million to $30 million per year to its bottom line. The money came not so much from fees as from the advance knowledge of Negara's trades. Negara traded big numbers. When it turned its attention to the pound, for example, bankers who executed Negara's orders say Negara bought or sold perhaps £100 million sterling per transaction, and made many transactions within minutes, often through several banks. When orders that size hit the market, the market moved. Most trading systems of the sort used by banks have rules that require prompt sales to cut losses when prices fall. Market sources say Negara specialized in exploiting these rules—selling short a currency in volumes big enough to trigger a wave of panic selling by bankers, for example, then buying back the currency in the midst of the panic to lock in profits. Bankers who knew what Bank Negara was about to do had valuable advance knowledge of which way the market was going to move. They could and frequently did place their own bets alongside those of the Malaysian speculator, and profit when Negara did.

"People treat Negara's trader as a king—provide him with every kind of information available," said a banker who had managed foreign exchange trading for both American and British banks and was very familiar with Negara. "Talk to the largest twenty banks in the world, they all want to go in with their heads down and try to get Negara's business," he said.[6]

However, Negara was a hard master for the banks that served it. In 1990, prior to Britain's entry into the European Exchange Rate Mechanism, Negara had been buying up the pound sterling. On September 21, almost five years to the day after the Plaza meeting, Negara suddenly sold between $500 million and $1 billion worth of pounds, driving the price of sterling down 4 cents against the dollar and inflicting heavy losses on the major British banks with which it did business. Whether Negara had deliberately torpedoed the pound just as it entered the ERM or was merely taking profits was never discovered. British banks attempted to form a currency trading cartel to protect themselves against future raids of this sort, but foreign competitors were more than willing to accommodate Negara at noncartel prices, and all that the British banks managed to do was to make themselves the object of an investigation by British antimonopoly regulators.[7]

No one had traded on the scale of Negara since Andy Krieger had leveraged the capital of Bankers Trust Company into massive speculative onslaughts against small currencies like the New Zealand dollar. Krieger was a sort of inspiration to Negara. He recalls that when he met several of Bank Negara's officers in New York, they asked for his autograph.[8] When Negara shot down the pound in 1990, market rumors said that Krieger was in fact the mastermind behind Negara's heavy bets. Britain's *Independent* newspaper published the rumors and prompted an angry retort from the Malaysians. "The existence of this rumor is a reflection of the condescending attitude of the Western media, which refuses to believe that a central bank in a developing country can do well in an area of the financial market which has previously been the preserve of the Western banks for so long," the bank said in a rare public statement.[9]

Negara's market manipulation was so egregious that one American central banker said, "If they tried this on any organized exchange in the world, they'd go to jail."[10] However, in the unregulated international currency markets, there were neither police nor jailers. The only rule was the rough justice of the vandals, and it was this rule that eventually brought Negara down.

In 1992, Negara took on a large pound sterling position, apparently expecting Britain to maintain the discipline required by the European Exchange Rate Mechanism. It was a bad economic and political judgment. Negara lost approximately $3.6 billion when Britain withdrew from the ERM, letting sterling collapse. The next year, Negara lost an additional $2.2 billion. By 1994, Bank Negara was technically insolvent and had to be bailed out by an infusion of fresh money from Malaysia's finance ministry. Jaffar attributed the $5.8 billion in losses to poor judgment and resigned. The opposition leader in the Malaysian parliament called for a Royal Commission of Inquiry into the "greatest financial scandal in Malaysia."

Bank Negara had used finance as a weapon. It conquered the core of the financial system—the interbank currency market—and held a commanding position there until the weapon blew up in its own hands. The risk represented by Negara is the risk that a major, well-capitalized entity could pursue a deliberate strategy to achieve certain political objectives through the equivalent of financial terrorism. The political objectives could be as simple as commanding attention and respect, as in Malaysia's case, but they might, in a future avatar, be considerably more sinister.

Hedge Funds

Although Negara's campaign of financial guerrilla war was dramatic, it was a threat whose source was known, and because it was known, it could be closely watched. By the early 1990s, Negara began to be eclipsed by a new phenomenon, the great concentration of speculative capital entrusted to hedge funds or commodity pools, and by the massive movements of funds by banks, pension funds, and insurance companies, about which very little is known.

The term *hedge fund* derives from American securities law. In its strict sense, it means a fund that is exempt from registration under federal securities laws and able to trade a broad range of financial products. Commodity pools and commodity funds were, as the names suggest, originally vehicles by which investors could participate in the commodity futures markets. They are regulated by the Commodity Futures Trading Commission (CFTC).

Financial market evolution during the 1970s and 1980s made those definitions and the regulatory turf they circumscribed moot. In hearings before the U.S. Congress in 1994, regulators from the SEC, the CFTC, and the Fed all attempted to define hedge funds and to measure their impact. Estimates of the number ranged from a low of eight hundred to a high of about three thousand if the similar commodity pools were included. Estimates of capital under management by hedge funds and similar investment pools are even harder to pin down. They range from a low of $7 billion[11] to a high of $47.967 billion.[12] It is not surprising that regulators are confused. Because U.S. regulations on investment managers tend to be strict, many of the biggest funds take care to register outside the United States, where disclosure requirements are less burdensome.

Yet to single out hedge funds as a source of financial risk is somewhat misleading, since most of the money invested with hedge funds comes from major financial institutions like banks, insurance companies, and pension funds. Ultimately, hedge funds are only one consequence of a far-reaching change in the structure of the international financial system described in previous chapters. The Bretton Woods system failed to provide stability in the risky world of international finance. Now the private markets sell stability. When a bank sells a customer a currency exchange or interest rate contract, the bank then assumes the risk that rates may change adversely. Managing this risk is crucial to the solvency of the bank, and most banks attempt to keep a neutral risk position in the business they do with customers. If they buy francs forward from one customer, they try to sell them forward to another customer, and make their trading profits on the spread between the price at which they buy and sell the franc risk. Often, hedge funds end up taking the risk that banks are laying off.

However, banks also speculate. Most big banks run a so-called proprietary trading operation that takes risk not on behalf of customers but simply in order to make a profit. This proprietary trading function usually accounts for only a fraction of bank trading activity, but it can be a large fraction. In an investigation conducted at the request of Congress, the General Accounting Office mentioned one bank where speculation accounted for 20 percent of its trading activity. Usually, proprietary trading is handled by a separate group from the one that provides risk management services to customers.

It is a simple matter for traders to avoid regulatory scrutiny. In 1992, the CFTC commissioner chaired a meeting of the Financial Products Advisory Committee, a special group of traders, bankers, finance professors, and other experts assembled to advise the agency on how the markets would react to proposed new regulations. An American banker who was organizing a derivatives trading operation for a large Japanese brokerage firm told her, bluntly, "We'll eventually be financial organizations headquartered on a ship floating mid-ocean."[13] This is hyperbole, of course, but not far removed from the truth. In 1994, when the U.S. Congress convened hearings into the development of the derivatives markets, the head of global derivatives trading at Bankers Trust quipped, "Sell your real estate in New York; buy real estate in London."[14] The threat is anything but idle. Bankers Trust already maintains extensive trading operations in London, as do many other major U.S. financial institutions, and it would be easy to move more trading out of New York if U.S. regulations became inconvenient. They could still trade with U.S. markets. Distance is no obstacle to the traders, because no matter where they are based, they can easily communicate with any market by phone, fax, or electronic mail and, if necessary, trade through brokers, bankers, and other intermediaries.

If geography is no barrier to traders, neither are the legal fictions that once defined and separated markets into neat compartments labeled stocks, bonds, commodities, currencies, and so on. From the establishment of the International Monetary Market at the Chicago Mercantile Exchange in 1971 onward, these regulatory barriers have become progressively more permeable. Regulators seem not to have noticed what was happening until it had already happened. The Presidential Task Force on Market Mechanisms that investigated the causes of the great stock market crash of 1987 noted with some surprise that instead of the distinct markets regulators thought had existed, there was really only one big market. Capital moved easily and swiftly between the Chicago futures markets, the options markets, and the New York Stock Exchange. Three years later, Japanese regulators were even more astonished at how easily their market controls were evaded by traders operating in Singapore.

While the regulators were surprised to learn about these linkages, traders had known for years that the regulatory barriers were, for practical purposes, virtually meaningless. Economic laws—supply and demand, the time value of money, the law of one price—were the only laws that really mattered. A trader makes money by taking risks. If it is possible to take the same risk in both New York and Chicago, then the price of that risk ought to be the same in both places.

For example, in 1982 the Chicago Mercantile Exchange invented a stock index futures contract on the Standard & Poor's 500, a list of five hundred stocks. A trader who wanted to buy these stocks could either place an order to purchase them on the New York Stock Exchange or buy the futures contract in Chicago and receive an economic return equivalent to that of the stocks in the index. The futures contract cost only 5 or 10 percent as much as actually buying the stocks, but the price of the futures contract and the price of the stocks in the index had to be mathematically related. If the stocks were much more expensive on the stock exchange than the ideal mathematical relationship suggested they ought to be, people could buy the futures contract, sell the stocks themselves, and pocket an immediate profit. If it was easier or cheaper to buy and sell futures than to buy and sell stocks, business would move from the stock exchange to the future markets. This is exactly what happened during the great stock market crash of 1987. The phenomenon is not limited to stocks. Currency futures in Chicago, currency options in Philadelphia, and currency forwards on the interbank market all moved up and down together for the same reason. This is the law of one price in action.

How did markets become so closely linked? In the currency markets, at least, some say that the single most important factor was Joe Ritchie, a graduate of an obscure West Coast Bible college who made his way to Chicago.

Ritchie's father was an ordained minister and an engineer. In 1957, he took his wife and five children to Afghanistan, where he spent four years teaching engineering and "living the Gospel."[15] They returned in 1961. Joe attended Wheaton College, a small Christian school in Illinois, where he majored in philosophy.

After graduating, Joe Ritchie found work in Chicago as a jail guard and later as a policeman. He won a citation for bravery when he walked up to a mentally disturbed man who had been threatening several other officers with a knife, and talked the man into putting down the weapon. Perhaps it's no wonder he didn't see much future in law enforcement, and left Chicago for Los Angeles when his brother-in-law helped him get a job with a silver trader.[16]

It was the kind of opportunity Ritchie had been hoping for. "I'd read a book on trading, and I felt like I understood what really made it work," he recalls. "I felt I understood it better than the guy writing the book. He was writing about the surface phenomenon, and I felt I could understand what was going on underneath."[17] From that moment, he wanted to trade, but it took money to break into the trading business, and Joe Ritchie didn't have money. He didn't even own a suit.

The silver dealer hired him as a researcher. There was only one other researcher in the department. Soon Ritchie began to come up with profitable trading ideas. After six months, the company moved him into the trading area, and he was soon running trading for it. Silver futures contracts were traded at exchanges in New York and Chicago, sometimes at different prices. Joe Ritchie decided that New York and Chicago prices differed enough to make an arbitrage operation profitable. An astute trader could buy on whatever exchange the price was lower, and sell where it was higher, making immediate profits with virtually no risk. However, to set up such an operation, he needed to have a membership—a seat on one of the exchanges.

Although Joe was running trading for the silver dealer, he was still far from rich. When he visited Chicago to inquire about the possibility of buying a seat on the Chicago Board of Trade, he still didn't have a suit. His brother, Mark, who was still working as a jail guard, happened to own two suits, both of them cheap, one new and the other quite shabby. He loaned Joe the better of the two, donned the shabby one himself, and together they went to pay a call on the world's biggest futures exchange.

When they walked into the president's office, an exchange official smirked. "You boys have got to be in the wrong place!" he said. They asked about memberships, and he responded derisively that the cost would probably be beyond their means. After a brief, strained conversation, they left.[18]

A few months later, Joe Ritchie's employer put up the money and he began to trade in the silver pits. He hired his brother as a telephone clerk. They weren't the only traders who had spotted the difference between New York and Chicago prices, but Joe demonstrated a rare ability to see mathematical relationships between time, prices, and probabilities that other traders missed. He also recognized the importance of timely information. Some of the other traders didn't even hire telephone clerks to keep in touch with the New York markets and notify them when prices changed. Joe and Mark Ritchie made sure they hired the best phone clerks and managed to get the most current market information five or six seconds before anyone else. With that slight advantage, they became the most aggressive traders in the pit.[19]

Soon they were making money and taking business away from the old-timers. Naturally, the other traders objected to the newcomers' success. They even tried to use an obscure, unenforced exchange regulation to throw the Ritchies out of the pit. The regulation required that any communication between telephone clerks and floor traders be in writing. The Ritchies were hauled up before a disciplinary committee because their phone clerks communicated with them verbally. They pointed out that the same rule was routinely violated by all of the other traders, and if the exchange had enforced it universally, orders would take so long to fill that people would stop using the Chicago silver contract. The exchange officials recognized that they couldn't enforce the rules against the Ritchies and not enforce them against anyone else, so Joe was able to keep trading.

Their success in silver was short-lived. They had started to trade silver during a period of great volatility. By 1974, silver prices had begun to calm down. Since traders don't make money in calm markets, Joe began to look for other opportunities. He soon found one in the soybean pit. He talked his former employer into supporting his diversification away from silver by promising him that if he succeeded, he would share profits 50-50, but if he failed, he would be responsible for the losses himself. The employer agreed to stake him.

In retrospect, the opportunity looks obvious. The Board of Trade had contracts on soybeans, soybean meal, and soybean oil. Soybean meal and soybean oil were called the "crush" because they were made by crushing beans. Obviously, there was a mathematical relationship between the price of whole beans and the price of the crush. However, prices often diverged from the mathematically correct relationship. They diverged frequently enough that Joe Ritchie and his brother, Mark, decided to build a business around them. They called their firm the Chicago Board Crushers, got a telephone listing, and started receiving phone calls from people who literally wanted to have boards, of all sizes and types, crushed. They changed the name to Chicago Research and Trading, or CRT.[20]

CRT made a small fortune from arbitraging the soybean crush, buying and selling soybean futures and meal or oil futures simultaneously when the prices diverged. It was strictly an arbitrage operation—CRT didn't take trading positions in order to make money when the market went up or down. This trading style linked markets that had previously operated more or less independently.

By 1982, the firm employed about thirty-five people and had about $5 million in capital.[21] From silver and soybeans, the Ritchies had moved on to bonds. But the failure of a government securities dealer named Drysdale had caused a crisis of confidence in the bond market. CRT had been trading about $30 million in bonds and bond futures daily, but the credit crisis killed the business. Many of its potential customers now had suspect credit, and the firm could not take the risk that it too might fail as Drysdale had. In June 1982, casting about for a new business to replace bonds, Joe Ritchie decided to take another look at options. In the mid-1970s, he had experimented with the stock options traded at the Chicago Board Options Exchange, but burdensome regulatory paperwork turned him away from the market. Now, in 1982, the options on futures were being introduced by the Chicago and New York commodity exchanges, and the Philadelphia Stock Exchange was developing options on currencies.

By August 1982, Ritchie had figured out pricing relationships between options on gold futures traded at New York's COMEX and options on treasury bond futures traded at the Chicago Board of Trade. Wherever options were introduced, CRT appeared. "In the early days, we were the market," recalls CRT partner Gary Ginter. "Our guys were the buyers and sellers of in excess of 80 percent of the trades made. In the early years, just one of our traders did 50 percent of the bond options market."

If the experience of Philadelphia is any indication, that's no idle boast. Arnie Staloff, who invented the currency option for the Philadelphia Stock Exchange, credits CRT with turning the market into a viable force. He got a phone call one day in 1983 from a CRT trader who was interested in the newly introduced currency options:

He comes down next day, said, "This seems interesting; do you have any price data?" I said, "Yes, I can show you every quote and every trade that ever took place since the first day of trading." I gave it all to him. He said, "This is phenomenal!" He spent about an hour looking over this data, and got on the phone and started reading prices off the computer sheet to somebody. I had a board meeting, returned at 7:00 p.m., and he was still reading these numbers. I said, "I know you're living in New York, so I guess you're not going to be able to start trading tomorrow." He said, "No, I'll be here; I just have to go home and change my shirt and come back." That's basically what he did, and he was in the next morning before me. That was a record day of trading for us that day, and from then on, it was like an explosion of that market. They became so active in trading, it encouraged a lot of other people to trade too.[22]

The major New York banks and investment banks also depended on CRT, because they were just beginning their own options business and needed to hedge their own risks through the exchanges.

CRT expanded internationally as new futures and options markets developed in London, Paris, Singapore, and elsewhere. "Because of Joe's abilities, CRT was at least two years ahead of everybody in August of 1982 and probably held that lead until 1986," says Ginter.[23] The lead faded eventually, though, as the mathematics of the pricing became more widely known. In the early years, the firm made money because Joe Ritchie had a better idea of what things were worth than his competitors and therefore was better at risk management. But when the rest of the world caught up, CRT's lead diminished. "We used to pick up dimes in front of bulldozers. Then we were picking up pennies and nickels," Ritchie says.[24] In 1993, the firm that had been started by a former jail guard in a borrowed suit was sold to NationsBank for $225 million. At the time of the sale, CRT had 750 employees.

NationsBank was not alone in its decision to expand in the lucrative trading business. For the seven largest banks in the United States, the so-called money center banks, average trading revenues more than doubled, from $557 million per quarter in the mid-1980s to $1.243 billion per quarter in the early 1990s.[25] Some industry experts and many bankers believed that the new business was, perhaps paradoxically, less risky than lending.

The biggest banking debacles of the 1970s and the 1980s had involved lending, not speculation. Changes in the financial system made it possible for big corporations to borrow money directly from investors in money market funds or in the Euromarkets much more cheaply and conveniently than they could borrow from banks. When these traditional customers of the biggest banks discovered that they no longer needed banks, the banks scrambled to find other customers to whom they could lend. Continental Illinois bank failed because it made too many loans to oil-well drillers. The Bank of New England failed because it made too many loans to real estate developers. The entire banking industry in the United States and Europe nearly failed because most banks made too many loans to governments in Latin America and Africa.

Although many disasters had been caused by loose lending, the United States had never experienced a major banking disaster caused by loose trading. In contrast to lending, trading seemed consistently profitable and relatively low-risk. Some analysts pointed out that trading allowed banks to do business once again with their traditional customers, the large and creditworthy corporations. Instead of borrowing money, the big corporations were now buying risk management products, like derivatives.

This argument was true, so far as it went, but it did not convince everyone. Regulators pointed out that as financial institutions moved aggressively into the trading business, they increased the linkages between markets and, consequently, the risk that a major shock in one market could reverberate dangerously through the entire financial system. In fact, trading had changed a familiar old workhorse of a system into a racehorse that was certainly faster and certainly more streamlined but might also be much more fragile.

In 1992, bank regulators in the United States and Europe began to speak publicly of their worries. In January, the president of the Federal Reserve Bank of New York addressed a congregation of top executives of New York's banks. In heated language, he suggested that perhaps their trading in derivatives did not serve a legitimate hedging purpose but instead merely fueled speculation.

Two months later, Alexandre Lamfalussy, general manager of the Bank for International Settlements (BIS), was even more explicit. In a lecture at the City University of London, Lamfalussy said that the growth of trading in futures and swaps "makes it increasingly difficult to assess the direct credit, liquidity and interest rate risks assumed by any individual financial firm." In addition, the growth of trading in such instruments had created new links between sectors of the financial industry that used to be separate. "We simply do not know the size of the indirect risks for the individual institution generated by this interdependence," Lamfalussy said. "These risks cannot easily be captured, even through very sophisticated risk assessment techniques."[26]

A week later in Paris, Richard H. Farrant, deputy head of banking supervision of the Bank of England, further admonished the derivatives traders who had gathered for the annual meeting of the International Swap Dealers Association. He focused on the dubious legality of certain trades and the questionable enforceability of contracts, both worrisome sources of risk. He noted that accounting standards could not cope with the new businesses, as accountants disagreed among themselves about how to measure the gains and losses on trading. He said that institutions often depended heavily on a few, highly skilled specialists who built risky portfolios their managers did not understand. These specialists were in short supply, highly paid, and fervently courted. Sometimes they left suddenly, and the problem of managing the risks they left behind was a troubling one.

In 1993, the prestigious Group of Thirty, a Washington-based think tank, issued a groundbreaking report that was the first major attempt to categorize and assess the risks of the new markets. The report identified four major categories of risk: credit, market, operational, and legal. In order to understand why regulators worry about the new hidden world of these markets, it helps to know what damage each of these risks has already caused.

Credit Risk and the Collapse of Drexel

The Drexel bankruptcy was a cataclysmic event that brought the world close to financial collapse—and forced regulators to face the fact of their near impotence.

Drexel was not a complicated investment bank. Most of its business was in relatively simple, straightforward, widely accepted, and liquid financial instruments. Junk bonds, per se, were not Drexel's problem. Junk bonds were merely bonds that paid a high rate of interest. Everyone knew how bonds worked. But when a combination of political and economic pressures caused the junk bond market to falter, Drexel's concentration in junk made it a questionable credit risk.

The firm's worsening financial condition was an open secret on Wall

Street for months before the investment bank declared bankruptcy.[27] Most major banks had stopped lending Drexel long-term money, and they extended credit only on a fully collateralized basis.

Drexel's problem was a simple liquidity problem. Although the firm had massive wealth in the form of junk bonds, it was short of ready cash. Because no one was willing to lend it long-term funds, Drexel had been financing its long-term investments in junk bonds with short-term borrowings. This is something like buying a car by paying with a credit card and paying off the credit card debt at the end of each month by using another credit card. Drexel simply ran out of credit cards to pay off its old short-term debt.

The crisis came to a head early in February, 1990 when Drexel had trouble rolling over about $30 million in short-term borrowings. Eleven major banks held about $1 billion of securities as collateral for Drexel's borrowings. The securities were held in accounts at the Depository Trust Corporation in New York. Under the rules of that institution, a bank could release securities only to the institution that had pledged them as collateral for a loan—in this case, Drexel. If the banks released the securities, Drexel could have sold them and repaid its loans to the banks. However, no one wanted to take the chance of delivering securities to a troubled investment bank. There was a good chance that instead of using the cash to repay loans to the bank, Drexel would use it for some other purpose. This was gridlock: Drexel did not have cash, so banks would not release the securities, and unless the banks released the securities, Drexel could not obtain cash.

The standoff lasted for several weeks. The banks met regularly at the offices of the Federal Reserve Bank of New York, where President Gerald Corrigan was spending his nights in the office, occasionally grabbing a few hours' sleep on the couch. Serious gridlocks threatened other markets. The Bank of England stepped in as an "honest broker" to assume responsibility for clearing Drexel's obligations in the London foreign exchange market. In New York, the Federal Reserve Bank prepared to play the same role in the Ginnie Mae securities market. Ginnie Maes, simple securitized mortgages that carry a government credit guarantee, constituted a hefty portion of Drexel's assets. Unlike the securities held at the Depository Trust Corporation (DTC), Ginnie Maes had no formal, institutionalized mechanism to deliver securities and payments. Thus, the Ginnie Mae market depended completely on trust and creditworthiness.

In order to prevent gridlock in Ginnie Maes from spreading to other parts of the financial system and precipitating a complete collapse of confidence, the Fed set up an emergency clearance operation in its gymnasium. Holders of Ginnie Mae securities could bring them to the Fed and exchange them immediately against payment from Drexel in the sight of a Fed official. The emergency operation was a last-ditch defense against systemic paralysis. Fortunately, it did not have to be used. At the last moment, another investment bank agreed to purchase Drexel's entire mortgage portfolio and thus eliminated Drexel's poor credit as a risk factor in the Ginnie Mae market.

Fed officials and others who worked through the Drexel collapse recall long nights and tense days cajoling payments and securities to move through the system. "Without the intervention of the U.S. authorities, the failure of Drexel Burnham Lambert might have blocked the [international] payments mechanism, with widespread repercussions," said Alexandre Lamfalussy.[28] That crisis was only narrowly averted. Yet Drexel was relatively simple, after all. "If you looked at the books of any of the major players today, and particularly the more esoteric parts, there isn't a prayer of a chance that we could have played the facilitative role that we played in Drexel," recalls one bank regulator closely involved with the Drexel situation. "It's too complicated."[29]

Market participants don't share regulators' worries. They consider the Drexel episode to be an example of how well private markets can contain such a problem. The banks were, after all, eventually able to reach an agreement among themselves to exchange securities and cash through the DTC. A private institution did buy Drexel's mortgage products, so the emergency clearing operation at the Fed was unnecessary.

However, Drexel was simple because only one real problem was involved—credit. People were unwilling to release securities because they were afraid that Drexel would not pay for them. No one had any doubts about what these securities were really worth. Yet the complexity of the new financial markets has made it difficult even for experts to figure out what securities are worth. Nowhere is this problem more acute than in the market for mortgage obligations.

Market Risk

Most mortgage loans made in the United States become fodder for the securitization industry. Buyers collect pools of mortgages and issue securities against these pools. The buyers of the securities receive a stream of principal and interest payments from the pool, made up of all the homeowners' monthly payments, combined together.

There is a risk to the buyer of a mortgage security. The risk is that a homeowner may pay off the mortgage prematurely—usually through a refinancing. Borrowers usually have the right to repay their mortgage at any time without penalty. In fact, in most states, this right is guaranteed by law. In effect, almost all mortgage borrowers have an option, and that option is one of the biggest sources of risk in the contemporary financial system.

Financial engineers treat mortgage payments as mathematical equations. A mortgage payment is the sum of a principal payment and an interest payment, and one of the first steps in the design of the contemporary mortgage security was to split the principal from the interest payment on some tranches. Interest payments went to investors who purchased "interest only" securities; principal payments went to investors who purchased "principal only" securities.

Other refinements of the basic mortgage security soon followed. "Inverse floaters," for example, are mortgage securities that pay investors more when interest rates go down, and less when interest rates go up. They are pegged to any of a variety of indices. "Residuals" are all the cash flows that are left over when more desirable securities have been created.

All of these securities and their multiple permutations are mathematically designed to balance each other and add up to the sum of payments from a given pool of mortgages. Some buyers of mortgage securities relied on the mathematical relationships between these securities to design elaborately balanced investment portfolios that would capture high returns with very low risk. Others used the same securities to make massive, highly leveraged bets on the direction of interest rates.

Unfortunately, the instruments themselves were so complex that even experts had trouble telling the difference between a safe, low-risk strategy and a highly speculative plunge. After studying the ways in which millions of homeowners paid or refinanced their mortgages for the prior few decades, Wall Street's scientists were pretty confident that the homeowner's threshold of pain was about 2 percent. Based on the rule of thumb that there had to be a 200-basis-point—or 2 percent—difference between the rate on a homeowner's existing mortgage and current rates to make refinancing economical, the financial scientists built, and brokers sold, billions of dollars of mortgage securities.

Then, suddenly, the old rule of thumb stopped working. When the financial scientists weren't looking, fee-hungry mortgage bankers made refinancing so easy that it took only a phone call to swing a deal, and homeowners were willing to refinance for as little as three-quarters of a percentage point in interest savings. When homeowners refinanced at a higher rate than Wall Street had anticipated, even the most carefully balanced portfolios turned out to have been a house of cards.

At Piper Capital in Minneapolis, money manager Worth Bruntjen was one of the most aggressive practitioners of the new financial science. "I think one of the great fallacies is the thesis that the only way you can increase return is by increasing risk," he said.[30] By analyzing the performance of high-risk mortgage securities and combining them appropriately in a portfolio, Bruntjen claimed to have a low-risk, high-return investment strategy. "IOs, for example, will be hurt by rising prepayments; POs will gain. The fund's interest rate exposure is fairly mild," he said in a letter to a magazine that criticized his reliance on complex derivatives to achieve high yields.[31] In fact, as much as 50 percent of his portfolio was invested in derivatives, over 20 percent in inverse floaters.

However, when interest rates began to rise late in 1993, Bruntjen's reliance on complex mathematical relationships between securities did not save him from disaster.

It turned out that the mathematical relationships between securities were no more than an untested and ultimately invalid hypothesis. By August 1994, he had lost an estimated $700 million of his investors' money, losses that threatened the very survival of his firm. "We got caught in a market that we thought we understood," Addison L. Piper, the firm's chairman and CEO, confessed ruefully.[32]

The shift in the markets that toppled Bruntjen also brought down one of the fastest-growing hedge funds in New York—Granite Capital Management. Like Bruntjen, managers of Granite had relied on mathematical relationships that proved to be considerably less stable in practice than in theory.

Major banks and industrial companies were among the investors who had believed Granite Capital's pitch about low-risk, high-return investment strategies. Fund managers familiar with Granite's portfolio say that it contained derivatives ten times more risky than an ordinary, interest-bearing treasury bond. "The underlying nature of these securities changes so dramatically when rates rise or when they fall that it's nearly impossible when you buy it to know exactly what your investment outcome will be," said Paul DaRosa, president of Eastbridge Capital.[33]

Operational Risk

Markets in risk had developed because some parties needed to get rid of risk, and others were willing to take a risk in order to make a profit. At first, only a few big banks and investment banks had the technology to take financial risks and trade for profit. They made a lot of money. Soon competitors rushed in to grab a piece of the action.

In order to keep ahead of their competitors, the risk takers had to develop ever more complex and subtle trading strategies. As soon as competitors found out about a strategy, they imitated it and sold it cheaply. In the early 1980s, simple swaps and options were lucrative. By the 1990s, such so-called plain vanilla products were no longer profitable. Banks offered them because it was a service customers demanded and expected, not because it was profitable. The real money could be made only in new, usually complicated feats of financial engineering. The banks endeavored to keep these feats secret from the competition and usually compensated the financial wizards who developed and traded the new risk-management products with a percentage of the money they made.

Banks, investment banks, and insurance companies at the core of the world's financial system were in a new and different business. No one was really sure what risks they were taking anymore. The environment was rife for abuse.

The first major scandal occurred in 1987, at Bankers Trust Company. The chairman of Bankers Trust, Charles Sanford, studied mathematics in college and came up through the traders' ranks to the top spot in the seventh largest bank holding company in the United States. He spent much of the decade of the 1980s turning his bank into a trading powerhouse. In recent years, Bankers Trust has relied on trading and derivatives for as much as two-thirds of its revenues.

When Bankers Trust decided to enter the options business, it hired a young Andy Krieger away from Salomon Brothers. Krieger earned hundreds of millions of dollars for Bankers Trust by trading currency options for a short period that began in 1986 and lasted just until the end of 1987. Then he abruptly quit. Press reports at the time suggested that he was dissatisfied with his paltry $3 million bonus. Krieger says that he was simply tired of the hours and the work and wanted a rest. He left on vacation.[34]

On January 20, 1988, the bank made a public announcement of its earnings for the prior year, claiming $593 million in foreign exchange trading profits, $338 million of which was earned during the last quarter of 1987. Most of this, Krieger says, came from his own foreign currency options trading. The bank does not dispute him.[35]

The earnings announcement was made in the morning. In the afternoon, the auditors finished checking the foreign currency options portfolio. They discovered some surprising discrepancies between the volatilities marked on options in the portfolio and the real volatilities in the market. At Bankers Trust, volatilities were usually marked by the traders themselves and by their assistants. The auditor checked them only periodically.[36]

Volatility is the most important part of options pricing. It is not a firm and precise measurement. Volatility is the probability of a change in price of the underlying currency on which the option is written. The party who sells an option takes a greater risk when prices are changing rapidly, because it is more probable that the price changes will result in the option being exercised and the seller incurring a loss. In calm markets, when prices are unlikely to change, options are cheaper than in turbulent, volatile times.

A federal bank regulator familiar with the "Andy Krieger affair" said that the volatilities on options in Krieger's portfolio were much higher than the volatilities on similar options then trading in the market. These were not small differences of judgment. A 5 or 10 percent difference might be attributed to a difference in judgment, he said, but not a difference of 25 percent.[37]

Andy Krieger has an attorney who returned calls from this author inquiring into the matter, and the attorney made it clear that any implication of Andy Krieger being involved in any questionable activity was unproven, unsubstantiated, and potentially libelous. So it is important to state here, as *Fortune* magazine also stated in a restrospective article on the Krieger affair, that no one has ever publicly accused Andy Krieger of any wrongdoing in connection with the Andy Krieger affair.[38] In a meeting with this author, Krieger said that he was out of the country when the options were valued and had left the bank when the scandal broke in January. Even some sources within Bankers Trust, speaking on background, deny that the Andy Krieger affair was Andy Krieger's fault. He was not prosecuted for or charged with any wrongdoing by any law enforcement authorities. Nothing was ever proven against him.

However, as a result of the curiously high volatilities, the profits of Bankers Trust currency options trading had been wildly overstated. The mismarking had added about $80 million to Bankers Trust Company's reported earnings for the year, $80 million that was nonexistent.

The bank did not want to publicize the fact that its controls were so slipshod that it was not even sure of its real earnings. So instead of immediately correcting the error in its reported earnings, Bankers Trust used an accounting device to avoid acknowledging it. Finally, under pressure from bank regulators, Bankers Trust reluctantly agreed to amend certain financial statements and publicly confess this serious lapse in its controls.

With an $80 million markdown in profits, yet with no one being blamed or taking the blame, the Andy Krieger affair remains an unsolved mystery in the financial world.

Other mysteries followed it.

Consider the case of AIG, the big insurance company that decided to plunge into the market for long-term, high-risk swaps and other financial hedges. AIG recruited former Drexel Burnham Lambert executives to create a new group, AIG Financial Products Corporation (AIGFP), in 1987. Howard Sosin, a former professor at the Columbia Business School who had established Drexel's swap group, led the new venture.

AIGFP quickly established a reputation as an organization willing to take risks no one else would touch. People developing mining and industrial projects looked to AIGFP for interest rate insurance policies. For most banks, seven to ten years was considered a long-term commitment for an interest rate swap. AIGFP was willing to offer interest rate protection for three decades and more.

AIGFP had few competitors, and prospered. By 1991, it had even established its own bank, Banque AIG, in Paris. However, not all was well with the group. Sosin's subordinates had begun to write memos to him warning of the high level of risk he was taking. According to press reports, Sosin ignored the warnings. Eventually, word reached AIG chairman Hank Greenberg. When Greenberg attempted to get an accounting of the risks the subsidiary was taking, Sosin rebuffed him. In order to find out what risks his own company was taking, Greenberg had to put together what the trade magazine *Investment Dealers Digest* called "a shadow unit: a covert operation of auditors, derivatives experts and other professionals to infiltrate Sosin's operation and learn what kind of risks were being taken."[39] The shadow group rented office space and put together a computer system similar to Sosin's. They surreptitiously obtained copies of all of AIGFP's computer tapes and ran their own analysis. Their findings were never made public, but Sosin left the company. In 1994, the consulting firm Capital Markets Risk Advisors, Inc., estimated AIG's pretax losses on swaps at $90 million.

Shortly after AIG's problems came to light, a disturbingly similar scenario played out at Metallgesellschaft, the German industrial group whose $1.3 billion in losses rang alarm bells throughout the European banking industry. To this day the facts of the Metallgesellschaft story are murky. There are two radically different versions of what went on. Was Metallgesellschaft's supervisory board deceived by a rogue trader, as the company and Deutsche Bank contend? Or was the rogue in fact a genius, as a group of American financial economists led by Nobel laureate Merton Miller maintain? Did the board's crisis-management team defuse a ticking time bomb by selling off the trader's derivative positions, or was his carefully balanced and profitable business wrecked by the board's ignorant and festinate actions? Who ruined Metallgesellschaft and risked an international financial crisis?

The whole truth of the Metallgesellschaft story is now unfolding piecemeal, behind closed doors, in courtrooms and confidential arbitration hearings. What has been made public is enough to raise serious questions about how well banks and corporate managers really understand the risks of the new financial market into which they have allowed their institutions to be led.

The obscure figure at the heart of the Metallgesellschaft saga was Art Benson, described as 5 feet 5 inches tall, 195 pounds, and a family man who employed his wife, brother, son, and daughter in his oil trading operation.[40] In a lawsuit filed in 1987, Benson had been sued by his brokerage firm for reneging on margin payments. His defense attorneys in that suit described him as an aggressive speculator "caught up in an addiction to the market . . . [whose] decisions became, with regard to the market, irrational."[41] His addiction was apparently no bar to employment.

According to *Euromoney* magazine, Benson marketed oil contracts for Metallgesellschaft during the 1980s and reportedly lost $50 million before being made "redundant" in 1988.[42] He then joined Louis Dreyfus Energy, where his luck changed. In August 1990, Benson had bought long-term oil futures and was losing money on them, when Saddam Hussein happened to invade Kuwait. Oil futures prices suddenly soared, and Benson reportedly made a quick $500 million.[43]

His old boss at Metallgesellschaft Refining and Marketing (MGRM), a U.S. subsidiary of the German multinational, invited him back and staked the whole net worth of Metallgesellschaft's worldwide operations on Benson's theory about the oil futures market. Benson reportedly believed that he had discovered a sure way to make money, by exploiting a phenomenon called *backwardation*. Longer-dated oil futures—those that will not expire for a while—usually sell for less money than do short-dated oil futures. So it is often possible to make money by purchasing a long-dated futures contract, holding it until it is about to expire, then selling it for a profit. "When a futures market is in backwardation, the market is in effect saying that the spot price is eventually going to fall. In the particular case of crude oil, the backwardation can be considered the market's judgment that OPEC's cartel pricing was unsustainable over the long run and prices would some day collapse," wrote Merton Miller and doctoral candidate Christopher Culp.[44]

MGRM reportedly used the basic idea of backwardation as the foundation for a unique business strategy. The company offered to supply gasoline and heating oil to customers under fixed-price contracts that ran as long as ten years. In order to hedge these commitments, MGRM bought *one-month* futures, sold them at the end of each month, and bought the next month's futures.[45] Hedging ten-year supply contracts with one-month futures is very unorthodox. According to Miller and Culp, it can work, provided the hedger has enough cash. Sometimes the hedger will lose money on futures contracts, but that's the nature of hedging. When the hedge loses money, it means that the underlying supply business is doing well.

In MGRM's case, if the theory of permanent backwardation proved correct, the company would always make money by selling the high-value, short-dated futures and buying cheaper, longer-dated futures. What's more, the futures contracts would protect the company from increases in oil prices that could otherwise make the long-term oil supply contracts unprofitable.

For a while everything seemed to work. Customers flocked to MGRM for the best long-term oil and gas contracts around. By November 1993, MGRM had committed to supply gas stations, mom and pop home heating oil delivery services, and other customers with diesel fuel, gasoline, and heating oil that added up to the equivalent of 160 million barrels of crude oil.[46]

It takes Kuwait almost three months to pump that much oil.

Success carried the seeds of disaster, however. MGRM needed to hedge all those contracts. Traders discovered that, regular as clockwork, MGRM came to market every month to sell immense volumes of very short-dated futures and buy immense volumes of slightly longer-dated futures. So the traders refused to buy the short-term futures unless the price came down, and refused to sell long-term futures unless the price went up.[47] Meanwhile, the market's doubts about OPEC's price discipline were justified. "As OPEC managers became deadlocked on reaching production quotas in late 1993, the spot price tumbled in accordance with the expectations reflected in the inverted market," Miller and Culp wrote.[48] Now prices on short-dated futures were lower than prices on longer-dated futures. There's a technical name for this situation: Instead of backwardation, the market was now in *contango*.

MGRM had expected to make money by buying longer-dated futures and holding them until they were about to expire, then selling them at a profit. But the contango meant that MGRM was instead buying longer-dated futures and then selling them for *less* money when they were about to expire. The company estimates that contango losses alone totaled $20 million to $30 million per month during the last quarter of 1993.[49]

On December 1, 1993, Ronaldo Schmitz, a board member of

Deutsche Bank and chairman of Metallgesellschaft's supervisory board, received a disturbing phone call from a reporter who was following up rumors of losses by the company's New York subsidiary. That, Schmitz says, was his first indication that something was amiss.[50] He wasted no time: by December 17, the supervisory board took control of MGRM and began to liquidate the futures contracts.

According to Nobel laureate Miller, that decision was disastrous. "Unfortunately for MGRM, the supervisory board and creditors of its parent may not have fully understood the nature and risks of the hedging strategy it chose."[51] When oil prices fell, MGRM's hedge lost money—but its underlying business was better off. By getting rid of the futures contracts, the board removed MGRM's only protection against a rise in oil prices. Remember, MGRM had signed contracts to deliver 160 million barrels of oil at fixed prices. As luck would have it, prices did rise. It now cost Metallgesellschaft more cash to buy oil to deliver to its customers according to the terms of those supply contracts. If Metallgesellschaft had stood behind the trader, this might not have been a problem, Miller says. In the long term, the trader's futures contracts would have protected the underlying cash business and the strategy would have been vindicated.[52] In other words, MGRM faced a classic gambler's-ruin problem. Although the company would have made money in the long run, it lost so much in the short run that it could not continue to play.

Within a month, one of the biggest financial salvage efforts in modern European history was lurching into place. Metallgesellschaft's lenders vied to distance themselves from the fiasco. Deutsche Bank and Dresdner, the company's biggest shareholder banks, put together a 3.4 billion deutsche mark ($1.97 billion) rescue package to keep the company out of bankruptcy, and twisted arms to get other banks and shareholders on board. Some banks refused to cooperate, and others challenged the deal in court, but eventually it went through.

Was Art Benson a rogue or a genius? The lesson of Metallgesellschaft is more than one in hedging mechanics. It is also a lesson about management. Metallgesellschaft's supervisory board claims not to have known about Benson's trades until their company was already teetering on the edge of insolvency. The bankers who financed Metallgesellschaft were even more in the dark. They had lent to what they thought was a solid, old industrial company, never imagining that they, too, were really backing a trader whose own attorneys had described him as irrationally addicted to the markets. Perhaps his irrationality was the divine madness—the genius—and perhaps Benson's subtle vision had eluded the less illumined souls in the higher bureaucracy of Metallgesellschaft. If Miller is correct, when Metallgesellschaft's management acted, they turned a management communication problem into an international financial disaster.

Close on the heels of the Metallgesellschaft crisis came a string of other, scarcely believable failures of management. More companies were discovered to have engaged in highly risky financial transactions without really understanding them, and losses mounted. Yet one of the most graphic demonstrations of inadequate management occurred at a distinguished Wall Street house long admired for its financial sophistication and market might.

In April 1994, General Electric Company's Kidder Peabody, the conglomerate's brokerage unit, revealed that fully $350 million of its reported revenues had never existed. According to a report commissioned by Kidder Peabody, they had been created out of thin air by a trader who had entered false data into the company's computers.[53]

In July 1991, after short stays as a junior trader with two other New York firms, Morgan Stanley and CS First Boston, Joseph Jett had joined Kidder. His colleagues dubbed him "the human piranha" for his aggressive pursuit of profits.[54] Soon he was promoted to head government bond trader and had received a $9 million bonus. His sudden change of luck apparently didn't strike anyone as in any way questionable. Jett has told reporters for several newspapers that he did not do anything that was not approved by his supervisors.

Legal Risk

Though operational risks were shocking, even well-managed institutions faced dangerous threats from sudden changes in law and the interpretation of laws. Traders may deceive their managers, or the competitive dynamic of the market may carry some institutions beyond the pale of safe and sound practice, but all finance depends on legally enforceable contracts. The foundations of the whole system could crumble if courts ruled these contracts illegal. In 1990, that very unthinkable nightmare began to come true.

Hammersmith and Fulham is a London borough with a population about the same as that of Dayton, Ohio, in the United States. When Maggie Thatcher swung her budget ax at local authorities in the 1980s, she cut off their power to raise taxes to fund social welfare spending. Hammersmith and Fulham didn't want to stop spending and devised an ingenious plan to replace the lost tax revenue.

British local authorities could borrow from the British government at special, low fixed interest rates. So Hammersmith and Fulham borrowed from the government, then went to banks and entered into interest rate swaps. It agreed to pay the banks a floating interest rate, and the banks agreed to pay Hammersmith and Fulham the fixed rate that prevailed in the markets. The township made money because the fixed rate it received from the bank was higher than the fixed rate it had to pay the government on its borrowings. The floating rate that Hammersmith and Fulham paid the bankers was even lower.

Hammersmith and Fulham found swaps so profitable that in 1986–87, the township put on approximately £5 billion worth, measured in notional principal. In fact, swap dealers credited Hammersmith and Fulham with generating about 25 percent of all the interest rate swaps in Great Britain.[55] Banks were delighted to get the business, and the local authority spread it around generously, using as many as fifty banks to execute its transactions.

Hammersmith and Fulham wasn't the only local authority pursuing this strategy. In fact, officials of local authorities were about the only people in England willing to make a commitment to receive fixed rates and pay floating rates. Everyone else thought this was too risky because British interest rates were likely to go up.

In 1988, interest rates did go up steeply, and continued to rise. Soon Hammersmith and Fulham owed the banks over £150 million on its swaps. Hammersmith and Fulham sought legal advice. Its lawyer said that the swaps were probably illegal. The British government had convened a panel to examine the swap activity of local authorities, and this panel had concluded that local authorities didn't have the power to enter swaps. In legal terminology, the swaps were *ultra vires*. So the district auditor took the township to court—in order to prevent Hammersmith and Fulham from paying the banks.

Jonathan Asquith, an attorney with the British bank Morgan Grenfell, recalled in a 1990 panel discussion, "Well, funny thing, this district auditor goes to court and says 'Hammersmith and Fulham's done wrong. Shouldn't have entered into all these contracts. Acted illegally.

Acted wrongly.' And what do Hammersmith and Fulham say? They're saying, 'Oh, it's a fair cop, guv'nor. You're absolutely right. We shouldn't a' done it. Shit!' "[56]

The judge ruled that not only were Hammersmith and Fulham's swaps illegal, but all swaps by all local authorities in England were illegal. Banks appealed the decision and won a partial reversal, but the local authority appealed again to the House of Lords. In 1991, the local authority established to the satisfaction of the House of Lords that it had engaged in a pattern of illegal conduct over a period of years. The House of Lords ruled that all swaps entered into by all local authorities were *ultra vires* and therefore void. International banks lost about £550 million on this decision, though it was good news for Hammersmith and Fulham's taxpayers, who would have faced additional taxes of as much as £1,700 each had the swaps been ruled legal.[57]

The lessons of Hammersmith and Fulham were not entirely lost on the industry, but, like the lessons of the Andy Krieger affair, they were not entirely taken to heart either. In the United States, in 1994 a smattering of lawsuits challenged the appropriateness of high-risk financial transactions for pension funds, municipalities, and even large multinational corporations. A report by the U.S. Government Accounting Office (GAO) noted that many derivatives contracts could be ruled illegal.[58] In other countries, a case could be made that some of the new financial contracts violated laws against gambling or fraud.

However, lobbying action by the industry was slowly and steadily winning victories and eliminating legal barriers to the enforceability of its contracts. Ernest Patrikis, executive vice president and chief counsel of the Federal Reserve Bank of New York, said, "The one thing I can see that's happening in a number of countries is there's competition in legislative action in trying to deal with these issues. Everyone wants their financial system to be safer and sounder, so statutes like those against fraud, bucket shops, and so forth, are slowly and steadily being addressed. We're having competition in legislation to make the legal foundation for these transactions more solid. That's a good thing, That's not competition in laxity—that's competition in developing a solid foundation of commercial law."[59]

Of course, nothing comes without a price. Making the world safe for financial transactions was not everyone's priority. Put to a vote, publicly and openly, financial interests would not always prevail over others. Lobbying by banks, trading houses, exchanges, corporations, and others with a vested interest in the new risk industry ensured that in some of the most important cases, people would pay the price without knowing that they were paying.

The most obvious example of this was the Arkansas Best story, which found the IRS engaged in an unlikely campaign to overrule a decision of the U.S. Supreme Court, circumvent congressional budget processes, and deliver a $2 billion tax break to America's biggest corporations.[60]

In 1988, the high court rejected an appeal of a tax levy against a holding company named Arkansas Best. The company had purchased a bank. As long as the bank stock was going up, the company claimed that the investment was a speculation in order to get capital gains treatment. At that time, capital gains taxes were lower than ordinary income taxes. However, after going up for a while, the bank stock suddenly went down. Arkansas Best then tried to deduct the losses, claiming that the investment in the bank was no longer speculative, but rather part of its overall business.

For thirty years, it had been the established practice of courts and the accepted policy of the IRS to allow companies to "whipsaw" the government thus. In his opinion on the Arkansas Best case, Justice Thurgood Marshall reversed thirty years of tax history with a stroke of his pen. He said that except in very narrowly defined circumstances, the law gave no tax breaks to hedging. He effectively defined almost all of the financial transactions associated with risk management as outright speculations. Incidentally, he gave the IRS a license to go after back taxes and penalties.

Oddly, uncharacteristically, the IRS did not leap at the chance to collect these taxes. Instead of aggressively moving against the corporations and banks that had hedged, the IRS policymakers tried to find a way to restore the old laissez-faire system of corporate taxation. "The policy perspective on this issue was that it would never have been appropriate to collect this tax," said one former IRS policymaker. "I have heard people say that if they went out and collected all of these deficiencies, they'd send people into bankruptcy."[61]

In fact, a preliminary survey by the IRS showed that companies faced tax adjustments of at least $2 billion as a result of the ruling. According to data obtained from IRS internal documents and published by *Corporate Finance* magazine in 1991, General Motors faced $654 million in tax adjustments, the Federal Home Loan Mortgage Corporation had a $582 million adjustment pending, and the Federal National Mortgage Association was fighting a $124 million adjustment.[62] Kellogg, the cereal maker, and Arkla, a utility whose chairman would later become President Bill Clinton's first chief of staff, were also on the hook for back taxes as a result of Arkansas Best.

Financial lobbyists worked on the Treasury Department and the Congress, trying to come up with some kind of legislative solution. Treasury and IRS officials drafted a regulation that would have interpreted Marshall's decision away and restored the status quo ante. However, they were unwilling to promulgate the regulation without congressional backup. Under the Bush administration, the Treasury Department was said to be acutely sensitive to the political appearance of engineering a tax break for big companies, particularly since Congress had just attacked an administration proposal to intensify tax collection efforts against individuals of modest means.

Congress, for its part, refused to offer a legislative solution. Under budget procedures mandated by the Gramm-Rudman-Hollings deficit reduction efforts, if Congress granted a tax break to anyone, it had to find a way to pay for it, either by cutting another program or by raising taxes. Politicians would find it difficult to explain to retirees that their social security payments were being cut to provide a tax break to General Motors.

So instead of devising a solution, both the IRS and Congress decided to let the matter be decided by the courts. Fannie Mae and Freddie Mac, the twin pillars of the American mortgage industry, both had massive tax liabilities as a result of the Supreme Court decision. Fannie Mae went to the U.S. Tax Court to contest the IRS auditor's opinion of its liabilities.

The IRS fought the suit, albeit tepidly. "I know the trial attorney on many occasions has thrown up his hands in frustration and said, 'What am I supposed to do? I don't know what our position is,'" recalled Kenneth Jones, formerly the large-case program manager at the IRS.[63]

In 1993, the tax court ruled that Fannie Mae was right. Seizing on the opinion, the IRS reacted as though the tax court had overturned the Supreme Court's Arkansas Best decision. Regulations issued after the Fannie Mae decision made it clear that most common business hedges would not be subject to the draconian tax treatment that a literal reading of Supreme Court justice Marshall's Arkansas Best decision would require.

The risk-management industry applauded. William J. Brodsky, chairman and chief executive officer of the Chicago Mercantile Exchange, boasted in the exchange's 1993 annual report that "in the Arkansas Best matter, finally resolved on October 19, we, along with a large coalition of financial institutions, corporations and agri-businesses, ultimately convinced key Washington policymakers, including Treasury Secretary Lloyd Bentsen, that the IRS should treat losses and gains related to hedging consistently as 'ordinary,' and not 'capital,' and therefore not subject to a $3,000 per year deduction limit. . . . We are now actively working on new rules that will harmonize the 'Fannie Mae' decision and the Treasury Department's revised guidelines with the interpretation we have long advocated."[64]

In the spring of 1994, the hidden risks and linkages between markets began to break through the surface at last. The Fed had raised interest rates slightly at the end of 1993. The ensuing market turmoil was far out of proportion to the magnitude of the rate hike and inflicted massive losses on hedge funds, banks, and other financial institutions. Regulators and market professionals were taken by surprise. The central bankers at the Fed had become accustomed to driving monetary policy like an old Ford. They knew from decades of experience that if they stepped on the accelerator by lowering short-term rates, they could eventually expect to see economic activity pick up. Similarly, if they pumped the brake by raising short-term interest rates, the economy would gradually slow. In 1993, the economy was growing fast enough to make inflation a real threat. As a consequence, investors in long-term bonds were beginning to demand higher interest rates to compensate them for the losses they expected inflation to cost them.

The Fed tapped the brakes by raising interest rates ever so slightly. Yet its passengers flew through the windshield. Both long- and short-term interest rates went up immediately. Ten-year treasury bond interest rates surged so high that they were only slightly lower than thirty-year rates.

In a forbidding, gray stone edifice on Liberty Street in lower Manhattan, economists were puzzled. They began to investigate the sudden strange behavior of the economy, and much to their surprise, they discovered that the key to the mystery was buried in the mortgage securities market.

In fact, the mortgage refinancing habits of American homeowners had so magnified the Fed's small adjustment in interest rates that even the government bond market trembled from the shock.[65]

Homeowners had been refinancing mortgages to save as little as a percentage point in interest payments. When the Fed raised short-term rates a notch, and signaled its willingness to raise them more, the markets looked immediately to the effect on mortgage prepayments. Odds were good that those savvy homeowners wouldn't be refinancing their homes with rates moving up. That meant that fewer mortgages would be prepaid. Investors who'd bought mortgage securities did some quick calculations. When interest rates had been headed down, a mortgage security may have had an average duration of two and a half to three years. Homeowners were likely to refinance faster as rates moved down, and when they refinanced, they effectively "retired" a lot of mortgage securities. Now, with rates headed up, the refinancing boom was probably over. Homeowners would be likely to hold on to their mortgages. That meant that mortgage securities would last longer.

Investors usually hedge their mortgage securities by selling treasury bonds short. To hedge their investment in short-duration mortgage securities, they'd sold short-term Treasury securities. Now that the mortgage securities looked more like long-term investments, they had to sell short the long-term treasury bonds.

So mortgage securities investors suddenly started shorting long-term treasury bonds en masse. A glut of long-term bonds hit the market at once. Lots of people wanting to sell, and not many people looking to buy meant that long-term bond prices dropped. When bond prices fell, interest rates rose, by definition. That's how a slight adjustment to short-term interest rates wreaked havoc on the markets.

The Fed economists had never seen anything like it. No one had really paid much attention to the mortgage securities market before. Now it was driving the monetary transmission mechanism.

Worse, the apparent breakdown in what everyone thought were well-understood relationships between financial markets confirmed a fear that had been gnawing at some regulators for years: that no one really understood how the financial system worked. After all, if an investor in long-term treasury bonds could be impoverished by some event in the mortgage derivative markets, how could anyone predict anything anymore?

The old rules no longer applied. It wasn't just that the markets had gotten bigger or more volatile. The markets were behaving in ways that no one had ever predicted they could. The financial system used to be a honeycomb of compartmentalized cells. The cells were labeled banks, insurance companies, hedge funds, mutual funds, pension funds, savings and loans, domestic markets, foreign markets, stock markets, bond markets, commodity markets, and so forth. Each cell contained a particular kind of institution that took particular, well-defined, and clearly understood risks.

Now the walls between the cells had broken down. No one really understood what risks any institution was taking.

The new markets had been designed to transfer risk from businesses and investors who sought safety to those willing and able to bear risk—ideally, sophisticated traders and financial institutions with the technology to manage it prudently. Yet the December 1994, Orange County, California, bankruptcy showed that risk moved just as easily to those least able to bear it. Like Hammersmith and Fulham, the British local authority that had rocked the international financial markets a few years earlier, Orange County had relied on a high-risk interest rate speculation to fund its ambitious spending programs. When interest rates shifted, the county's portfolio suddenly lost about 27 percent of its value, or about $2 billion. County officials estimated that as many as 1,700 jobs would have to be eliminated. Much of the money lost had belonged to school districts and agencies required by law to invest in the county's fund. So the risk shed by others was borne by the schoolchildren, workers, and taxpayers of Orange County. If they did not fully understand the risk they were taking, they were hardly alone.

Financial reports had once been very useful to people who wanted to understand whether or not a particular institution was financially healthy. Now the old financial reports weren't very useful. They had been designed to cope with a whole different environment. Regulators worried about the lack of "transparency" in the financial system. Not only was it difficult for them to figure out what was happening inside the banks and other institutions they regulated. Clearly, in many cases, the chief executives of the biggest institutions couldn't themselves understand what risks they were taking.

In 1993, an extraordinary series of coincidences opened a window on the foreign exchange operations of a major options trading bank, ABN

Amro. A trader who had been brought on by the bank to establish its presence in the New York market went to trial on criminal charges for falsifying options volatilities in order to conceal losses from his managers. Because the trader had been taped discussing this fraud with his trading assistant, it was fully documented. In fact, the ABN Amro case shows more clearly than any other the weaknesses of a financial system that is more efficient than any financial system in history, but may also be more vulnerable to moral hazard than ever before.

The following account of the fraud at ABN Amro draws material from transcripts of those taped conversations, from statements of witnesses who testified under oath at the trader's trial, and from interviews the author subsequently conducted with the trader, his assistant, and lawyers involved in the case.

EPILOGUE

IT AIN'T NO BIG THING
(BUT IT'S GROWING)

U.S. v. James Martignoni, 92 Cr. 1097 (JFK). They called him Elvis because he did a really wicked Elvis impersonation in New York's karaoke bars. When he wasn't doing Elvis, he was wheeling and dealing and joking to her in his soft Australian accent. He was tall, glamorous, dashing, and as good as rich. He defended her and sheltered her when the rough New York Italians on the trading floor made cutting remarks about her. When he was mad, he could string together obscenities in ways she'd never heard before. Yet he said he needed her, she was his lifeline, he depended on her, and when she wanted to leave for another job, he asked her not to go. He was a big gambler, she said. Currencies were the biggest casino in the world, he said.

It had been a very good year for him, trading currency options for one of the world's biggest banks, ABN Amro of the Netherlands. He was ABN Amro in New York, when it came to options. Life is funny sometimes. He'd joined the bank late in 1990, only twenty-six years old with hardly any experience, just a year at Bankers Trust in Australia and then a couple of years at a bank in Boston that really wasn't much of a trading bank. He didn't like the bank in Boston because they didn't let him take much risk there. He felt stifled. He left by mutual agreement after he made a mistake pricing a corporate trade. The

259

mistake cost the bank about $10,000, he says. He went to California for several months, thought about dropping out, but came back to join ABN Amro as a vice president making a six-figure salary with a chance for big bonuses. ABN Amro's brass wanted Elvis to put them on the New York map, make them a force in currency options in the Big Apple, because they were known for currency options worldwide, but not in New York yet.

Elvis wanted to gamble. He was hooked on trading, he admits it, but he won so big that his boss said proudly, "We've got our own little Andy Krieger here." He pushed around big numbers, he was a real heavy trader, brokers were always calling to take him out to dinner, and sometimes she got to go along.

Treat Me Nice

She was just plain Kristen, a clerk with a weight problem and a bachelor's degree in anthropology from a college in New Jersey who had followed instructions all her life. She followed them well enough to be moved from the bank's back office to the actual trading floor. When Elvis joined the bank, she was assigned to be his trading assistant. She did his paperwork for him, kept track of the trading tickets and the calls, and fed the computer a daily blizzard of numbers. The computer was called FENICS, short for Foreign Exchange Nuclear Interstellar Computer System. She was diffident and acutely self-conscious because she had a terrible, terrible disorder, something like dyslexia, that caused her to occasionally reverse the order of numbers. In June 1991, she put an options trade in backwards and cost the bank a half million dollars just like that. Everyone knew that she made a lot of mistakes, but she was honest and meant well, and options clerks were hard to find, so she just went on being painfully aware of her faults. That was, in its way, very useful.

One day, Elvis turned to Kristen in his likable way and said she should run a quick program to check the value of his options portfolio. She ran it, and it showed a $20 million loss. This was in September 1991. He saw the loss and said, Kristen, this is terrible, don't tell anyone, people will lose their jobs if you do. She knew that "people" meant Elvis and Kristen.

Big Boss Man

The boss was an old-fashioned, seat-of-the-pants spot trader, not too educated. Kristen used to chuckle to herself when the boss tried to use big words and they came out wrong. But she was really scared of him. He weighed almost three hundred pounds, she said, and one day when his assistant was out, she had to substitute. She told him she didn't understand spot trading jargon, so he should just say "buy" when he wanted her to buy and "sell" when he wanted her to sell. The markets got hot. He said "give" when the dollar moved; she bought, but he meant just the opposite. "Give" meant sell in spot trading jargon, and now the dollar crashed and crashed. He grabbed the desk and screamed, his knuckles white, his face all red. She was afraid he'd hit her, so she ran and ran and ran.

Later, the boss apologized. He always came back and tried to make it up, she says. He joked to her, saying, Kristen, we ought to go on a diet together.

She says: Some people are sensitive and some people aren't, and you get the line that if you're sensitive, then what are you doing in a trading room? But there's no reason for that; he knew how I felt about him. One day, the boss came and said, Kristen, you think I'm a prick, don't you, and she said, Yes, I do.

Now she feared in her heart that she herself had caused this problem with Elvis's portfolio, because she knew she had trouble with numbers, and now there was a $20 million loss.

All Shook Up

Elvis knew how to fix it, though. The most important factor in valuing an option is a judgment called volatility. Volatility is the probability of a change in the price. For example, an option that gave Elvis the right to sell guilders for dollars was worth more if the prices were jumping around than if they were constant. Volatility is a slippery number. Since nobody knows the future, nobody can be sure what is the chance that an option price will change in the future. So Elvis decided to fix the $20 million loss by raising his estimate of volatility, so the bank's computer model would use the high volatility to calculate a high price for the options, and thus eliminate any evidence of the loss. No one would know what the options were really worth until he sold them, and he could just hang on to them and not sell them until the market changed, went his way again. That's the ticket. That's what he did. That's what Kristen had to tell the court, and that's what the prosecutors proved to the jury.

Elvis remembers it differently. Yes, he inflated volatilities, he says, but he had a good reason. He still doesn't think he lost money. Even the day before he began his jail sentence, on June 29, 1994, he was asking, Why won't the bank just show me how I lost? Then I could sleep at night. He was a trader, not an accountant. Accounting was the job of the back office. His job was to make money trading. He thought he was making money all along. Even when the $20 million loss turned to $70 million.

When My Blue Moon Turns to Gold Again

But Kristen said under oath he'd told her to throw away the report with the $20 million loss. He gave Kristen high volatility numbers, and she entered them into the reports, and she turned the reports in to the usual people, and the loss disappeared like magic, and Kristen was happy because she had after all not caused Elvis to lose his job, and Elvis was happy.

Even the bosses at ABN Amro were happy. They didn't understand options at all, they admitted under oath later, but they saw that Elvis was making a lot of money in the options trading business. It was right there in black and white on Kristen's reports.

They were so happy that one day the boss called him aside for one of those talks bosses like to have with promising young employees. He told Elvis that he had done so well the bank was going to award him a $200,000 bonus. Not only that, but the boss wanted Elvis to accompany him to headquarters in Amsterdam, to take it easy for two weeks, meeting the top management of the bank. Elvis was a star.

It's Now or Never

Only one thing, the boss said. Since we're going to be gone for a while, why don't you sell your options now, take the profits, and then we won't have anything to worry about when we're gone.

Elvis returned to his desk, still smiling, but inwardly, who knows how he felt? He never testified at his trial. There had been a problem not long ago with a young accountant who had gotten curious about the high volatility numbers on the deutsche mark and guilder options. Elvis had told him, patiently, with a soft accent and a cocked smile, in the nicest possible way, that after all, there was this computer problem and somehow the computer program the bank was using just didn't produce results anything like the real market prices, so if Elvis used low volatility numbers, well, the books would not really be accurate, because nobody bought or sold options for such low prices as that. So in order to make the results come out realistic, he just used a higher volatility estimate, that's all. The young accountant was charmed, and went away reassured. Everybody liked Elvis, everybody trusted him.

I Really Don't Want to Know

After all, who was there to question him? ABN Amro may have been one of the world's most sophisticated dealers in currency options, but Elvis's boss didn't even read the foot-high stack of papers he got each day from the back office. Elvis says everything he did was in those papers all along. He says he never made any secret of his volatility estimates. He told the accountant, and he told his boss, and he put in those papers that the estimates were high. He even gave them the phone numbers of three outside brokers they could call if they wanted to check his volatilities. They never made the calls. The prosecutors conceded all of this at the trial. Of course, the bank was negligent, they said. As to those things, there really is no dispute. ABN Amro's accounting department could have prevented much of the damage. But, ladies and gentlemen, that does not excuse Mr. Martignoni. Don't fall into the trap of blaming the victim, the prosecutor told the jury at last.

Elvis never knew whether or not he was making money, he says. It was their job to tell him. But the boss never read any of the papers. This all came out at the trial. Also, it came out that Elvis and Kristen marked with a special code the reports they kept on their desks, using asterisks and triangles instead of zeros to hide the size of his cash trades and make them appear hedged against options, just in case the boss walked around the room and looked over their shoulders. Elvis was trading way beyond his trading limit, but nobody noticed or seemed to care, even though there was no way to hide the size of his cash trades from the accountants in the back office if they'd bothered to look, or from his boss if he'd bothered to read the reports. But the boss never read those.

Money Honey

Poor Kristen. It was all her fault.

Elvis knew his boss wanted him to get rid of the options, and almost all of the high volatility options were deutsche mark options, and those were the ones the young accountant had asked about, so Elvis sold them, got rid of them all, out the door, poof. He bought at the same time about a billion pounds of sterling options, though. Pound sterling options weren't very volatile before Elvis bought them. Then he marked up the vol. He paid about $4 million for the options, but when he marked up the vol, they looked to be worth almost $45 million on his books. The sudden gain in his pound sterling options more than wiped out the losses he had taken on getting rid of the overvalued deutsche mark options.

Poor Kristen. She was out sick when he put on the sterling options. When she came back, she noticed them on the FENICS. There was no time to talk with Elvis; he was about to leave with his boss for the headquarters in Amsterdam.

It was being a lovely trip. But then poor Kristen, alone in New York, who didn't know how to trade, got a call from the boss, the loud man with the violent temper who broke a telephone every week because he just exploded.

Suspicious Minds

The accountants had noticed the new sterling trades, and they were curious about the high volatilities. They were talking to the boss. The boss hadn't read the reports, he was a seat-of-the-pants guy, so he said, Look, if they just sell one of these options at a value close to what's in the book, then that should prove what we need to know. Since Elvis was gone, Kristen had to sell the options. Where to sell them? Elvis had written in such high volatility numbers, no one in the world would buy for those prices. She called Elvis, tearful, hysterical almost, in a panic about the options she had to sell—what could she do, it was all her fault, maybe she should just quit the bank and take responsibility for it all herself, maybe that would save him. She offered to be his scapegoat.

No, no, he said.

I Slipped, I Stumbled, I Fell

He had to stall for time; he couldn't let the bank find out about those losses now. He said: Put the sterling closing rate in at the guilder vol. Move the long-end U.S. interest rates up. Move the spot up.

She did it. Later, they talked again. There's a 20 million dollar loss, she said.

Well, why don't you just do what I told you to.

It's down twenty-two . . . which is what I expected when I moved the sterling vols down. I told you it would be down about twenty-two, she said. Do you want me to move Canada up a bit? They're not even looking at that.

No, that's not going to be enough, he said, Um, those sterling options that we did today, what are they showing, higher losses?

Well, not with . . . my creative inputting . . . that's going to have to show up tomorrow . . . someone's going to say . . . You put the premium in wrong . . . I figure the back office is not going to check out with Bankers Trust tonight if I wait long enough . . . maybe I should move the decimal point on the premium, she said.

She'd recently made a mistake, moving the decimal point on a sales ticket. Rather than correcting it, she realized that if she just made the same mistake on five additional sales tickets, she could continue to hide the loss. It would look as if she'd sold the options for ten times what they were really worth, just by moving the decimal point.

Don't worry, just relax, he said.

I can't relax, she said. If I lose my job, I don't have any money, I don't have anything.

That's Alright

Kristen, I'll give you money, don't worry about that, he said, I've got money for you, alright? I told you I've got fifty grand for—I've already got the money for you . . . don't cry. Please compose your—if they come and see you crying, they'll know something's wrong. . . .

Um, do you know what I'm going to do? I'm going to say, Shoot, I screwed these up on the decimal points, on the sterling, or I'm just going to have to misinput something, or something, I don't know, she said, I'm going to have to misinput a trade somehow in a different currency. What if I misinput a mark trade?

No, he said, misinput a sterling one. Can you do that? Put in like a—put in like a wrong premium, he said.

Elvis said she should talk to a girl in the back office who sends out confirmations, and get her to agree to the phony number without trying to confirm it.

Hound Dog

Elvis was panicking. Things were unraveling. The boss, all 275 pounds of mad Italian boss, livid and crazed, stood inches from his face, screaming You scum of the earth, You scum of the earth, over and over, so close spit sprayed on Elvis's face.

Back in New York, the girl in the back office said she wouldn't go along with them. She said she'd lose her job if she did that.

Poor Kristen. I'm just loyal, she said, I'm like a golden retriever, throw me a bone and I'm loyal for life.

Heartbreak Hotel

The boss and Elvis flew back to New York, and stayed up all night in a hotel room, on the telephone all night, then went into the office the next day to clean up the book.

Elvis made a motion that he had to go out for cigarettes. He left the office, flew back to Boston to his wife and home. His wife works in the district attorney's office there, she's a prosecutor, she knew a good defense lawyer. The next time the boss heard from Elvis, it was through his lawyer, he says.

The bank filed a form reporting that a crime had happened. The bank didn't want to file the form. It just happened that a bank regulator had been sniffing around, trying to get information, because the bank wanted to acquire an S&L and he heard about the options problem and said they had to file the form. So, reluctantly, they did.

The case of *U.S.* v. *James Martignoni* had begun. No one called him Elvis anymore.

In the Ghetto

It was a curious bank, ABN Amro. The U.S. attorney who prosecuted Elvis and Kristen for bank fraud didn't make any argument in defense of ABN Amro. It had hired a green, inexperienced trader and had let him violate its policies on trading and marking to market, it hadn't followed up or double-checked, its controls were terrible.

The prosecutor summed up, saying, Look, if you live in a bad neighborhood and never lock the door and one night someone just walks in and steals something or even just goes to sleep on the couch, trespassing, well, of course it's negligent, but does that mean the thief or trespasser is not guilty? Of course not.

By the time ABN Amro realized that the options on James Martignoni's books wouldn't sell for what he said they were worth, the original $20 million loss had turned into a $50 million loss. ABN Amro fired James Martignoni, and fired Kristen, and fired the boss, and brought in an expert from Europe to unwind the book. The ABN Amro expert turned the $50 million loss into a $70 million loss in less than thirty days.

I Forgot to Remember to Forget

James Martignoni went to trial in New York, for bank fraud. The jury listened to the tapes and convicted him in November 1993. He didn't have a chance, really. All those conversations had been on taped lines to the trading floor.

Kristen cooperated fully with the prosecutor. The prosecutor said she had a personal relationship with Martignoni that made it difficult for her to cooperate at first but she quickly overcame the difficulty.

Kristen refuses to discuss the personal relationship. I don't want to hurt his wife, she says.

James Martignoni says Kristen wanted more than a professional relationship, it was obvious several times, but he refused. He has a wonderful wife, he says, an extraordinary woman, if it weren't for her, he might have committed suicide after this.

Jailhouse Rock

Kristen pleaded guilty. The prosecutor wrote a letter to the judge to help her get a lenient sentence. She testified for four full days, the letter said. Her testimony was the culmination of a twenty-two-month investigation. She reviewed the many hours of tapes and hundreds of pages of transcripts approximately a dozen times, explained scores of documents and dozens of complicated foreign exchange options transactions. She constantly made herself available to the government on short notice late at night and on weekends. On occasion, when she had an idea or a lead that she thought might be helpful, she called unsolicited, even after her trial testimony had been completed. She recommended foreign exchange options texts the government used to learn about the business, and at one point, unsolicited, did research to find newspaper articles relating to a person who she believed might be a potential defense witness.

Elvis refused to testify, choosing to exercise his right not to incriminate himself. Kristen got off with two years' probation, but she became very depressed. (I did not feel good about testifying against James, she said, very agitated, when a reporter spoke with her afterward, I still get flashbacks in the middle of the night, it's hell. But I had to do it because I did something wrong and this was the only way I knew to put it right, I couldn't go back in time to fix it.)

James Martignoni went to jail. The prosecutor said that usually somebody who causes a $70 million loss should go to jail for eight to ten years, but give the guy a break. He didn't make any money by causing this loss, the $70 million didn't go into his pocket. He just wanted to hide the loss to keep his job and bonus. So, the prosecutor said, figure his ill-gotten gains were the salary and bonus, not the $70 million. That's why James Martignoni was sentenced to only twenty-one months in prison on sixteen counts of bank fraud.

In June 1994, James Martignoni was packing up to go to Otisville, New York, and do his time. He wanted to appeal his case but said the lawyer was ransacking him, demanding over $100,000 just to file the appeal brief.

The lawyer said it would probably be OK for a writer to write the story as though there would be no appeal.

Kristen was trying to pull her life back together. It's very hard to admit that you've been manipulated, she said, at times I really want to hate him for making me go through what I went through, but sometimes I can and sometimes I can't. My psychiatrist gets paid $130 an hour to try to deal with this with me.

She found a new job, was working on a degree in library science, and taking voice lessons in New York. Five years from now, I want to sing with the Metropolitan Opera, she said. She wants to sing *Carmen*. Or maybe run a library.

So the story isn't over yet.

The boss got a job running foreign exchange for another big European bank in New York.

The accountant got promoted.

Odd. ABN Amro was one of the biggest and most sophisticated banks in the world and one of the most respected dealers in currency options, and yet a green trader nicknamed Elvis and his dyslexic, diffident trading assistant were all it took to hit Holland's biggest bank with a massive loss on options. Where were the controls? Where was the safe, prudent, Dutch bankerly discipline?

———————

This is the Achilles' heel of the new financial order.

James Martignoni called this writer the day before he began his prison sentence.

Look at the volumes that go through the currency markets on a daily basis. Trillions. Trillions of dollars are changing hands. There's no need for that amount of money to change hands. It's the biggest casino in the world. If I'm alleged to lose $70 million as a one-man show where I'm disclosing everything, what's going to happen in a big fund?

The market usually takes care of its own, he said. People stuff trading tickets in drawers, lie, get fired, and get hired somewhere else, all the time. He, on the other hand, disclosed everything. It was all in the papers no one read. He said, Why I was singled out, not even given a chance to see what the bottom line was, I don't know.

The End of the Beginning

Elvis went away, but the rockin' didn't stop.

As James Martignoni was standing trial in Manhattan, a financially unsophisticated school administrator in Chicago sank nearly all of the community college system's $100 million investment fund into mortgage derivative securities so risky that they are called "toxic waste" by finance industry pros. Within months, the fund had lost nearly $39 million. In Texas, another publicly supported junior college lost $22 million on similar investments, leading to the cancellation of sports programs, a 20 percent increase in tuition, a $2 million cut in the budget, and a tax hike for the surrounding community. Even the Shoshone Indian tribe on Wyoming's Wind River reservation was devastated by derivative investment losses.

Elvis was found guilty of committing a fraud against his employers. Over the course of 1994, more frauds were alleged to have been committed by bankers against their *customers*. Not all the alleged victims were unsophisticated. Gibson Greetings, Inc., and Procter & Gamble Company both sued Bankers Trust Company, claiming that the bank had misled them about the safety of the complex hedges they had purchased. Federal securities regulators also launched an investigation of the bank. Bankers Trust denied any wrongdoing, claiming that the companies had been fully informed about the risks of the instruments. Nonetheless, on November 14, the bank announced that five executives involved in the transactions had been "reassigned." On December 23, Bankers Trust agreed to pay a $10 million fine as part of a consent decree with federal securities regulators to settle charges of fraud in connection with the Gibson Greetings transaction.

The world is volatile, and at its best the new financial system that replaced Bretton Woods transfers risk from those unwilling to bear it to those most able to take it on. Yet the markets can also be used to transfer risk to those too ignorant or too greedy to bear it responsibly—sometimes with serious consequences for innocent parties. As news reports of inappropriate investments by school districts, county governments, and other less sophisticated investors proliferated, legislative interest in the new markets grew more intense. It seemed that the markets could be relied upon to enforce one law only—the law of one price—and that morality and ethics were superfluous.

So even before the Orange County debacle, five separate bills had been drafted by congressmen eager to legislate order into the new financial markets. "It has become clear to me that we can't rely on the industry to police itself. Rather, legislation is urgently needed to regulate derivatives,"[1] said Congressman Henry Gonzalez, then-chairman of the House Committee on Banking, Finance and Urban Affairs. Two bills contained an outright ban on derivatives trading by banks unless they established separately capitalized trading companies. Congressmen Gonzalez and Jim Leach co-authored a somewhat less onerous bill that did not require banks to establish separate trading companies, but prohibited them from trading derivatives without a written management plan approved by the board of directors. The Gonzalez-Leach bill also required public disclosure of the reasons why institutions held derivatives, stipulated that all gains and losses on derivatives portfolios should be reported to regulators, and mandated a study of the prospects for international cooperation in regulating the derivative markets, among other requirements. All of the bills died when the 103rd Congress adjourned, but neither Gonzalez nor Leach showed any intention of abandoning the effort to legislate controls for the new markets.

For the most part, the banks and trading houses have strenuously opposed legislation, as have most financial regulators. They argue that the volatile markets in financial risk are evolving so quickly that any legislation written would likely be outdated before the ink was dry. Moreover, the financial system is surprisingly fragile, despite its strength. Some of the more draconian legislative "fixes" could cause a crisis by suddenly removing important participants from the international financial system's risk-transfer mechanism.

Federal Reserve Board Chairman Alan Greenspan spoke with uncharacteristic frankness when he told reporters in London that financial institutions would have to be "self-regulated, largely because government regulators cannot do that job."[2] In New Zealand, the central bank announced a radically new regulatory model. Central bankers usually work behind the scenes to encourage each bank to meet standards of safety and soundness, but New Zealand's innovative policy requires banks to publish openly the information previously provided in confidence to the central bank. In the United States, Federal Reserve Bank of New York President William J. McDonough also called for "reexamination of the division between proprietary and public information."[3] Regulators believed that once full information about risks was publicly available, markets themselves could discipline those institutions that were taking inappropriate risks.

In the autumn of 1994, signs emerged that market discipline was indeed beginning to cause a reappraisal of risk. The bluest of blue-chip banks, J. P. Morgan, offered to share, free of charge, the proprietary model it used to evaluate and control its own financial risk. At large industrial corporations, boards of directors began to look carefully at the policies, procedures, and management practices that governed their use of the new financial technologies. Kodak abandoned its long-standing strategic hedging program, despite the program's historical advantages, without publicly explaining its reasons for doing so. No corporate executive wanted to repeat the experience of Procter & Gamble or Metallgesellschaft, so bankers in New York reported a slowdown in business for the most exotic of the new risk-transfer devices. They hoped it would be temporary.

These are small beginnings, hopeful signs perhaps that the chaos of conquest is subsiding. The vandals have conquered—now it is up to them to rule.

NOTES

Prologue: Rumors of War

1. See Andrew Krieger, *The Money Bazaar* (New York: Times Books, 1992), pp. 61–81.

Chapter 1: The Vandals' Crown

1. Peter L. Bernstein, *Capital Ideas: The Improbable Origins of Modern Wall Street* (New York: Free Press, 1992), p. 203.
2. Arnie Staloff, interviews, August and September 1993.
3. Ibid.
4. Ibid.
5. Ibid.
6. Ibid.
7. Ibid.
8. Arnold F. Staloff, memo to Nicholas A. Giordano regarding options on foreign currencies, February 16, 1982.
9. Gregory J. Millman, *The Floating Battlefield: Corporate Strategies in the Currency Wars* (New York: AMACOM, 1990), p. 52.
10. Staloff interviews.

11. Ibid.

12. Lisa Polsky, interview, November 8, 1993.

13. Ibid.

14. Ibid.

15. Background interview, Bankers Trust Company, November 8, 1993.

16. Background interviews, former Citibank bankers, October 1992, November 1993.

17. Polsky interview.

18. Ibid.

19. Ibid.

20. Andrew Krieger, *The Money Bazaar* (New York: Times Books, 1992), p. 6.

21. Peter Koenig, "A Maverick Breaks into the Forex Club: Malaysia's Central Bank Is Now an Influential Player in Foreign Exchange Markets," *Independent*, November 4, 1990, p. 10.

22. Dominic Casserley, *Facing up to the Risks* (New York: HarperBusiness, 1991), p. 197.

23. Krieger, *Money Bazaar*, p. 104.

24. "Foreign Exchange Outlook," *International Reports*, November 9, 1990, p. 19.

25. Carol Loomis, "How Bankers Trust Lied about $80 Million," *Fortune*, September 7, 1992, p. 78.

26. Fischer Black, interview, August 31, 1993.

27. Ibid.

28. Ibid.

29. Ibid.

30. Paul A. Volcker and Toyoo Gyohten, *Changing Fortunes* (New York: Times Books, 1992), p. 293.

Chapter 2: Cheaters

1. H. Montgomery Hyde, *John Law: The History of an Honest Adventurer* (London: W. H. Allen, 1969), p. 26.

2. Ibid.

3. Ibid.

4. Ibid.

5. Ibid., p. 27.

6. Edgar Faure, *La Banqueroute de Law* (Paris: Editions Gallimard, 1977), p. 12.

7. Robert Minton, *John Law: The Father of Paper Money* (New York: Association Press, 1975), p. 38.

8. Joseph A. Schumpeter, *History of Economic Analysis* (New York: Oxford University Press, 1954), pp. 294–296 and 321–322.

9. Charles P. Kindleberger, *A Financial History of Western Europe* (New York: Oxford University Press, 1993), p. 24.

10. Nathan Sussman, "Debasements, Royal Revenues, and Inflation in France during the Hundred Years' War, 1415–1422," *Journal of Economic History*, vol. 53, no. 1 (March 1993), p. 47.

11. Ibid., p. 44.

12. Ibid., p. 48.

13. Ibid., p. 56.

14. Ibid., p. 45.

15. Ibid., p. 63.

16. Sir Albert Feaveryear, *The Pound Sterling: A History of British Money* (Oxford: Clarendon Press, 1963), p. 84.

17. Angela Redish, "Anchors Aweigh: The Transition from Commodity Money to Fiat Money in Western Economies" (unpublished paper, University of British Columbia, Vancouver, June 1993), pp. 4–5.

18. Feaveryear, *Pound Sterling*, p. 63.

19. Ibid., p. 64.

20. Debra Glassman and Angela Redish, "Currency Depreciation in Early Modern England and France" (Discussion Paper no. 86-04, Department of Economics, University of British Columbia, Vancouver, February 1986), pp. 8–10.

21. Marcello de Cecco, "Gold Standard," in *The New Palgrave: A Dictionary of Economics*, ed. John Eatwell, Murray Milgate, and Peter Newman (London: Macmillan/New York: Stockton Press, 1987), p. 539.

22. Charles Mackay, *Extraordinary Popular Delusions and the Madness of Crowds* (New York: Noonday Press, 1932), p. 6.

23. Hyde, *John Law*, p. 83.

24. Antoin E. Murphy, *Richard Cantillon: Entrepreneur and Economist* (Oxford: Clarendon Press, 1986), p. 77.

25. Ibid., p. 147.

26. Ibid., pp. 149–150.

27. Mackay, *Popular Delusions*, p. 31.

28. Ibid., p. 20.

29. Kindleberger, *Financial History*, p. 100.

30. Michael D. Bordo, "The Gold Standard, Bretton Woods and Other Monetary Regimes: An Historical Appraisal" (Working Paper no. 4310, National Bureau of Economic Research, Cambridge, Mass., April 1993), p. 20.

31. Warren H. Carroll, *The Guillotine and the Cross* (Manassas, Va.: Christendom Press, 1991), p. 139. See also John McManners, *The French Revolution and the Church* (London: Talbot Press [S.P.C.K.], 1969), pp. 100–101.

32. Feaveryear, *Pound Sterling*, p. 193.

33. G. de Vivo, "Ricardo, David," in *The New Palgrave*, p. 540.
34. Charles Dickens, *Oliver Twist* (New York: Marboro Books/Barnes & Noble, 1992), p. 28.
35. Barry Eichengreen, *Golden Fetters: The Gold Standard and the Great Depression, 1919–1939* (New York: Oxford University Press, 1992), p. 6.
36. Ibid., p. 9.
37. Ibid., p. 172.
38. Emile Moreau, *The Golden Franc*, trans. Stephen D. Stoller and Trevor C. Roberts (Boulder, Colo.: Westview Press, 1991), p. 503.
39. Ibid., p. 126.
40. Ibid., p. xi.
41. "Morgenthau's Talk to Monetary Conference," *New York Times*, July 2, 1944.
42. Edward Bernstein, interview, September 13 and 14, 1993.
43. "The Mount Washington," *Bugle of Bretton Woods*, October 1, 1902.
44. John H. Crider, "Delegates Search for Warm Clothes," *New York Times*, July 2, 1944.
45. Stanley W. Black, *A Levite among the Priests: Edward M. Bernstein and the Origins of the Bretton Woods System* (Boulder, Colo.: Westview Press, 1991), p. 37.
46. Ibid., p. 38.
47. Allan Meltzer, interview, August 26, 1993.
48. Richard N. Gardner, *Sterling-Dollar Diplomacy in Current Perspective* (New York: Columbia University Press, 1980), p. 73.
49. Ibid., p. 76.

Interregnum: The Attack on the European Monetary System, Part I

1. Background interviews, fund manager in New York, November 1993.
2. "Gaddum Skeptical of Soros Pronouncements," Reuters, August 18, 1993.
3. Background interview, former Pittsburgh National Bank employee, July 21, 1994.
4. Jack D. Schwager, *The New Market Wizards: Conversations with America's Top Traders* (New York: HarperBusiness, 1992), p. 189.
5. Thomas Dick, Nicholas Nilsen, and Donald Pettler, Pittsburgh National Bank, interviews, August 27, 1994.
6. Schwager, *New Market Wizards*, p. 193.
7. Ibid., p. 201.
8. Michael Lewis, "The Speculator," *New Republic*, January 10 and 17, 1994, pp. 22–23.
9. "The Man Who Moves the Markets," *Business Week*, August 23, 1993, p. 35.

10. Lewis, "Speculator," p. 28.

11. Grant N. Smith, Millburn Ridgefield Corp., interview, September 7, 1993.

Chapter 3: The Golden Vanity

1. Immanuel Kant, *Zum Ewigen Frieden Ein Philsophischer Entwurf*, cited in Brian J. Benestad, *The Pursuit of a Just Social Order* (Lanham, Md.: Ethics and Public Policy Center, 1982), p. 123.

2. See Alasdair MacIntyre, *After Virtue*, 2nd ed. (Notre Dame, Ind.: University of Notre Dame Press, 1984), pp. 14–15.

3. Robert Skidelsky, *John Maynard Keynes*, vol. I, *Hopes Betrayed: 1883–1920* (New York: Viking, 1986), p. xxii.

4. Skidelsky, *John Maynard Keynes*, vol. II, *The Economist as Savior: 1920–1937* (New York: Penguin, 1994), p. 8.

5. Ibid., p. 234.

6. D. E. Moggridge, *Maynard Keynes: An Economist's Biography* (New York: Routledge, 1992), p. 219.

7. Skidelsky, vol. I, p. 220.

8. Skidelsky, vol. II, p. 161.

9. Moggridge, *Maynard Keynes*, p. 727.

10. R. F. Harrod, *The Life of John Maynard Keynes* (New York: St. Martin's Press, 1966), p. 557.

11. Richard N. Gardner, *Sterling-Dollar Diplomacy in Current Perspective* (New York: Columbia University Press, 1980), p. 73.

12. Harrod, *Life of Keynes*, p. 558.

13. Stanley W. Black, *A Levite among the Priests: Edward M. Bernstein and the Origins of the Bretton Woods System* (Boulder, Colo.: Westview Press, 1991), p. 39.

14. Moggridge, *Maynard Keynes*, pp. 727–728.

15. Michael Bordo, "The Bretton Woods International Monetary System: An Historical Overview," in *A Retrospective on the Bretton Woods System*, ed. Michael D. Bordo and Barry Eichengreen (Chicago: University of Chicago Press, 1993), p. 38.

16. Gardner, *Sterling-Dollar Diplomacy*, pp. 9–10.

17. Ibid., p. 26.

18. Ibid., p. 31.

19. Black, *Levite*, p. 43.

20. Edward M. Bernstein, "The Soviet Union and Bretton Woods," in *A Retrospective on the Bretton Woods System*, p. 197.

21. Ibid., p. 198.

22. Gardner, *Sterling-Dollar Diplomacy*, p. 7.
23. Robert Solomon, *The International Monetary System 1945–1981* (New York: Harper & Row, 1982), p. 15.
24. Black, *Levite*, p. 66.
25. W. H. Auden and Louis Kronenberger, *The Viking Book of Aphorisms* (New York: Dorset Press, 1981), p. 327.
26. Solomon, *International Monetary System*, p. 18.
27. Ibid., p. 19.
28. Ibid., p. 28.
29. Ibid., p. 35.
30. Ibid., p. 36.
31. Ibid., p. 39.
32. Paul A. Volcker and Toyoo Gyohten, *Changing Fortunes* (New York: Times Books, 1992), p. 33.
33. Julian Walmsley, *The Foreign Exchange and Money Markets Guide* (New York: John Wiley & Sons, 1992), p. 32.
34. Ibid., p. 31.
35. DC Gardner Group PLC, *The DC Gardner Guide to the International Capital Markets* (New York: John Wiley & Sons, 1993), p. 16.
36. Walmsley, *Foreign Exchange Guide*, pp. 38–39.
37. Solomon, *International Monetary System*, pp. 41–42.
38. Allan H. Meltzer, "U.S. Policy in the Bretton Woods Era," Fifth Annual Homer Jones Memorial Lecture, delivered at Washington University, April 8, 1991 (St. Louis, Mo.: Federal Reserve Bank of St. Louis, May/June 1991), p. 63.
39. Solomon, *International Monetary System*, p. 48.
40. Ibid., p. 55.
41. Michael D. Bordo, Dominique Simard, and Eugene White, "France and the Bretton Woods International Monetary System: 1960–1968" (Working Paper no. 4642, National Bureau of Economic Research, Cambridge, Mass., February 1994), p. 3.
42. Solomon, *International Monetary System*, p. 24.
43. Bordo, Simard, and White, "France and the Bretton Woods International Monetary System: 1960–1968, p. 9.
44. Ibid., p. 10.
45. Solomon, *International Monetary System*, p. 43.
46. Bordo, Simard, and White, "France and Bretton Woods," p. 12.
47. Ibid., p. 19.
48. Ibid., p. 20.

49. Solomon, *International Monetary System*, p. 155.

50. Ibid., p. 153.

51. Ibid., p. 161.

52. Ibid., p. 186.

Chapter 4: Power Pits

1. Graham Greene, *Travels with My Aunt* (New York: Viking Press, 1969), pp. 55–56.

2. See Milton Friedman, foreword to *Leo Melamed on the Markets*, by Leo Melamed (New York: John Wiley & Sons, 1993), p. x.

3. Milton Friedman, interview, April 6, 1994.

4. Alan Walters, "Friedman, Milton," in *The New Palgrave: A Dictionary of Economics*, ed. John Eatwell, Murray Milgate, and Peter Newman (London: Macmillan/New York: Stockton Press, 1987), p. 425.

5. Alfred T. Andreas, *History of Chicago* (Chicago: 1886), vol. 2, p. 337.

6. Ibid., p. 325.

7. Ibid., p. 331.

8. Ibid.

9. Kevin Koy, *The Big Hitters* (Chicago: Intermarket Publishing, 1986), p. 119.

10. Mike O'Connel, (Chicago Board of Trade), interview, April 12, 1994.

11. Leo Melamed, interviews, September 24 and 30 and October 8, 1992.

12. Ibid.

13. Ibid.

14. Ibid.

15. Ibid.

16. Ibid.

17. Bob Tamarkin, *The Merc: The Emergence of a Global Financial Powerhouse* (New York: HarperBusiness, 1993), p. 203.

18. Melamed interviews.

19. Peter L. Bernstein, *Capital Ideas: The Improbable Origins of Modern Wall Street* (New York: Free Press, 1992), pp. 256–257.

20. Richard Sandor, interview, October 8, 1992.

21. Ibid.

22. Ibid.

23. Ibid.

24. Ibid.

25. Ibid.

26. Background interview with Italian financial regulator, May 1992.

27. Background interview with German financial regulator, May 1992.
28. Michael Hoffman, interview, May 1992.
29. Charles Kindleberger, telephone interviews, February 3 and 4, 1992.

Interregnum: The Attack on the European Monetary System, Part II

1. Charles Wyplosz, interview, September 29, 1993.
2. Dave Williams, interview, September 1994.
3. Ibid.
4. Robert Sinche, interview, September 1994.

Chapter 5: Eastern Sunset

1. Asia Development Bank, news release, October 8, 1993. Mitsuo Sato was elected president of the ADB and began his term November 24, 1993. A spokesman for the Tokyo Stock Exchange said Sato was unable to answer questions or meet with this author prior to his departure in the fall of 1993. The spokesman also declined the author's request to interview other officials of the exchange during a visit to Japan in January and February 1994.
2. See, for example, Peter Tasker, *Inside Japan* (London: Penguin Books, 1989), pp. 285–286.
3. Background interview, Singapore International Monetary Exchange, March 1993 and April 1994.
4. Ang Swee Tian, interview, March 1993.
5. Background interview, Singapore International Monetary Exchange staff.
6. Tian interview.
7. Minerva Lau, "Simex Resists Call to Restrain Nikkei Futures," *Nikkei Weekly*, May 16, 1992.
8. Edwin O. Reischauer, *The Japanese* (Tokyo: Charles E. Tuttle, 1977), p. 38.
9. Samuel L. Hayes III and Philip M. Hubbard, *Investment Banking: A Tale of Three Cities* (Boston: Harvard Business School Press, 1990), p. 138.
10. Takuma Takahashi (Nomura Research Institute), interview, February 1994.
11. Reischauer, *The Japanese*, p. 83.
12. Hayes and Hubbard, *Investment Banking*, p. 140.
13. Ibid., p. 138.
14. Ibid., p. 139.
15. Oland D. Russell, *House of Mitsui* (Boston: Little, Brown, 1939), p. 222.
16. Ibid., pp. 225–226.

17. Ibid., p. 247.
18. Ibid., p. 249.
19. Hayes and Hubbard, *Investment Banking*, p. 149.
20. Ibid., p. 150.
21. Quentin Hardy, "Tokyo Bounce: Japanese Stocks Surge but Reasons for Rise Make Some Queasy," *Wall Street Journal*, March 14, 1993, p. 1.
22. Hayes and Hubbard, *Investment Banking*, p. 153.
23. Takahashi interview.
24. Hayes and Hubbard, *Investment Banking*, p. 157.
25. Takahashi interview.
26. Michael T. Jacobs, *Short Term America: The Causes and Cures of Our Business Myopia* (Boston: Harvard Business School Press, 1991), p. 156.
27. See Richard C. Marston, "Pricing to Market in Japanese Manufacturing" (Working Paper no. 2905, National Bureau of Economic Research, Cambridge, Mass.: March 1989).
28. Quoted in G. Bennett Stewart III, *The Quest for Value* (New York: HarperBusiness, 1990), p. 56.
29. Ibid., p. 67.
30. See Martin Feldstein, ed., *The Risk of Economic Crisis* (Chicago: University of Chicago Press, 1991), pp. 1–3.
31. Charles P. Kindleberger, *A Financial History of Western Europe* (New York: Oxford University Press, 1993), p. 361.
32. Jeffrey Bardos, "The Risk-Based Capital Agreement: A Further Step Towards Policy Convergence," *Federal Reserve Bank of New York Quarterly*, Winter 1987–1988, p. 29.
33. Jacobs, *Short Term America*, p. 176.
34. Stella Danker, "Fewer Fools in Paradise," *Risk*, August–September 1988, pp. 46–47.
35. Lillian Chew, "The Great Unease over Zaitech Zeal," *Risk*, December 1987, p. 24.
36. William P. Sterling, "The Leveraging of Japan," *International Economy*, May/June 1988, p. 69.
37. Ibid.
38. Ibid., p. 70.
39. Ibid.
40. Shinichi Muroi and Yukihiko Endo, "Japan's Capital Markets in the 1990's," *NRI Quarterly*, Winter 1993, p. 56.
41. Keith K. H. Park and Steven A. Schoenfeld, *The Pacific Rim Futures and Options Markets* (Chicago: Probus, 1992), p. 161.

42. Keikichi Honda, interview, January 1994.

43. Ibid.

44. Ibid.

45. Ibid.

46. Takaki Wakasugi (professor, Tokyo University, and cofounder, Mitsui Life Financial Research Center at the University of Michigan), interview, January 1994.

47. Background interview with trader, January 1994.

48. Mary L. Schapiro (commissioner, U.S. Securities and Exchange Commission), "The Growth of the Synthetic Derivative Market: Risks and Benefits," speech delivered to the National Options and Futures Society, Washington, D.C., November 13, 1991.

49. Ivers Riley, interviews, Spring–Summer 1992 and February 1994.

50. "Kingdom of Denmark 6,000,000 Nikkei Stock Average Put Warrants Expiring January 3, 1993. Underwriters Goldman, Sachs & Co., Paine Webber Incorporated, Dean Witter Reynolds Inc.," prospectus, January 12, 1990, p. 8.

51. Yoshio Suzuki (Nomura Research Institute), interview, January 1994.

52. "Volatility in U.S. and Japanese Stock Markets: A Symposium," *Continental Bank Journal of Applied Corporate Finance*, vol. 5, no. 1 (Spring 1992), p. 14.

53. Ibid., p. 16.

54. Ibid.

55. Riley interviews.

56. Ibid.

57. Ibid.

58. Ibid.

59. Thomas P. O'Toole, "Nikkei Futures Arbitrage Trade Shifting from Osaka to Simex," *Nikkei Weekly*, April 25, 1992.

60. Riley interviews.

Chapter 6: The Secret Life of the Fortune 500

1. Greenwich Associates' annual survey of treasury practices of large companies in the United States and Canada, May–July 1993.

2. Walter Dolde, "Use of Foreign Exchange and Interest Rate Risk Management in Large Firms" (Working Paper no. 93-042, School of Business Administration, University of Connecticut, November 1993), p. 1.

3. Ibid., p. 13.

4. Group of Ten, *International Capital Movements and Foreign Exchange Markets: A Report to the Ministers and Governors by the Group of Deputies*, April 1993, p. 13.

5. Estimates by Capital Market Risk Advisors, Inc., 420 Lexington Avenue, New York, NY 10170; all losses stated in pretax amounts.

6. "Another Two Bite the Dust," *Derivatives Strategy*, May 16, 1994, p. 7.

7. David Schlang and Michael Craig v. Joseph R. Canion, Benjamin M. Rosin and Compaq Computer Corporation, U.S. District Court for the Southern District of Texas, Houston Division, Case H-91-9191 (out-of-court settlement, June 1994).

8. *Moody's Industrial Manual 1994* (New York: Moody's Investment Service, Inc., 1994), vol. I, A-I, p. 1053.

9. See Gregory J. Millman, "Dow's Dance of the Seven Veils," *Corporate Finance*, July 1990, pp. 50–54.

10. Ibid.

11. See Donald R. Lessard, "Finance and Global Competition: Exploiting Financial Scope and Coping with Volatile Exchange Rates," in *New Developments in International Finance*, ed. Joel M. Stern and Donald H. Chew, Jr. (New York: Basil Blackwell, 1988), pp. 3–23.

12. Ibid., p. 4.

13. Ibid., p. 17.

14. *The Jerusalem Bible: Readers Edition* (New York: Doubleday, 1968), Matt. 25:14–30.

15. Charles P. Kindleberger, *A Financial History of Western Europe* (New York: Oxford University Press, 1993), p. 190.

16. Shakespeare, *Merchant of Venice*, act 1, lines 42–45.

17. Charles Smithson, interview, January 24, 1992.

18. See also Clifford W. Smith, Jr., Charles Smithson, and D. Sykes Wilford, *Managing Financial Risk* (New York: Harper & Row, 1990), pp. 1–19.

19. Smithson interview.

20. Paul A. Volcker and Toyoo Gyohten, *Changing Fortunes* (New York: Times Books, 1992), p. 171.

21. Ibid.

22. Ibid., p. 173.

23. Ibid., p. 174.

24. I. M. Dester and C. Randall Henning, *Dollar Politics: Exchange Rate Policymaking in the United States* (Washington, D.C.: Institute for International Economics, 1989), p. 20.

25. Ibid., p. 23.

26. Stephen Cooney, *New Directions for U.S. Trade: Manufacturing Is the Key to Eliminating the Trade Deficit* (Washington, D.C.: National Association of Manufacturers, December 1988), Figure 7.

27. George Anders, "European Multinational Concerns Profit from the U.S. Currency's Surging Ways," *Wall Street Journal*, September 20, 1984.

28. Allen J. Lenz, "A Sectoral Assessment of the U.S. Current Account Deficit: Performance and Prospects," in *International Adjustment and Financing: The Lessons of 1985–1991*, ed. C. Fred Bergsten (Washington, D.C.: Institute for International Economics, 1991), p. 58.

29. Smithson interview.

30. Dester and Henning, *Dollar Politics*, p. 125.

31. Ibid., p. 126.

32. See Richard C. Marston, "Pricing to Market in Japanese Manufacturing" (Working Paper no. 2905, National Bureau of Economic Research, Cambridge, March 1989).

33. Gregory J. Millman, *The Floating Battlefield: Corporate Strategies in the Currency Wars* (New York: AMACOM, 1990), p. 112.

34. Ibid., pp. 107–121.

35. Judy C. Lewent and A. John Kearney, "Identifying, Measuring and Hedging Currency Risk at Merck," *Continental Bank Journal of Applied Corporate Finance*, vol. 2, no. 4 (Winter 1990), pp. 19–28. See also Gregory J. Millman, "Merck Hedges Currencies to Protect Its R&D Budget," *Corporate Finance*, April 1990, pp. 71–72.

36. Mark J. Ahn and William D. Falloon, *Strategic Risk Management* (Chicago: Probus, 1991), p. 116.

37. Smithson interview.

38. Ahn and Falloon, *Risk Management*, p. 116.

39. Ibid., pp. 111–146.

40. Gregory J. Millman, "Shareholders Applaud Risk Management," *Corporate Finance*, June/July 1992, p. 20.

41. Portia Richardson, "Put on Your Thinking Cap," *Intermarket*, March 1989, p. 11.

42. Eugene A. Rotberg, interview, September 13, 1993, and unpublished paper, "The Currency Swap: In the Beginning."

43. John Dizard, "The Swap Market Shrugs Off Its First Defaults," *Corporate Finance*, May 1989, p. 29.

44. *Financial Derivatives: Actions Needed to Protect the Financial System*, U.S. General Accounting Office Report to Congressional Requesters, May 1994, p. 36.

45. Gregory J. Millman, "Qualex Hedges Gasoline and Silver," *Corporate Finance*, April 1991, p. 66.

46. Gregory J. Millman, "Kaiser and Union Carbide Hedge Their Bets with Their Banks," *Corporate Finance*, June 1991, p. 95.

47. "Swaptions," *Intermarket*, January 1989, p. 27.
48. Gregory J. Millman, "A Maverick Hedger," *Corporate Finance*, June/July 1992, pp. 26–29.
49. Gregory J. Millman, "How Albany International Cuts Its Interest Cost to Less than Zero," *Corporate Finance*, June 1990, p. 54.
50. Gregory J. Millman, "Trader in the Dell," *Corporate Finance*, February 1993, p. 36.
51. Estimates by Capital Market Risk Advisors, Inc.
52. Ibid.
53. Unpublished letter to shareholders, May 3, 1991.
54. Eli Bartov, Gordon M. Bodnar, and Aditya Kaul, "Exchange Rate Variability and the Riskiness of U.S. Multinational Firms: Evidence from the Breakdown of the Bretton Woods System" (Working Paper no. 94-6, Weiss Center for International Financial Research, Wharton School, University of Pennsylvania, Philadelphia, August 1994), p. 4.

Interregnum: The Attack on the European Monetary System, Part III

1. Jon Peabody, interviews, September 29 and 30, 1993, and July 13, 1994.
2. Interview with French banker, September 30, 1993.
3. Ibid.
4. Peabody interviews.

Chapter 7: Nuclear Finance

1. Douglas Williams, interview, September 16, 1993.
2. Grant N. Smith, interviews, September 1993.
3. Malcolm Wiener, interview, May 18, 1994.
4. Dave Allman (director of research, Prechter's Elliott Wave International), interview, June 4, 1994.
5. Joseph Granville, interview, June 1994.
6. Peter L. Bernstein, *Capital Ideas: The Improbable Origins of Modern Wall Street* (New York: Free Press, 1992), pp. 18–23.
7. Ibid., p. 33.
8. Ibid., p. 34.
9. Ibid., p. 36.
10. Ibid., p. 190.
11. *Brancato Report*, vol. 1, edition 2 (Fairfax, Va.: The Victoria Group, Inc., April 1994), p. 47.

12. Josef Lakonishok, Andrei Shleifer, and Robert W. Vishny, "The Structure and Performance of the Money Management Industry," *Brookings Papers: Microeconomics 1992* (Washington, D.C.: Brookings Institution, 1992), pp. 348–349.

13. Ibid., p. 379.

14. Gregory J. Millman, "Sheep in Wolf's Clothing," *Corporate Finance*, February 1993, p. 18.

15. Bernstein, *Capital Ideas*, p. 247.

16. *Brancato Report*, p. 31.

17. According to a spokesman for the Virginia Retirement System, the program began in 1990 with a decision to allocate 1 percent of the system's portfolio to managed futures. In December 1993 the allocation was increased to 4 percent. The program was controversial, however; in June 1994 a newly appointed board of trustees terminated it.

18. "Inside Long Term Capital," *Derivatives Strategy*, April 4, 1994, p. 9.

19. Lawrence Hilibrand and Eric Rosenfeld, interview.

20. Gregory J. Millman, "The Junk Currency Play," *Forbes*, June 21, 1993, pp. 218–219

21. Ezra Zask, interviews, February 1 and April 18, 1993.

22. Ezra Zask, interviews, May 27, 1994.

23. William Aronin, interviews, May 1993.

Chapter 8: Hidden Risks

1. Paul A. Volcker and Toyoo Gyohten, *Changing Fortunes* (New York: Times Books, 1992), p. 252.

2. Ibid., p. 256.

3. Ibid., p. 255.

4. Tan Sri Dato' Jaffar bin Hussein, "Central Banking in an Era of Change: XI Industrial Finance Corporation of India (IFCI) Silver Jubilee Memorial Lecture," December 5, 1988, collected in *Central Banking in an Era of Change: Landmark Speeches 1959–1988* (Kuala Lumpur: Bank Negara Malaysia, 1989), pp. 381–383.

5. Reuters report, November 6, 1990.

6. Background interview with banker, February 19, 1993.

7. Peter Koenig, "A Maverick Breaks into the Forex Club: Malaysia's Central Bank Is Now an Influential Player in Foreign Exchange Markets," *Independent*, November 4, 1990, p. 10.

8. Andrew Krieger, interviews, March 24 and 27, 1992.

9. Reuters report.

10. Background interview, U.S. financial regulator.

11. Group of Ten, *International Capital Movements and Foreign Exchange Markets: A Report to the Ministers and Governors by the Group of Deputies*, April 1993, p. 7.

12. Barbara Pederson Holum (acting chairman, Commodity Futures Trading Commission), testimony before the House Committee on Banking, Finance and Urban Affairs, April 13, 1994, table summary.

13. Transcript of meeting, Financial Products Advisory Committee, Commodity Futures Trading Commission, March 12, 1992, p. 42.

14. Brian Walsh, interview, May 17, 1994.

15. Joe Ritchie, interview, November 10, 1994.

16. Gary Ginter, interviews, October–November 1993.

17. Joe Ritchie interview.

18. Mark A. Ritchie, *God in the Pits: Confessions of a Commodities Trader* (Nashville: Thomas Nelson Publishers, 1989), p. 146.

19. Jack D. Schwager, *The New Market Wizards: Conversations with America's Top Traders* (New York: HarperBusiness, 1992), p. 345.

20. Ibid., p. 347.

21. Ginter interview.

22. Arnie Staloff, interviews, August and September 1993.

23. Ginter interview.

24. Joe Ritchie interview.

25. See David S. Berry, "Perspectives on Trading Revenues," *KBW Bank Industry Issues* (Keefe, Bruyette & Woods, Inc.), July 29, 1993.

26. Alexandre Lamfalussy, "The Restructuring of the Financial Industry: A Central Banking Perspective," SUERF lecture, delivered at City University, London, March 5, 1992, p. 4.

27. Background interviews with financial regulators.

28. Lamfalussy, p. 11.

29. Background interview with U.S. bank regulator.

30. Worth Bruntjen, interviews, July 1993. See Gregory J. Millman, "Bond Funds on Steroids," *Worth*, October 1993, pp. 68–72.

31. Quotation taken from letter before it was edited by *Worth* for publication.

32. G. Bruce Knecht, "Piper Manager's Losses May Total $700 Million," *Wall Street Journal*, August 25, 1994, section C, p. 1.

33. Paul DaRosa, interview, May 6, 1994.

34. Krieger interview.

35. Carol Loomis, "How Bankers Trust Lied about $80 Million," *Forbes*, September 7, 1992, p. 78.

36. Ibid.

37. Background interview with U.S. bank regulator.

38. Loomis, "How Bankers Trust Lied about $80 Million."

39. Cheryl Strauss Einhorn, "The Shadow War at AIG," *Investment Dealers Digest*, September 6, 1993, p. 14.

40. William Falloon, "Who Is Arthur Benson?" *Energy Risk*, vol. 1, no. 9 (October 1994), p. 19.

41. Rick Raber and Vaughan Scully, "Metallgesellschaft Says Oil Trader Benson Was Speculative Addict," Bloomberg News Service, October 14, 1994.

42. David Shirreff, "In the Line of Fire," *Euromoney*, March 1994, p. 42.

43. Ibid.

44. Christopher Culp and Merton H. Miller, "Hedging a Flow of Commodity Derivatives with Futures: Lessons from Metallgesellschaft," *Derivatives Quarterly*, vol. 1, no. 1 (September 1994), p. 12.

45. Shirreff, "In the Line of Fire," p. 42.

46. Ibid. See also Culp and Miller, "Hedging a Flow of Commodity Derivatives," p. 2.

47. Shirreff, "In the Line of Fire," p. 42.

48. Ibid., p. 12.

49. Prepared statement by Michael J. Hutchinson, Jr., managing director of Metallgesellschaft Ltd. in London, "The Metallgesellschaft Affair: Risk Management in the Real World," October 10, 1994, p. 2.

50. Shirreff, "In the Line of Fire," p. 43.

51. Culp and Miller, "Hedging a Flow of Commodity Derivatives," p. 2.

52. Metallgesellschaft strongly disputed Miller's argument that their lack of understanding and premature action caused the $1.33 billion loss. "This assessment is as unrealistic as it is misinformed," said Michael J. Hutchinson, Jr., in the prepared statement he delivered on October 10, 1994 (see note 49 above). He noted that many customers who had committed to buy oil from MGRM weren't creditworthy and might not have honored their contracts. He also said that the company had eliminated many of the oil supply contracts while they were eliminating futures contracts. Citing litigation and commercial considerations, he refused, however, to divulge the information that might substantiate his claims.

53. Gary Lynch, *Report of Inquiry into False Trading Profits at Kidder, Peabody & Co., Incorporated* (New York: Davis Polk & Wardwell, August 4, 1994), p. 3.

54. Michael Siconolfi, "Kidder Discloses Phony Trade, Fires Trader," *Wall Street Journal*, April 18, 1994, p. 1.
55. Panel presentation by Jonathan Asquith of Morgan Grenfell, at the ISDA Annual Meeting, Montreal, March 15, 1990.
56. Ibid.
57. Anatole Kaletsky, "Banks Face Bill of £550 m after Swaps Decision," *Financial Times*, May 8, 1991.
58. *Financial Derivatives: Actions Needed to Protect the Financial System*, U.S. General Accounting Office Report to Congressional Requesters, May 1994, pp. 64–66.
59. Ernest Patrikis, interview, June 24, 1994.
60. See Gregory J. Millman, "The $2 Billion Tax Boomerang," *Corporate Finance*, September 1991, p. 50. See also Millman, "The Tale of Arkansas Best," *Barrons*, November 9, 1992, p. 10.
61. Millman, "$2 Billion Tax Boomerang," p. 50.
62. Ibid., pp. 46–47.
63. Ibid., p. 47.
64. Annual Report, Chicago Mercantile Exchange, 1993.
65. Patricia C. Mosser, interview, April 25, 1994. See also Julia Fernald, Frank Keane, and Patricia C. Mosser, "Mortgage Security Hedging and the Yield Curve" (Research Paper no. 9411, Federal Reserve Bank of New York), August 1994.

Epilogue: It Ain't No Big Thing (But It's Growing)

1. Press release, U.S. House of Representatives, Committee on Banking, Finance and Urban Affairs, Washington, D.C., September 13, 1994.
2. "Greenspan Warns Banks of Need for Self-Regulation," *Financial Times*, June 9, 1994, p. 1.
3. "Financial Market Innovations—Practical Concerns," remarks by William J. McDonough, president, Federal Reserve Bank of New York, before the Money Marketeers of New York University, June 16, 1994, p. 18.

GLOSSARY

Arbitrage. Buying something that seems relatively cheap and selling a related, higher-priced item in order to profit from the price difference, or spread, between the two. Securities and derivative instruments offer arbitrage opportunities when they are priced differently on different exchanges or by different traders.

Arkansas Best. Colloquial term for a 1988 Supreme Court decision that threatened to restrict the tax deductibility of hedging losses.

Black, Fischer. Co-inventor of the Black–Scholes option pricing model.

Black–Scholes option pricing model. A differential equation used to determine the correct theoretical value for an option, given the spot price of the underlying asset, its price volatility, the interest rate, the strike price of the option, and the time until the option expires.

Bretton Woods. (1) A 1944 conference at the Mount Washington Hotel in New Hampshire where 700 representatives of 44 nations met to map out a new economic order for the postwar world. (2) The international monetary system agreed to by the conferees.

Brokers. Traders who buy and sell on behalf of customers, not for their own accounts.

Capital markets. (1) Collective term for the individual and institutional investors who invest their savings, or capital, in order to earn a return. (2) The institutions and mechanisms that channel capital from investors to investments.

Capital standards. Rules established by international and national regulators to keep the international financial system from collapsing as a result of bad decisions by bankers and other financiers. These rules, or standards, require financial institutions to maintain adequate capital to absorb most anticipated losses.

290

Central banks. Institutions that establish and/or implement national monetary policies. Examples: Bank of England, Bank of France, Bundesbank.

Chaos theory. A theory of systems that produce apparently random results which are, in fact, strictly determined.

Convergence trade. A trade in which investors bought high-yielding European currencies and hedged themselves with lower-yielding currencies, in the expectation that regulators would maintain a certain relationship among the currency values.

Corporate hedging. Taking measures to protect a corporation's cash flows against currency and interest rate risks. These may be operational measures, such as purchasing materials from suppliers in various countries, or financial measures, such as buying or selling financial instruments like options.

Currency debasement. Originally accomplished by mixing base metals into gold and silver coins, currency debasement is the policy of cheapening currency without admitting it.

Derivative. (1) A contract or security whose value is closely related to and to a large extent determined by the value of a related security, commodity, or index. (2) Any bond or security that includes one or more derivatives in its structure.

Druckenmiller, Stanley. Trader credited with devising the strategy that won a billion dollars for George Soros in 1992.

Efficiency. The degree to which market pricer reflect all information that might affect the value of a security.

Exchange. An organized marketplace for trading securities, futures contract, or physical commodities, usually under the jurisdiction of a regulatory body.

Euromarkets. Currency and securities markets that are beyond the jurisdiction of the government whose currency is traded. In a typical Euromarket transaction. a Japanese bank may use its U.S. dollar deposits in London to purchase dollar-denominated securities issued in London by a corporation headquartered in Mexico City.

European Monetary System (EMS). The EMS established the currency unit (European Currency Unit, or ECU) and Exchange Rate Mechanism (see below) that would lay the foundation for the European Monetary Union.

Exchange Rate Mechanism (ERM). The framework that defines the value of European currencies relative to each other.

Floating currency, floating exchange rate. A currency or exchange rate whose value is set by market forces rather than by government decisions.

Group of Five (G-5). Finance ministers and central bankers of the world's five strongest economic powers: the United States, Japan, France, Germany, and Great Britian.

Group of Ten (G-10). The G-5 plus finance ministers and central bankers of Canada, Italy, Belgium, the Netherlands, and Sweden.

Hedge. An asset, liability, or financial commitment that protects against adverse changes in the value of or cash flows from another investment or liability. An unhedged investment or liability is called an "exposure." A perfectly matched hedge will gain in value what the underlying exposure loses, or lose what the underlying exposure gains.

Hedge funds. Private investment pools that invest aggressively in all types of markets, with managers of the fund receiving a percentage of the investment profits. Some hedge funds actually hedge, but in general a hedge fund manager makes money by taking a great deal of risk.

Hybrid bonds. Debt securities whose payments are determined by an equity, currency, or commodity derivative incorporated in the bond's structure.

Indexing. Investing to mimic the performance of an index of prices rather than to beat the index.

Institutional investors. Pension funds, banks, insurance companies, mutual funds, and other financial institutions that accumulate savings and invest them on behalf of savers.

Interbank market. The market in which banks and other big investors trade currencies and securities among themselves.

International Monetary Fund (IMF). An institution originally established to maintain currency values in accordance with the Bretton Woods agreements.

International Monetary Market. The market in currency and other financial futures contracts traded at the Chicago Mercantile Exchange.

Inverse floaters. Securities designed to pay investors more when an interest rate index falls, and less when the index rate rises.

Keiretsu. Groups of closely related Japanese financial and industrial companies.

Keynes, John Maynard. An economist and author of *The General Theory of Employment, Interest and Money.* His ideas provided the intellectual foundation for the Bretton Woods system of international financial institutions.

Krieger, Andrew. A trader reported to have earned hundreds of millions of dollars for Bankers Trust Company in 1987. After his departure, regulators required the bank to adjust its earnings downward.

Law, John. An adventurer and economist. See "Mississippi Company."

Leading and lagging. A technique of timing payments and receipts in order to protect against or profit from currency depreciation.

Linkages. Relationships between markets.

M&M theory. A hypothesis that won the 1990 Nobel Prize for Franco Modigliani and Merton Miller, M&M theory states that in an efficient market with no taxes, merely changing the proportion of debt to equity in the capital structure of a firm will not change the value of the firm.

Mark to market. To record the value of an investment or liability at current market prices.

Market neutral. An investment approach that seeks to insulate capital against general market moves in order to profit from arbitrage opportunities or other market inefficiencies.

Market risk. Uncertainty about the direction in which the market will move; also, the possibility of damage if the market moves the wrong way.

Markowitz, Harry. 1990 Nobel laureate who discovered and explained how rational investors should think about risk.

Melamed, Leo. Founder, International Monetary Market.

Merton, Robert. Together with Fischer Black and Myron Scholes, refined the Black–Scholes option pricing model.

Miller, Merton. 1990 Nobel laureate who, with Franco Modigliani, advanced a theory of firm value popularly called "M&M theory."

Mississippi Company. Founded by John Law in eighteenth-century France to exploit the mineral wealth of Louisiana, the Mississippi Company occasioned one of the biggest speculative manias in financial history.

Monetary transmission mechanism. The means whereby monetary policy affects the economy.

Mortgage securities. Securities that entitle holders to payments from a pool of mortgages.

Neural networks. Computer systems more or less modeled on the human brain and allegedly capable of "learning."

Nikkei. The most widely referenced index of Japanese stock prices.

Option. The right to choose whether or not to buy or sell something for a specified price, or to begin or end a financial agreement, at a specified time or period of time. In the United States, the most familiar option is the right of a homeowner to prepay a mortgage. Other options—for example, on currency, on futures contracts, on swaps—are traded on exchanges and in the interbank market.

Portfolio insurance. A program of trading that aims to protect a portfolio against loss by buying and selling in timely response to market movements.

Program trading. Trading large portfolios according to mathematical rules, usually for purposes of arbitrage or portfolio insurance.

Proprietary trading. Trading for one's own account, rather than on behalf of customers.

Quantitative arbitrage. A form of arbitrage that relies on intensive analysis of the mathematics of pricing.

Reserves. (1) Gold or foreign exchange held by a central bank in order to settle international payments. (2) That portion of commercial bank deposits that is not loaned out by the bank but rather placed on deposit with the central bank.

Risk. Uncertainty that asset values, cash flows, or business objectives may be achieved or maintained.

Risk management. A program undertaken by a corporation to assess the nature of risks the corporation is exposed to and to select the best method of hedging these risks.

Risk premium. The value that investors demand in return for making risky investments; the price of risk.

Ritchie, Joe. Co-founder, Chicago Research and Trading (CRT).

Sandor, Richard. Established the first interest rate futures contracts at the Chicago Board of Trade.

Saturday Night Massacre. The market turmoil that followed Federal Reserve Board Chairman Paul Volcker's announcement on Saturday, October 6, 1979, that the Fed would aim to manage the money supply rather than interest rates.

Sharpe, William. 1990 Nobel laureate for the capital asset pricing model (CAPM); he discovered that investors can best minimize risk and maximize returns by owning a representative cross section of the whole market. See also "Indexing."

Soros, George. Trader who drew international press attention to hedge funds by making a billion dollars when Great Britain withdrew from the European Monetary System's Exchange Rate Mechanism in 1992.

Speculation/speculators. Taking risk in order to reap rewards; those who do so.

Staloff, Arnie. Philadelphia Stock Exchange official who invented the currency option.

Strength of currency. The relative value of currency. A strong dollar buys more yen, marks, or francs than a weak dollar.

Strike price. The price at which an option buyer may buy the underlying security, commodity, currency, or other asset. Also referred to as the "exercise price."

Swap. An agreement in which two parties commit themselves to exchange a stream of payments over a specified time period. Typically, one party pays a fixed rate while the other pays a floating rate determined by some index, or one party pays in one currency while the other party pays in another currency.

Swaption. The right, but not the obligation, to enter into a swap agreement.

Tokkin funds. Japanese investment pools for purposes of stock market speculation by Japanese corporate and institutional investors.

Triffin's dilemma: The fatal flaw in the Bretton Woods international monetary system. The world needed U.S. deficits in order to assure abundant dollars, but dollars were officially convertible into gold at $35.00 per ounce. Over time, U.S. deficits made the dollar worth much less on the market than the official gold price dictated. Solving the deficit problem would have meant choking the world's money supply, but not solving the deficit problem meant further erosion of the gold price.

Volatility. A measure of the variability of price over time; roughly, the probability of a change in price.

World Bank. International Bank of Reconstruction and Development, an international investment institution established at the Bretton Woods Conference to aid the postwar recovery of Europe.

Yield Curve. A graph showing the relationship of interest rates to time. In a normal yield curve, interest rates on short-term investments are lower than rates on long-term investments. In an inverted yield curve, the converse is true. In a flat yield curve, interest rates on longer-term investments are not much if at all higher than rates on shorter-term investments.

Zaitech. Japanese term that literally means "financial engineering" but that connotes wild and irresponsible speculation.

ACKNOWLEDGMENTS

This book is based on nearly eight years of reporting on financial markets. In 1992, the Alicia Patterson Foundation provided financial support in the form of a fellowship that enabled me to spend a year researching and writing about these markets from the perspective of readers who were not finance professionals. Without that fellowship and the personal friendship of Margaret Engel, this book would not have been possible. Thank you.

I would like to acknowledge the assistance of numerous sources in banks, corporations, exchanges, central banks, regulatory agencies, and universities who contributed to my understanding of the radical changes in the international financial system. Special thanks are due to Professors Takaki Wakasugi of Tokyo University and Charles Wyplosz of INSEAD, who introduced me to some of their own sources in Tokyo and Paris, respectively. Some of the most helpful and informative of my sources have requested that their names not be published. Thanks to all of them nonetheless.

I owe a particular debt of gratitude to those people who took the time to review the manuscript prior to publication and whose suggestions helped me to keep the book both accurate and readable. Thanks to journalists Elizabeth Bailey, Peter Bernstein, Aloysius Ehrbar,

William Falloon, and James Jubak and to Professors Gordon Bodnar at Wharton, Michael Bordo at Rutgers, Charles Kindleberger at Massachusetts Institute of Technology, Merton Miller at the University of Chicago, and Antoin E. Murphy at Trinity College, Dublin. Any errors of fact that may remain are my own fault.

I would like to thank Susan Hawrusik and Carolyn Della Sala of the reference department of the Plainfield Public Library. They were both ingenious and indefatigable in locating materials I requested, no matter how arcane or remote.

I very much appreciate the assistance provided by Bruce Nichols, Norah Vincent, and Edith Lewis of The Free Press, who saw the work through the editing process.

Thanks to my agent, Gail Ross.

Thanks to my children, Bridget, Anna, Magdalen, and William, who have tolerated my odd hours and near-total immersion in this project when I ought to have been playing with them.

Thanks to my brother Jim, who arranged a fishing vacation at precisely the time it was most needed, and to my father and mother.

Most of all, I thank my wife Martine, to whom this book is dedicated, for help that I cannot begin to describe adequately.

INDEX